Messages from the Deep: the West Encounters the Rig-veda

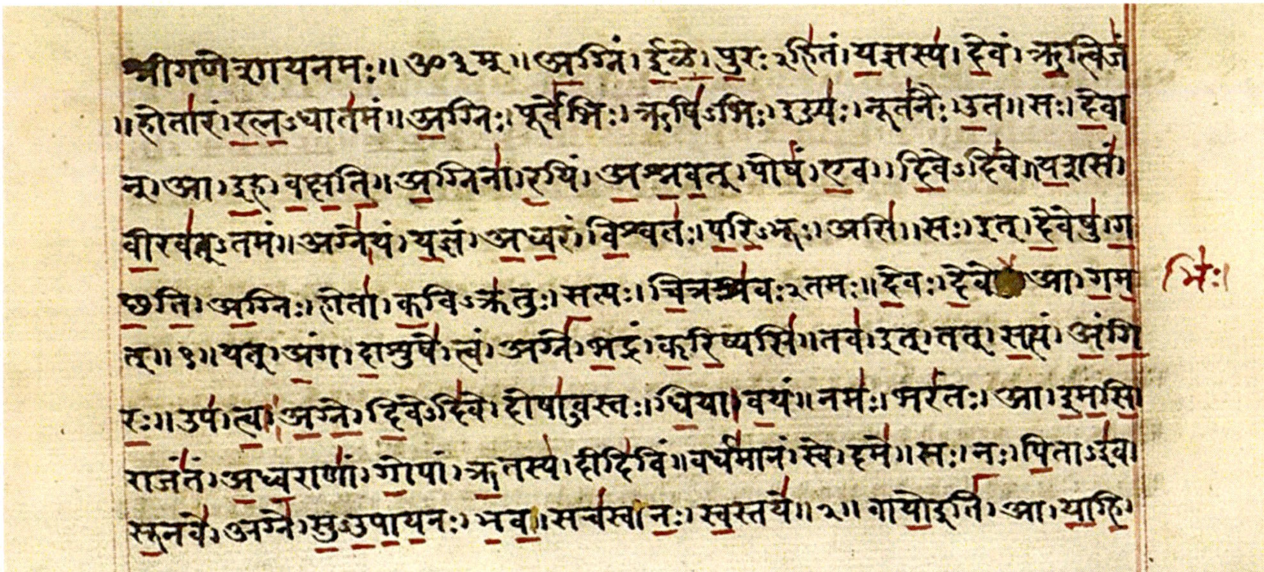

MSS (2097) image : First Sukta in Rig-Veda with Padapātha markings

Messages from the Deep
The West Encounters the Rig-veda

Sati Chatterjee

The National Council of Education, Bengal
in collaboration with
MAHA BODHI BOOK AGENCY

Messages from the Deep
The West Encounters the Rig-veda

by

Sati Chatterjee

First published : 2016

Published by

The National Council of Education, Bengal

In collaboration with

D.L.S. Jayawardana

MAHA BODHI BOOK AGENCY

4A, Bankim Chatterjee Street,

College Square, Kolkata-700 073

Phone : +9831529452, 9831077368

Email : mahabodhibookagency@hotmail.com

Cover design : Monita Chatterjee

DTP by Amar Sapui, NCE, Bengal

Printed by

Sagarika Press, Kolkata-700 009

ISBN 978-93-84721-48-0

₹ 650/-

in memory of
my parents and my husband
to
my children, with me all the way

Messages from the Deep : the West Encounters the Rig-veda

Publisher's Note

When, in 1905-06, the formation of the National Council of Education, Bengal was planned, the motivation had been to offer an alternative model of education for the Indian youth — moving away from the Western model impregnated with the imperial design of Anglicizing and de-nationalizing the colonized people of the land. The gesture had marked an extension of the nationalist upsurge against colonial domination, defining yet another trajectory of the anti-imperial movement. What followed is history : the decades of freedom movement and the formal de-colonization of the country.

Almost after a century and a decade after the inception of the National Council of Education, one of the early efforts at postcolonial reassessment of the Western scholars' interpretation of the ancient culture of India begins in the research wing of the National Council of Education. We bring out *Messages from the Deep : the West Encounters the Rig-veda* by Professor Sati Chatterjee, formerly of the Department of English, Jadavpur University and Life Member, National Council of Education, Bengal.

After the attainment of political independence, particularly after the emergence of Jadavpur University in 1955-56, the parent body, the National Council of Education, has remained engaged in conducting several educational institutions and educational schemes suited to the changing needs of our developing community and in research projects of pioneering importance in areas related to education, literature, religion and culture studies. Postcolonial research, as scholars in the field, like Ania Loomba for instance, note, yet remains confined to the Western academia; the approach is yet to emerge as a mainstream research in the study of the colonial experience in India. Professor Sati Chatterjee's work is one of the early efforts at a postcolonial assessment of the Western construct designated "Indology". The volume we publish engages in a probing analysis of the subtle contrarieties in the new discipline : its text and its sub-text, the Euro-centric world-view and the imperial compulsions interwoven into the texture of the West's new knowledge of the Orient.

In a way, it is in the fitness of things that the investigation is carried out under the aegis of the National Council of Education. The work opens up a field of enquiry vital to the understanding of the complex event of colonization and culture-confrontation and offers a wider sense of perspective so urgently needed in the present days of growing dissension and divisive discord.

We gratefully acknowledge the support, appreciation and encouragement received from eminent scholars.

We offer thanks for the logistic support from technicians in the Council and outside. Sri Amar Sapui composed and formatted the typescript with infinite care; the publication of the volume is indebted to him.

We are thankful to Mahabodhi Book Agency for collaboration in the publication of the volume.

Ananda Deb Mukherjee

(Ananda Deb Mukherjee)
General Secretary

The National Council
of Education, Bengal
Kolkata, April 2016

Foreword

Messages from the Deep: the West Encounters the Rigveda by Professor Sati Chatterjee, attempts a re-viewing from a postcolonial point of view of the culture confrontation between the colonizing modern West and India, the land of a millennia-old ancient tradition.

Focused on the Western scholars' reading of the Rigveda, particularly on Max Müller's mammoth interpretive effort and his formulation of the "historical approach" and the comparative method, Chatterjee's explorations bring out deeper complexities and contrarieties in the West's encounter with the ancient Veda and the vedic modality of perception. Chatterjee questions the West's assessment of the Rigveda as a collection of "helpless utterances" of primitive people in the infancy of human civilization. The work engages in unraveling the intermingling of the forces of epistemic domination with the imperial in the construction of an empire of the mind; it analyses the interplay of cognitive perception and positional compulsions on the side of the colonizer as well as the colonized

As chroniclers of civilization studies in recent times note, Postcolonial studies as yet remain entrenched in the Anglo-American Universities. Although in the Western academia it is already moving out of the "post"- phase into the perspective of a "trans-National" community, borderless and global, postcolonial study of the colonization experience in India is yet to emerge as a mainstream in the field of culture studies. The present author argues that the colonization of India by the West — the colonizing West triumphant in its expansionist adventure and ancient India past its peak-point of maturation and in deep decline at that point of time — had been a major event in the history of colonization. Its cultural ramifications were deeper and more complex than was the case in other colonies. India's vast and undeniably rich (although obscure and difficult to access for various reasons) tradition and her apparent social stagnation at the time of the colonial experience, placed before the West an almost unique interpretive challenge. Probing studies in the nature and the impact of the experience on both the colonizer and the colonized, the author believes, is of vital importance in our understanding of the historical process of colonization and the way it continues to shape our identity and understanding of our pre-colonial heritage.

Chatterjee's competent and commendable effort marks a belated, and for this reason all the more welcome, beginning of a postcolonial approach to the Euro-centric interpretation of the ancient culture of India and explores ways of release from the grip of established epistemic domination.

Kolkata
2016

D.P. Chattopadhyaya

Preamble

I have gone through the work entitled *Messages from the Deep: The West Encounters the Rigveda* written by Sati Chatterjee. The title of the monograph is fascinating as it deals with the Rigveda, the 'oldest book' in human history and Max Müller's designation of it as reflecting the child mind of the human race in its 'infantia'. The author does not support the view of Max Müller as she finds in the Rigveda deeper levels of meditation and human understanding. Such assertions strike at the roots of the learned German Professor's discovery in the Rigveda of 'the helpless utterances of the primitive man in the infancy of civilization'. The primitive profile portrayed by the Western scholars does not take into account the underlying deeper truth enshrined in the Rigveda—asserts the author.

The present work has been divided into six chapters.

Chapter I: 'The West meets India' makes an assessment of the slow expansion and consolidation of British power in India, which happens to be the period during which Indology or Indic Studies came into existence. In this era, the Western scholars discovered Vedic India in their new field of research. In their opinion, Oriental studies can serve both ends–conquering the territory and bringing under domination the mind of the conquered.

The author takes a fresh look at the recent archaeological excavations, which reveal untold stories in the history of man's journey on earth and calls for a fresh initiative into the archaeological findings carried out from time to time. Modern linguists on the other hand negate the validity of theoretical speculation about language development and rapid growth in ancient times unless supported by archaeological evidence. In the opinion of the author, Indian antiquity emerges as the receptacle of an ancient account of human experience, enquiry and knowledge. According to the author, the ancient Vedic texts appear as rich harvest of a full-grown ancient civilization which had assimilated the complexities of physical existence, of mental needs, along with dreams and aspirations, and record the dizzy height they had attained in the field of metaphysical and spiritual realization. The author does not subscribe to the view that the Aryans who came from outside India, settled down to compose the Rigveda, a poem of more than 10,000 verses in the course of a couple of centuries.

The second chapter demonstrates how in his own time Max Müller and his effort to decipher the Rigveda can be best described as an individual commitment inspired by a collective missionary zeal.

Chapter III named 'Contrary pulls' articulates the tug of war between the colonizer and the colonized country i.e. India. It shows imperial interest urgently felt in the expansion of Oriental Studies in the interest of ruling a vast empire. It envisions linear progress towards Western location points: journey from infancy recorded in the Rigveda towards the more developed Hellenic mythology and from primitive nature worship towards Christianity, the one 'true' religion—so argues the author.

The fourth chapter entitled 'The idiom of yore and Sāyana, the guide' delves deep into the West's wrong entry and the incomplete inner translation of the Rigveda. In the author's opinion, the Western scholars miss altogether the metaphorical, symbolical, ritualistic and the holistic interpretations ingrained in it. The Westerners' study of the Rigveda does not take into account the long history of linguistic semantic enquiry in ancient India from the time of the Brāhmanas to the rhetoricians like Ānandavardhana, and Abhinavagupta.

Sāyana, in his renowned commentary of the Rigveda, named *Vedārthaprakāśa*, belonged to the 14th century AD; he presented an exposition of the mantras mostly from the sacrificial point of view. According to the author, Sāyana's position in a long tradition actually represents one section of scholars in an elaborate exegetical process.

Max Müller, however, has been eager to accept Sāyana's commentary as a representative native interpretation of the Rigveda, which the author opines does not make a good decision in utter disregard of the larger total perspective. Chatterjee believes that being shorn off from the long tradition of Vedic exegesis, the Bhāsya of Sāyana could do justice neither to Vedic interpretation nor to itself. In the same breath, the modern erudite Vedicist, Chatterjee, remarks that reading the Rigveda with the help of Sāyana's commentary is like meeting ancient India in decadence, not in the best but in the worst of her time. The author takes the Westerner's criticism of the Veda, especially the Rigveda, as the triumph of 'imperial knowledge'.

The penultimate chapter titled 'Voices of dissent' brings out the dissenting views from three Indian stalwarts, Bankim Chandra, Tilak and Aurobindo, who provide a post-colonial critique from within the colonial framework, so to say. Bankim Chandra in his 'Krishna Charitra' (1886) and Bal Gangadhar Tilak in his 'Orion' (1893) have proposed a greater antiquity for the hymns of the Rigveda. Sri Aurobindo in his 'The Secret of the Veda' (1914-1916)', rejected the viewpoints of the Western scholars, especially Max Müller. To quote his own view,

> "thus there emerged in my mind, revealing itself as it were out of the ancient verses, a Veda which was throughout the Scripture of a great and antique religion already equipped with a profound psychological

> discipline — a Scripture not confusing in thought or primitive in its substance, not a medley of heterogeneous or barbarous elements, but one, complete and self-conscious in its purpose and its purport, veiled indeed by the cover, sometimes thick, sometimes transparent, of another and material sense, but never losing sight even for a single moment of its high spiritual aim and tendency."

The concluding chapter styled 'Comparative Engagement — changing tropes, the stable premise' throws light on Max Müller's essay 'Comparative Mythology' (1856) and analyses how down the ages tropes change and comparative discussion becomes increasingly sophisticated. The author is of the opinion that the ground premise, however, remains stable i.e. India is for Europe, as Max Müller had known.

A perennial question has been posed by the author at the end: Where does the non-West stand? And when does it find its voice? Now, it is time for a post-modernist, post-colonial, multi-vocal, trans-nation, borderless man to provide the real answer from a truly global perspective as far as Veda text is concerned.

The work is marked by scholarly analysis, profound penetration into original texts, application of comparative method and freshness of thought and approach. I congratulate the author for her bold initiative in rejecting the Westerners' especially Bharat Bandhu Max Müller's, unsavoury utterances against the Rigveda with valid reasons and convincing arguments. The author, in her impeccable English has brought to the fore the hidden thought-currents of the ancient *risi*s contradicting the biased view of the European scholars regarding the Vedic text. Besides the chapters mentioned above, there are two appendices: "Appendix A: Commentators and their contexts" and "Appendix B: Indology and its reception in India", which will go a long way in enhancing the pristine quality of this magnificent work. My impression of the treatise is extremely favourable and I cannot but admire the author for her enormous labour, critical acumen and astounding thoroughness in preparing this work. I am confident, the book when published, will be received with a warm welcome by critical readers, both in the East and the West.

Bhabani Prasad Bhattacharya

04.12.2015

Bhabani Prasad Bhattacharya
Formerly Professor and
Head of the Department of Sanskrit
Jadavpur University

Preface

In the 1990's I was studying the Upanishads and the Dharma Sastras. At opposing ends — the Upanishads absorbed in the contemplation of transcendental monism, the Smriti Sastras engaged in enunciating orthodox social ethics in practice — the ancient texts revealed a mind mature beyond the estimate in popular currency. Beneath expository accounts, adulatory and hyper-critical, the ancient voices spoke from the depths of wisdom born of stored experience accumulated over ages. This aroused in my mind fresh curiosity about the older Rig Veda text. The Rig Veda, we had learnt in our school days, and we had learnt from encyclopaedias and handbooks, is the "oldest book" in human history; it records the earliest infancy of human civilization. Does it, really?

The question led into territory I knew little about; and it took years. My studies revealed a fascinating spectacle spread out on many levels, nuanced and laden with messages of historical import. Max Müller in the 1840's had been reading "helpless utterances" of the primitive man in the Veda text. The ancient text does offer worshipful appreciation to all the bounty in the universe, the forces in the mortal abode; and it voices the numerous needs of earthly existence. But, beneath the surface recognition of the perceptual world and its compulsive pragmatics, it projects a mind on a quest, a mind in moments of penetrative realization. The questing mind asks: whence comes all this? What had been the source when nothing was there? Is there anyone who knows? To whom should we offer our worship? What is this "mind" that asks, questions? The conviction arising out of accumulating experience, long meditation and persistent questioning, is that the truth behind, beneath, or beyond, is one, manifest in the many – and called by different names.

The vision in the oldest book extends into the Upanishads; the Rig Veda reaches into the Vedanta.

Whence then did the fable that the Rig Veda represents the "infantia" in the story of human civilization emerge? What forces had shaped this reading? Did it grow out of the event of the colonizer meeting the colonized, of the Hellenic mind meeting the Un-Hellenic, of Europe as the enlightened "self", facing the rest as the "other"? How authoritative is the mandate, how long is its validity? The present enquiry is intended to explore these and suchlike questions.

Rig Veda text cited here tallies with the edition published by the Vedic Samshodhanamandal, Pune, 1933.

The translation of Sanskrit texts, unless mentioned otherwise, is mine.

Rig-veda MSS images : UNESCO Memory of the World website. MSS preserved in Archives, Bhandarkar Oriental Research Institute, Pune.

Kolkata
April, 2016

Sati Chatterjee

Acknowledgment

A student of English literature, I started my explorations in the field of Indology with trepidation and hesitancy; every bit of encouragement counted.

An early formulation of the query, a tentative introduction to the work then taking shape in my mind, had been published in the Journal of The Asiatic Society (Volume LI, No. 3, 2009). In retrospect I feel grateful for the confidence the publication had brought.

Eminent Sanskritists and Vedicists, Ramaranjan Mukherji and Sitanath Goswami encouraged the work, Swami Probhanandaji Maharaj of Sri Ramakrishna Math and Mission lent intellectual support. Professor Ramaranjan Mukherji read through part of the manuscript and advised me to set aside other things and give priority to completion of this work. It is a matter of deep regret that progress was slow and the work could not be completed before he left us. Professor Sitanath Goswami placed before me his own work related to the field made in the nineteen-sixties and readily offered valuable suggestions.

Professor Shikha Mukherji stood by me all the way, checking factual details and Sanskrit citations. Professor Madhusudan Pati, Sanskritist and comparatist, looked through the plan of the work; fruitful discussions with him were instructive. But for their invaluable support and guidance, the work could not have continued. The debt is too large for formal expression of gratitude.

Professor Swapan Chakravarti looked through the typescript and offered invaluable advice. Professor Radharaman Chakravarti offered critical comments and detailed advice. Encouraging appreciation from them sustained and I remain deeply beholden.

Professor Debi Prasad Chattopadhyaya, founder Chairperson, Indian Council of Philosophical Research (ICPR) and Centre for Studies in Civilizations (CSC), New Delhi and President, National Council of Education, Bengal, Kolkata, writes a Foreword to the volume. Grateful thanks to him.

Professor Bhabani Prasad Bhattacharya, eminent Veda scholar, former Head, Department of Sanskrit, Jadavpur University and currently in the team of scholars engaged in the State Government's project at Sri Ramakrishna Institute of Culture of translating Veda and Vedic texts into Bengali, writes a Preamble to the work. This is a matter of deep gratification to me.

At the National Council of Education, Bengal, Sri Himendu Biswas, Professor Ramaprasad De, Professor Ananda Deb Mukherjee proved unfailing sources of support to the present work. Professor Madhabendranath Mitra went over the draft proposal, made comments and gave constructive suggestions. I remain indebted to all of them.

Dr. Maya Bhattacharya and Ms. Debi Rani Ghosh provided fresh inputs and extended help at every step. Dr. Sanjit Bhattacharya helped with Sanskrit texts and variant editions. Sri Amar Sapui composed and formatted the typescript. I offer grateful thanks to them.

My daughter Monita Chatterjee and her husband Shubhashish Kundu in the United States procured books and journals for me, assisted me (an old-timer used to the manual process) accessing archival material on-line and formatting the typescript. They gave me listening time, shared my explorations, offered criticism and advice. Somdev and Tamali Chatterjee had been my constant support; Somdev read through the work at different stages, came to share, helped in editing. Sri Tapan J. Chakravarti extended technological support. Srimati Anita Bhandary remained a supportive pillar of strength all along. Sri Rabin Chakrabarti, Sri Diptimoy Chanda, Sri Saurav Chanda helped in countless ways. They have all been drawn into my explorations, to my benefit. I stand obliged.

Hours of consultation with my former pupils, now senior college teachers, Indrani Choudhuri Dutt, Srimanti Chowdhuri, Parna Ghosh, Malobika Sarkar and Piku Chowdhury, are memories to cherish.

Sati Chatterjee

Contents

These ancient hymns represent the lowest stratum in the growth of the human mind which can be reached anywhere ...

The bridge of thoughts and sights that spans the whole history of the Aryan world has its first arch in the Veda, its last in Kant's Critique of Pure Reason .... *While in the Veda we may study the childhood, we may study in Kant's* Critique *the perfect manhood of the Aryan mind.*

... at present and for some time to come Sanskrit scholarship means discovery and conquest ...

Max Müller

Introduction

Katarāpurvā katarāparāyoh kathā
jāte kavayoh ko vi veda (Rig-veda I; 185:1)
कतरा पूर्वा कतरापरायोः कथा जाते कवयः को वि वेद।
(Who came first; who next? Oh sages and seers,
who is there who knows?)

Nāsad āsinna sadāsittadāning
nāsidrajo no vyomāparo yat (10; 129:1)
नासदासीन्नो सदासीत्तदानीं नासीद्रजो नो व्योमापरो यत् ।
(There was neither existence, nor non-existence then;
neither terrestrial dust nor the vast sky above.)

Asatosadajāyata (10; 72:2)
असतः सदजायत॥
(existence grew from non-existence)

Ekamsad viprāh bahudhābadanti (1; 164:46)
एकं सद्विप्रावहुधा वदन्ति।
(existence / reality / truth is one; sages call it by many names)

Do we hear in the questions and assertions cited above, as we had been taught to do by Western scholars in the mid-nineteenth century, the voice of man in his infancy? Is the primitive mind haunted by questions like these, does it glimpse truth in this form? Does the early infancy of human civilization speak in this idiom, does it question reality from these angles and project perception in this modality?

Max Müller stated in the Preface to the fourth volume of his *Rig-veda Sanhita with Sayana Bhasya* (1862) that the Rig-veda revealed "the lowest stratum" of the primitive human mind; in his autobiography he noted that the "oldest book that ever was composed", the Veda, preserved "a picture of what man was in his most primitive state"; in his 1882 Cambridge lecture "India, What Can it Teach Us?" he told his audience — would-be administrators preparing to sail for India — that the Vedic hymns recorded "the childish age of the human race", they "revived the recollections of the childhood which seemed to have vanished for ever". In his 1896 Oxford lecture on "Contributions to the Science of Mythology", he used the designation "infantia".[1]

This had been the basic perception in nineteenth-century Indology and this had been embedded in the culture history, the grand narrative, constructed during the colonial regime. The discourse of Comparative Mythology and Comparative Religion which Max Müller had formulated in his 1856 Oxford essay[2] and which, over the decades of the twentieth century, grew each into an enormous edifice, primarily stands on this idea of a linear growth in the story of man, growth from "infancy" to adulthood, from the primitive state to the modern.

The rhythm in the primitive mind's response to life, life with its enchanting pleasures and perilous hazards, is recorded in the twelve volumes (1890-1915) of *The Golden Bough,* a pioneering exploration by J.G. Frazer[3]. This response humans share at the instinctual level of survival strategies with all forms of animal life; it remains imprinted in the age-old lores

---

[1] *Rig-veda Sanhita with Sayana Bhasya* (1862), p. LXXX; *My Autobiography, a fragment*, 1901 (New Delhi, Asean Educational Service, 1993), p. 194; *India, What Can it Teach Us?* (London, Longmans, Green & Co. new edition, 1892), p. 109, p. 30; *Contributions to the Science of Mythology*, (Oxford, 1897), p. 72.

[2] *Essay on Comparative Mythology* (Edinburgh, Routledge and Sons, Ballantyne Press).

[3] London, Macmillan.

and rituals in different cultures and different climes. The pattern studied in the growing field of Comparative Religion and Comparative Mythology, suggests a mind floundering against the challenges: first, of physical survival, then of acquiring and wielding power, asserting dominance. Man striving to come to terms with the forces of the physical world and with the contending cravings in his own self for togetherness and for mastery, is a profile easy to recognize as the racial ancestry of modern man.

The voices recorded in the Rig-veda, however, speak of a different position, they speak in a different idiom. At one level they reflect the elemental, as all formal articulation does. At another level the metaphors the rishis use embody perception at deeper levels of awareness. The Veda utterances communicate mature self-reflexivity, abstractive pre-occupation with problems of existence man is still engaged with.

Are we then right in accepting the guidance of the nineteenth-century Western Indologists? Does the Rig-veda indeed record, as Max Müller assured us, the infancy that the adult civilized West had long left behind and lost sight of, the infancy that India in her cultural stagnation had preserved and, in the miasma of cultural-intellectual retardation, continued to cling to even in the heyday of "progress" in the mid-nineteenth century?

Again, must the remote past be threaded to the present in a single sequential order? Is the logic of the grand narrative compulsive? Might not the story of man, instead, be viewed as a spectacle of multiple growth-lines in different parts of the planet, reaching distinct peaks along divergent tracks at different points of time, meeting different destinies — of decline or death, of attenuated or vibrant continuity?

Questions like these started the present enquiry.

The study undertaken reveals a complex process of confrontation, interaction and interweaving of cross-cultural trends. Two different ways of relating to existence, two different modalities of self-perception, had met; and the consequent interaction had moved apace with the march of political history across two hemispheres.

The West's discovery of the mind of ancient India, synchronizes with the acquisition of an empire and effects a concurrence and convergence of distinct sets of interest: the cognitive and the imperial. Indology, the West's reading of the mind of the ancient land, constitutes an enunciatory site of colonial forces operative in the sphere of cultural expansion. The event demonstrates the constructive, shaping impact of the colonization experience on the colonized as well as the colonizer.

Studies in the fields of Comparative Religion and Comparative Mythology start with the nineteenth-century Orientalists' reading of the East. Max Müller's essay on Comparative Mythology had come out in 1856, Heinrich Zimmer studied the philosophy and the aesthetics of ancient India in the war-torn forties of the twentieth century and Joseph Campbell continued his elaborate exploration from the late forties to the late eighties[4]. This deep probing into the past proceeds under

---

[4] Heinrich R Zimmer (1890–1943), posthumous publications include *Myths and Symbols in Indian Art and Civilization* (Bolingen Paperback 1972), *The King and the Corpse: Tales of the Soul's Conquest of Evil* (Bolingen Foundation, 1948), *Philosophies of India* (Princeton University Press, 1952).

Joseph Campbell, *The Hero with a Thousand Faces* (Bolingen Foundation, Princeton Univ. Press), 1949; *Primitive Mythology* (Viking Penguin Inc.), 1959; *Oriental Mythology* (Viking Press, USA), 1962; *Occidental Mythology* (Viking Press USA), 1964; Creative Mythology (Viking Press, USA), 1968.

changing situations, responds to altering urgencies and takes on newer emphases; yet it basically follows the track of Occidental historiography and extends it in the emerging field of culture studies. The perspective had been defined from the Western point of view. The European and the non-European, the Hellenic and the non-Hellenic stand demarcated. The "subject" formulated by Foucault structures and shapes. "India" as Max Müller had assured fellow explorers, administrators and rulers of the time, "belongs to Europe".

II

After the long stretch of colonial rule, decades after the termination of the colonial regime as a political event, it is time to return to the questions posed in the beginning of the present study. The basic question — whether existing formulations in Indology claim indubitable authority— gains urgency as time moves forward. The twentieth century had faced challenges inconceivable in the nineteenth-century ambience of unshakeable confidence and certitude. The third millennium CE begins as an era of rejections, revisions, alterations; it is time to open up enclosures, move out of the "self-other" binary into a third space, perhaps of the "trans-National".

One area in which new findings challenge old assumptions on the level of ground reality, is archaeology. New excavations reveal untold stories in the history of man's progress on earth, call for a fresh look and new assessment.

New sites uncovered reveal earlier phases of Mayan civilization, excavations in sub-Saharan fields bring to light thriving centres of civilized existence like the cities named Kerma and Kush, satellite surveys trace the obliterated course of the mighty river mentioned in Rig-veda, the Saraswati, once running into the Arabian Sea. Water collected from the thin stream buried underneath desert sand, on chemical tests, we are told, date several thousand years back. Marine archaeology has detected man-made structures hidden in the Bay of Bengal and in the Arabian Sea near the Ranne of Kutch; relics and fossils on carbon dating have been found to relate back to the period after the end of the last Ice Age, around 8000 BC.

In 1991 investigations in marine archaeology conducted by the Indian National Institute of Oceanography under the leadership of S.R. Rao located a man-made structure 23 metres beneath the rolling waves of the Bay of Bengal offshore Tranquebar-Poompuhar coast of Tamilnadu. In 2000 Graham Hancock joined the NIO team to visit the remnants of the old lost city of Dwarka at the bottom of the Arabian Sea. Hancock explores sea-beds around the coastal contour of the landmass on the planet. Geologists work out that the landmass had been shorn of 5% of its span at the end of the last Ice Age, the "last Glacial Maximum". The "Holy Grail" in marine archaeology Hancock pursues is signature of lost civilizations in an antediluvian past. Hancock's recorded interviews with S. R. Rao, the marine archaeologist in NIO, delve deep into the past. Photographed pictures of submerged urban remains, supposedly 8000 years old, of artefacts and human remains recovered from them — from the Bay of Bengal off Poompuhar— presented in *Underworld: Flooded Kingdoms of the Ice Age* (*Penguin* 2002) and televised on BBC Channel Four, bring to our gage relics of forgotten time. All these indications, Hancock expects, would turn out to be the tip of an iceberg, the discovery of an earlier, forgotten phase of human civilization.[5]

[5] Referring to the discovery of the urban complexes deep under the waters of the Gulf of Cambay, Hancock notes, "More work must be done to establish the date exactly....Yet we know already by the very extent of the ruins, that they represent something that orthodox historians and

The excavation work started in 1974 under the leadership of J. F. Jarrige dug up pre-Harappan sites including Mehergarh; the work unearthed numerous sites spread out over about 200 hectares of land on the bank of the Bolan river in the Kachhi plain of Baluchistan. Findings in Mehergarh and other sites in this "Oxus-Indus intersection zone"[6] have brought to light a long stretch of agrarian civilization behind the Harappa-Mohenjo-daro pattern of existence. Dholavira, Kalibangan, Mehergarh, Banwali, Mitathal, Saraikhola etc. and classic Indus civilization sites (138 sites in the count published in 1984) indicate continuous occupation by communities in advanced stages of organized social life. The uninterrupted sequence of occupation layers here, extending to 7000 BC, pushes the chronology back by several millennia; civilizations in this part of the world now appear to be older than the Babylonian, Assyrian, Mesopotamian antiquity. Archaeologist D.K, Chakrabarti notes this "as a marked shift in the geographical focus of Indian archaeology"[7]. Hancock considers this a "historical breakthrough" and he quotes Gregory Possehl's comment that civilization studies before the

---

archaeologists have never accepted — the possibility that a lost civilization lies concealed in Indian pre-history. "*Underworld: Flooded Kingdoms* (Penguin 2002, imprint Michael Joseph), p. 677.

He winds up the volume with a "Stop Press" notice carrying a report released by the Indian Ministry of Science and Technology, a report that carbon dating of the artifacts recovered places these at a time "9500 years ago — 5000 years older than any city so far recognized by archaeologists", p. 677.

Hancock's is an experience of awesome thrill as he notes that "A city 9 kilo-metres in extent and more than 3000 years older than Harappa and Mohenjo-daro would re-write not only the history of the Indian subcontinent, but of the world." p. 306.

[6] D. K. Chakrabarti, *India, an Archaeological History* (New Delhi, OUP 1999), p. 119.

[7] Ibid., pp. 119-21.

excavation of the Mehergarh sites are now all amenable to radical revision.[8]

The Indian peninsula and the larger landmass including part of Baluchistan and Afganistan, the Oxus-Indus and the Saraswati-Indus regions are now perceived as the land of the oldest continuous growth of human civilization. Mehergarh displays remains of a pattern of life already in an advanced stage of agrarian culture; Gregory Possehl assumes earlier phases yet undiscovered. Mohenjo-daro and Harappa, thus, no longer count as relics of a pre-Vedic, non-Aryan civilization which had supposedly reached maturity between 2500 BC and 1900 BC, and had been subjugated and destroyed as a result of the "Aryan Invasion" sometime between 1500 and 1200 BC. The theory of the Aryan Invasion now faces significant challenges[9]. In the light of new discoveries the Harappan pattern of life appears to mark a phase in civilized existence spreading over several millennia in the Indus-Saraswati valley — the civilization which, with the drying up of the Saraswati under geo-climatic changes, moved eastward and came to be relocated in the Ganges-Jamuna valley. As closer kinship

[8] *Underworld: Flooded Kingdoms*. pp. 176-80.

[9] See: J.M. Kennoyer, *Ancient Cities of the Indus Valley civilization*, (American Institute of Pakistan Studies, Oxford, 1998), p. 38.

G.L.Possehl, in *Indus Age: the Beginnings* (University of Pennsylvania Press, 1999), p. 6, notes, "In the end there is no reason to believe today that there ever was an Aryan race that spoke Indo-European languages and was possessed of a coherent or well defined set of Aryan or Indo-European cultural features." Cited, Graham Hancock, *Underworld Flooded Kingdoms,* pp. 97-99.

See, David Frawley, *The Myth of Aryan Invasion* (New Delhi, Voice of India, 1994), *Rig Veda and the History of India* (New Delhi, Aditya Prakashan, 2001), Georg Feuerstein, S. Kak and D. Frawley, *In Search of the Cradle of Civilization* (USA 1995, Indian edn., Delhi, Motilal Banarasi Dass, 1999) p. 52ff.

comes to light between the yet un-deciphered Harappa script and the Brahmi Lipi, the script used in Asoka's inscriptions, Mehergarh—Mohenjo-daro—Mathura—Benares are in the process of being linked up in a continuous story of civilization indigenous to the land.[10]

Modern linguistics discount the validity of theoretical speculation about language development and proliferation in ancient times unless supported by archaeological evidence. The nineteenth-century theory of Indo-European language families and Proto-Indo-European roots, unrelated to material grounding, no longer enjoys ready acceptability.[11] Developments in genetics and micro-biological anthropology proceed eliminating old notions of the roots of ethnicity and narrow down the ancestry of humankind to a few DNA groups.[12] The idea of "race" has no genetic basis. The older divides between human groups recede.

The contour of Indian antiquity now, is significantly different from the one developed in nineteenth-century Orientalist discourse. Indian antiquity now emerges as the repository of a millennia-old account of human experience, human puzzlement, enquiry and understanding, a massive quantum, which alone perhaps can explain the articulations in the

---

[10] See, *The Cradle of Civilization*, p. 152ff.; S. P. Gupta, "Longer Chronology of the Indus-Saraswati Civilization", *Puratatva : Bulletin of the Indian Archaeological Society*, no. 23 (1992-93), pp. 21-29.

[11] Different models of speculation in this area are presented in *In Search of the Cradle of Civilization,* p. 55ff.
See, C. Renfrew, *Archaeology and Language: the Puzzle of Indo-European Origins* (Cambridge Univ. Press 1987); J.P. Mallory, *In Search of the Indo-Europeans: Language, Archaeology and Myth* (NY, Thames and Hudson, 1991); S. Piggott, *Pre-historic India* (Penguin Books, 1950).

[12] BBC Channel Four show, "The story of India, the beginning", displays part of its impact.

ancient texts in our hand. The old Veda texts now appear as precious harvest of a full-grown ancient civilization that had matured over thousands of years, assimilated the complex accents of physical existence, of mortal needs, along with dreams and aspirations, and had reached out towards transcendence in the realm of metaphysical and spiritual speculation.

The idea that the Aryans from outside, a horde of nomadic herdsmen in the primitive migratory stage seeking out better climates and greener pastures, competitive and aggressive in the struggle of existence, settled down to compose in the course of a couple of centuries the *Suktas,* the verses of the Rig-veda, is an assumption against the logic of cultural development. To argue that they composed the Rig-veda,"the epic of antiquity", and proceeded to work out the highly complex system of doxology in the Vedangas and reached the contemplative level in the Upanishads, is a premise in absurdity in the study of civilization. Extensive experience of living on the physical level, long tenure of existence on the material plane, slowly reaches into the domain of contemplation; existence extends itself, and only in that process gains the space for self-perception. Life lived to an adequate measure becomes the substance of reflections on life; the self is formed before it becomes self-reflexive. Aryans, a group of invaders, blonde and blue-eyed, light-skinned and sharp-nosed, on horse-drawn chariots, but only a group of nomadic plunderers, who were nowhere near the elevation illustrated in the relics of the earlier Indus civilization, cannot have been an exception to the tenor of the historical process; and they were not.

Bala Gangadhara Tilak noted this. Bankim Chandra Chatterjee and Sri Aurobindo noted this. Bankim Chandra in *Krishna*

Charitra (1886), engaged in complicated computations in terms of time measurements used in ancient discourse — related to the earth's rotation and the changes in the positioning of stars—and arrived at the conclusion that 1430 BC might be taken as the most acceptable date of the Mahabharata war. The Vedas, in that case, would be placed thousands of years earlier. In late nineteenth century Tilak in *Orion* (1893) placed the Rig-veda between 6000 and 4000 BC on the basis of astronomical calculations of stellar positions mentioned in the Veda text. In their own time and beyond, these could easily be pushed aside as over-zealous chauvinistic efforts at self-glorification. Bones rattling beneath waves of the seas, fossils below sand dunes, however, do not lie; these have a tell-tale validity of their own.

III

If archaeology calls for a re-writing of the early history of the land, the postcolonial proposal to glance back, to analyse and to understand the nature of the colonial experience on another plane calls for a close study of the situation in India.

Colonization is the historical experience of the majority of the world population—more than 75%, scholars assure[13]— having been at some point of time subjected to domination by a minority of less than 25%. In this long and chequered story of power assertion, the situation in India offers one of the most significant illustrative sites. To both major waves of colonization — from the Islamic "near East" ("near West"

---

13 Edward Said, *Orientalism* (Routledge & Kegan Paul 1978, New Delhi, Penguin Books India, 2001); Homi K. Bhabha, *The Location of Culture* (Routledge 1994, Second Indian Reprint 2009); Bill Ashcroft, Gareth Griffiths and Helen Tiffin, *The Empire Writes Back* (Routledge 1989, Indian Reprint 2005) among others.

viewed from India), and from the Christian West — India had been a territory with a legacy of ancient civilization. It had been a land inhabited by a human community bearing, albeit in an attenuated/decadent form, a millennia-old tradition, a tradition much older than that of the colonizer. In this part of the planet, more directly than anywhere else (and this is an aspect waiting for adequate critical attention) colonization had meant a major confrontation between cultures. The Islamic onslaught deserves separate consideration on the grounds that (a) it came from within the continent of Asia, or the region designated the East and (b) the incursion, proceeding through occupation, commingling and co-existence, led to inclusion in a broad sense. The modern chapter of the colonization of India refers to the advent of the West. "Post-colonial", the phase beginning in colonization, in the present context, would refer to the time period stretching from the European conquest of the land, through the British Raj, to date, covering the decades after August 1947.

Europe meeting India, it is good to remember, had started a process operating at two levels:

1) The level of material expansion—economic to political, trade expansion to the acquisition of an empire, and
2) The epistemic level— modern Europe coming to uncover and to encounter an "other" modality of existence, and of enquiry. The "other" had been a cultural identity of undecipherable antiquity — yet alive in the present, massive in measure and formidable in cognitive power.

The event was a true confrontation of two full grown cultures — an ancient one and a modern. The logic of material expansion prevailing, the logistic wherewithal amply provided by science and technology, imperial success surfaced the historical narrative; the epistemic encounter adding colours to the festival of triumph was shelved in the cloisters assigned to antiquarian interest.

If it remains there, even in times of flourishing postcolonial critique(s) — Ania Loomba in *Postcolonial Studies and Beyond* (2005) notes that while postcolonial critiques are "firmly entrenched in Anglo-US universities", "comparatively few scholars in places like India and South Africa ... see themselves as postcolonialists"—, the reasons mostly are:

1) Most of the lore is in a language which is ancient and unfamiliar.
2) The inheritors of the legacy themselves, thanks to the experience of colonial conditioning, are distanced from it.

Ngugi wa Thiongo talks of the colonization of the mind and the soul[14]; the process in the case of India had been complex and nuanced. Gayatri Chakravorty Spivak focuses on the implications of colonial conditioning, and she adopts the Freudian-Lacanian term, "fore-closure" to signify the impact on the colonized people. The process of conditioning, she reminds us, operates "embodying two complementary operations: 'the ...introduction into the subject, and the ... expulsion from the subject'. The Real is or carries the mark of that expulsion". She uses the term "native informant", which in ethnography, she tells us, stands "as a mark of that expulsion", "a blank, though generative of a text of cultural identity that only the West ... could inscribe."[15]

14 *Decolonising the Mind (1981; Bookland Publishing 2007).*

15 *A Critique of Postcolonial Reason* (Harvard Univ. Press 1999, Calcutta, Seagull Books, 1999), pp. 5-6.

The epistemic encounter enforcing the inner conditioning, had generated the discourse of Oriental scholarship, Indology an area-specific section. Discourse, as ever, functioned as an instrument of control. Indology grew into the West's inner dialogue with itself and also its public statement to the world, to future times. The public statement shaped the West's construct of cultural history, which steadily assumed encyclopaedic authority. Meanwhile the inner dialogue, the West's attempt at deciphering the 'other', coming to terms with it, witnessed contrary pulls: of pure intellection and of imperial interests. Colonization proved to be a shaping experience of inclusive range.

Ronald Inden in *Imagining India*[16] analyses the process through which the West effectively denied "agency" to the people of India. While the denial had worked as a political strategy at the surface level, it had been following complex courses at the deeper level of epistemic "intervention"/ "subjugation". At this deeper level it grew into a dual strategy of owning and disowning the strange, the non-self, the "other".

The theory of a proto-Indo-Aryan past, an account of shared origin and forgotten kinship, which William Jones had initiated and Max Müller had developed into the discipline of Comparative Philology, lent base support to the strategy of cognitive claim. Based on scattered instances of linguistic similarity and now generally pushed aside as a matter of speculation rather than decisive evidence, the idea of common linguistic ancestry had been a major discovery of revolutionary importance in its own time. It had been a gesture of self-assurance, self-persuasion and in course of time, a declaration purporting that the older civilization— substantial as it turned out to be — had once been part of a shared past. Kinship

[16] U.K. Blackwell 1990, Paperback 1992.

authorizes, endorses claims. "India for the future belongs to Europe.", Max Müller in the Cambridge lectures (1882) assured the West with the confidence of enormous erudition.[17]

But the corpus—the Vedas, the Upanishads, the Dharmashastras, the Buddhist texts—it all stood alien. The otherness of the other could be accommodated, safely placed, habilitated only in a temporal sequence ever flowing forward, toward adult phases in the story of Man. The story, it had to be told, moves towards maturity, leaving the past, the phase of infancy behind. The enlightened, rational West at the helm, the flow of time, the narrative spelt, had left behind the Indian way of life in isolated, land-locked stagnation, and to a miraculous destiny of preservation in the interest of the West. In the second half of the nineteenth century it all proved of enormous use for a better, fuller understanding of the West's own self. The detour, dexterously negotiated, was complete. A grand narrative was constructed in due course, enunciated in Encyclopaedic sites of new knowledge. The Empire stretched, shutting out sunsets.

Mircea Eliade in *Patterns of Comparative Religion* (1958) explains the gap between the modern Western temperament and the archaic; he enunciates the two modalities of experiencing the "sacred"—the iconic and the aniconic. This had indeed been a major stumbling block way back at the time the West had come to read the Rig-veda.

Culture relates to intellection as well as to faith; the ancient Rig-veda is an instance. In its literal sense it encodes modalities of a polytheistic nature worship, whereas in its symbolic signification it records reflections on human experience, on man's position in relation to the universe, his

---

17 *India, What Can It Teach Us?* p. 14.

dreams and aspirations – the inner response of the human mind at a much higher level of perception. The literal meaning endorsing ritualistic practice in its own time had played its role in generating and nurturing an ambience in which a sense of piety prevailed, the common man had been enabled to perceive patterns of symbiosis in the physical world and to relate to it in a wholesome manner. The sacramental vision had ensured respect for ecological stability too, while the symbolical message operated at higher levels of intellection-intuition. The total thought-structure in its dual signification thus could lend a support — ethical-intellectual/intuitive — to the entire community. The logic of it all, the logic that had evolved through many thousand years of human experience and wisdom born of experience, remained largely inaccessible to the Westerners.

In the effort at deciphering the ancient Veda text Western scholars had accepted the guidance of Sayana Acharya, Indian Veda exegetist of more recent past, the fourteenth century CE. Max Müller walked the same path, turning away from the rich field of linguistic studies and studies in hermeneutics in ancient India. The Westerners' selection of Sayana Bhasya as the representative native interpretation of the Rig-veda had been in total disregard of the position of Sayana Acharya in the long tradition of Veda studies in India. The razor-sharp analyses of multi-valence and obliquity or indirection in verbal signification, the perception of the inclusive range of multiple tiers of meaning in communication, the work of Yaska, of Panini, of the Sphota school, of Anandabardhana and Abhinava Gupta — all remained unheeded. The nineteenth century in the West, until the time of positivist thinking, had been a season of literalism, of trust in equivalence between idea and expression. Max Müller read in language the biography of nations; he engaged in two-dimensional cartography, leaving aside the intricacies of ancient linguistics in India. This long story Western scholars are just coming to appreciate and relate to in modernist and post-modernist linguistic pre-occupations today.[18]

Again, inheritors of a dualistic perspective, Christian and Cartesian, the Westerners failed to respond to and consequently missed the message of inclusive monism, the spirit of pervasive togetherness. The inner acts of "translation" required for empathically comprehending the unfamiliar proved difficult, remained mostly un-accomplished. The Western Vedicists could not truly enter into the conceptual world of the alien community. To the European scholars the Rig-veda was a string of cryptically formulated archaic incantations, riddle-like rhythmic accompaniment to primitive worship of the forces of nature – worship originating in fear of the uncontrollable and in the craving for the comforts of mortal life. The iconicity in the imagery of the text could be easily corroborated in the iconic modes of worship prevailing in the contemporary colonial scene; it all presented a system of heathen idolatry to the aniconic West. Sayana Acharya's ritualistic reading offered indigenous support to the literal interpretation. Rig-veda rescued by the Western scholars was taken as a curiously preserved record of polytheism, the fountainhead of a specific religion, Hinduism, alienated from the conquering Christian culture — even as it had been alienated from the earlier conquering force of Islam. Iconic Indian culture faced for the second time the antipathy of the Abrahamic tradition of revealed religion; cultural distance and incomprehension remained the brand of the colonial situation. Political powers deciding destinies, Christian colonizers

[18] See for instance, Harold G. Coward, *The Sphota Theory of Language* (Delhi, Motilal Banarasidass, 1980).

assumed the pious mission of converting the heathens to the one and the only true religion.

Europe facing ancient India in a situation of manifold alienation, presents an epic moment in the story of cultural confrontations. The import is much minimized in the constructed story of a discovery of the "infancy" of man — a retrospect, as it were.

Truly it happens to be a meeting of giant forces, both in full maturity: the adventurous, younger nineteenth-century Europe in full height of power, command and confidence; the earlier in time, the Indian culture, past its peak moment, long in political suppression and deep in decline, yet laden with the precious harvest of a millennia-old civilization, the oldest continuing civilization on the planet. It had been a meeting of two modalities, two idioms, two ways of relating to the universe. The conversation that started is not co-terminus with the event of political colonization. What one gains, or did gain, or may gain from the other is another story, an unending one in many folds. It is laden with messages from the depths of human experience — to be decoded in each phase, under the pressure of positionality.

IV

Of the dual strategy of disowning and owning the "other" perception, the first one: keeping the other apart, shouldering the task of civilizing it, bringing it up and the rest of the lore, effectively constructed and sustained the edifice of colonial administration. The second strand of strategy, the search for common origin, for forgotten ancestry and lost kinship, the strategy Max Müller had wrought to near perfection in his "historical" approach to religion and mythology, proves effective in another area. It comes to offer valuable help, offer a viable option, even a hundred years later when the West faces the challenge of an intellectual-cultural crisis, particularly in the post-World-War-II situation.

Max Müller's essay on "Comparative Mythology" had been published in 1856; the editor, A. Smythe Palmer, had felt convinced that the ideas initiated in the essay would generate new enquiries and shape out newer epistemic channels. The expectation proved prophetic. The essay became the genesis text introducing the comparative mode in the study of religion, mythology and culture. Mircea Eliade, about a hundred years later, with his commitment to the Christian faith, recommended widening acquaintance with the "archaic". Heinrich Zimmer in the early nineteen-forties and Joseph Campbell studying the making and re-making of the masks of God all his life, pleaded for a re-turn to the "antique" mode. A re-visit to the "infancy", if it had been one, in search of the relatedness missing in the world of Cartesian division and Christian duality, and world-war devastation, it seemed, held a promise.

The return, Zimmer knew and Campbell confirms, need not be a regression; God is not for borrowing, as Zimmer said. Renewing conversation with the other modality might help find a new way beyond prevailing binaries and oppositions. For Max Müller in 1856, there was the shade of the Indo-European, Proto-Indo-Aryan infancy. In the second half of the twentieth century Campbell recollects and reminds the world that in the beginning it had been a single tree in the garden where God walks in the cool of the day, a tree which later on in its growth had thrown up two branches: the tree of knowledge and the tree of eternal life, growing apart, one for the West, one for the East.[19] To recall the past before the split,

[19] *Oriental Mythology* (Penguin Books 1976), p. 9.

to harken to the pre- and the ante-, proves urgent from diverse points, in different situations.

The twentieth century advanced with a growing awareness of indeterminacy and instability. The War experience, Freudian psycho-analysis, Marxian philosophy of economic compulsions, findings in Quantum Physics, Wittgenstein's questioning of language and the logos, Derrida and his de-construction of the entire edifice — all had an unsettling effect on the Enlightenment legacy consolidated in an invincible confidence profile during the nineteenth century. Eliade, Jung, Zimmer, Campbell search for the missing hold of a spiritual anchorage, the factor of "soul", for the modern man. The counsel of turning to India and her ancient mind, the project of opening fresh dialogue with all that had been relegated to the category of the "archaic", broadly speaking, start here, in this need for a new redemption of the Occident. Max Müller to Campbell, the lineation and the lineament are the same. The West is the locus definitive, the rest, the other(s), are of use.

V

The post-colonial critique brings centre-stage the colonized three-fourths of humanity. However, as yet, as Homi K. Bhabha admits, the post-colonial, like the post-modernist, places the position in a beyond, in a post-situation, difficult to define, or to designate. Colonial strategies and constructs are analysed, laid threadbare; new alterities are yet to emerge.

Re-definition of course is not an easy process. As the authors of *In Search of the Cradle of Civilization* note,

> To lift the veil of the past, we must first lift the veil of our own minds. Our preconceptions tend to cloud our perceptions. We can see clearly only when we are willing to suspend our judgment as

> much as humanly possible and allow the evidence to speak for itself.[20]

Graham Hancock glances over the slow process of the West moving out of the Aryan Invasion account enshrined in the Encyclopaedias and handbooks of cultural history.[21] Habitual modalities grow roots reaching far and deep. Establishment is a powerful construct, and paradigm shift a formidable challenge. Again, disciplines of culture studies, area studies, carve out specializations which not only claim intellectual priority, but also enjoy high commodity value in the context of shifting global crises and conflict situations. Edward Said in *Orientalism* studies some of the constraints and sub-surface pulls.[22] Homi K. Bhabha in *The Location of Culture* looks deeper.

If the Western culture had been the conquering one at the functional level from the time of the expeditors to that of the imperial Crown, it continues as the dominant culture, endowed with the benefits of science and technology, the one modern, rational, scientific culture profile. The pattern of reading had been set by the makers of history—Hegel to Smith, to A.L. Basham, Indian historians fitting in between. Deviating attempts to re-read the ancient culture are fraught with risks. Such attempts face double misconstruction: one is the risk of being branded "reactionary" and, on that ground being pushed aside; the other is the risk of being hailed as a "nationalist" approach and being welcomed with unauthorized, misplaced and motivated gestures of gratulation.[23]

---

20 P. 4.

21 *Underworld Flooded Kingdoms*, pp. 102-105.

22 P. 10ff.

23 In the "Afterward to the 1995 Printing" of *Orientalism*, 18 years after the publication of the volume, Edward Said mentions experience of the kind. p. 331.

Yet, as India comes to be recognized as the land of the "oldest known continuing civilization on earth", one has to wake up to the need for re-appraisals. It is imperative to engage in a live process of re-defining and re-affirming the ancient tradition– relating it to the contemporary pattern of existence, its emerging sets of priorities and points of emphasis.

Unbroken continuity over millennia poses a challenge. Indian antiquity on Indian soil, we know, is not left behind. The Rig-veda is not among the defunct relics of a past dead and buried; it lives in the daily rituals performed by the Hindus, the largest religious community in India, the multi-faith subcontinent of the present day. The *homa*, the fire sacrifice Hindus perform in their *puja*, the ceremonial worship, begins with the chanting of *"Om Agnimide purohitam yajnasya devamritwijam* ....." (I worship the god Agni in the fore, the leading figure in the sacrifice ...), the first verse line in the Rig-veda. The Rig-veda, the Dharma Sutras and Sastras and the *Purohitadarpanam*, the priests' manual in use today, with elements of Tantra Sastra incorporated in it, are in a direct line of descent.[24]

Rootedness is a complex proposition. Roots knotted and gnarled, preserve strange vitality, hold secret powers of survival. They spread out at subsoil levels far and wide, preserve antique sap through hundreds of thousands of years, withstanding the rise and fall of empires, waves of cultural

---

[24] On the unbroken continuity Graham Hancock comments, "Unlike the cultures of ancient Egypt, Mesopotamia, China and the Americas, where only spectacular fossils of architecture and language remain, the culture of ancient India is still vibrantly alive today in the subcontinent and offers as its gift to the present a vast library of archaic ritual dances, games, ceremonies, festivals and customs as well as an immense oral literature... that is ... celebrated, rehearsed ... in thousands of Hindu villages from the Himalayas to the sea," *Underworld Flooded Kingdoms*, pp. 94-95.

re-orientations and upheavals in historical time. In the case of civilizations that grew, flourished and died — Sumer, Babylon, Mesopotamia, Egypt — it is a closed chapter; it all belongs to the lore of the past. With civilizations that survive, it is a fantastic story of continuity, of making and re-making, modalities of perception ceaselessly adjusting and re-adjusting to widening areas of human experience. They retain their relevance, resist forces of dysfunction — by virtue of the simple fact that they relate to the basic, the problematics of man's position in the universe.

"Tradition" is heritage; "tradition" is responsibility of a historical import too. While breaks in the history of human groups or communities are revolutionary, spectacular, continuity is a deeper running stream of vitality amenable to be channelized in the right directions. The term "right" of course denotes the positive, the significant — objectively perceived in each particular point of time. Relating and re-relating the past to the fabric of contemporary social existence, acknowledging the bond that arches over the antic and the modern, is a task which gains urgency in evolving a sense of perspective and defining a meaningful course of progress. A sense of history, as the traditionalist poet, T. S. Eliot tells us, alone can act as a de-personalizing–we might add, de-particularizing, de-essentializing—agent. This alone can effectively operate as an antidote to exclusivist orthodoxy, can truly historicize regional and ethnic and denominational specificities. De-particularization, of course, is a progressive process; historicization, as Foucault asserts, carries its own limitations in terms of dispassionate objectivity.

Reading the story of the human race in the account of one's ancestors, viewing the history of one's own group as part of the larger event of the march of man, is a major channel of liberalization, truly emancipatory in times of cultural exclusivity and growing dissension. R. Champakalakshmi and S. Gopal in their Introduction to *Tradition, Dissent and Ideology* note,

> At a time when traditions are misappropriated in a variety of ways, historical explorations into the making of traditions become urgent.[25]

Amartya Sen mentions the contribution that "reasoned assessments" can make to the "troubled world we live in."[26]

The idea of the "trans-Nation" as a position, the credo which in the 1990's, Bill Ashcroft tells us, freed the drive of "globalization" from its political-economic denominators and gave it, "a cultural turn"[27], basically aims at de-essentialization. The idea of the interpenetration of the global and the local described as the "transformation" of the global by the local, the idea of the circulation of the local in the global, the "flow" between the two, Ashcroft assures, grows on the "understanding of the complexities of imperial relationships."[28] In the present phase of post-colonial study, the idea of trans-nationality seeks to delete the "self-other" binary in a global engagement.

The trans-national position promotes de-essentialization; it promises to assist colonized population on earth to develop newer modes of self-reflexivity in which to transcend the impact of colonial conditioning, or "fore-closure". Joseph

---

25 Essays in honour of Romila Thapar, (New Delhi, OUP, 1996).

26 *The Argumentative Indian*, (Penguin Books, 2005), p. XV.

27 "Globalization, the Transnation and Utopia", Krishna Sen and Sudeshna Chakravarti (eds.), *Narrating the (Trans) Nation : The Dialectics of Culture and Identity* (Kolkata, Dasgupta & Co., 2008), p. 1.

28 Ibid., p. 2.

Campbell talks about "invisible players", counting India among them, in the drama of the growth of civilization — invisibility referring to the Westerners' gaze. An open-eyed, truly self-aware India could emerge as a visible player.

From pre-colonial, pre-modern phases India had been a home of trans-nationality. As Tagore celebrates in the language of emotive adulation, it had experienced the confluence of many identities. It has been, Bill Ashcroft appreciates, "the example *par excellence* of the excessive plenitude of the trans-nation."[29]

A growing sense of perspective, a deepening comprehension of the historical forces at play, could prove therapeutic in its remedial effect; it could dispel much of the crippling impact of colonial conditioning. India, fully aware of her load of experience, of her share of what Pierre Bourdieu designates "culture capital"[30], India, self-reflexive and articulate, could voice the past experience and the present perception in the case of the once-colonized.

That could initiate a counter discourse, not, as H.K. Bhabha cautions, as an "Occidentalism", but as an articulation of the so-far un-noticed point of view, the neglected modality, the un-heeded accent, to balance and, tentatively, to complete.

Not just "writing back", empires could find their voice, could begin to speak, among themselves, and to the world.

[29] Ibid., p. 13.

[30] See, *Distinction: A social Critique of the Judgment of Taste* (Harvard University Press, 1979).

One

The West meets India

The discovery of that new intellectual hemisphere is, to my mind, a far greater discovery than that of Vasco da Gama.

India for the future belongs to Europe.

Max Müller

From the cultural point of view, I do not think that we have much to fear now from the oriental influences. It is not unknown to us…. The real question in such matters is to digest. But that has always been… the great specialty of the European mind through the ages. Our role is therefore to maintain this power of choice, of universal comprehension, of the transformation of everything into our substance, powers which have made us what we are.

Paul Valery

Sir William Jones established the Asiatic Society in 1784. This played an important role in facilitating modern man's acquaintance with ancient India; and the giant effort of Max Müller starting in the 1840's, continuing over the entire second half of the nineteenth century, effectively uncovered the remote past. The West's earlier contacts with the East had been occasional and tentative in nature. William Jones and Max Müller started a process which shaped into a consistent movement. The time was ripe in terms of nineteenth-century intellectual liberalism, also in terms of imperial stakes. Western scholars discovered new territories, uncovered to the wondering world antique treasures wrapped in veneration, preserved over millennia with zealous piety and purist care in an obscure corner of the planet.

We might, for a moment, glance over known facts of history. The West's incursion into the subcontinent, of much earlier dates, primarily pursuant to commercial expansion, naturally had taken time establishing a paramount power centre and shaping a definitive cultural profile in the Orient. The construction of imperial modules in the East, we know, had been a slow process. Again, the West's contact with ancient India, India of the Vedic times, did call for an effort at reaching backward, across centuries. Europeans arrived at the end of a period during which another culture, the Islamic, had been in dominance on the land. The trade contacts since the 1500's made by commercial syndicates with the royal permission and patronage, from Portugal, Holland, France, England, had been with the Mahommedan rulers of the time.[1] The political authority the Western trade companies interacted with was in the hands of Islamic rulers. Sir Thomas Roe at the court of Emperor Jehangir, Sir Thomas Child in conflict with Aurangjeb, the Company seeking from Sultan Shuja *formans* granting lease of land in the eastern province of Bengal — all were engrossed in trade facilities and regional control, engaged in strategic games of persuasion with Muslim rulers. For the Westerners it was Islamic power to manipulate and geo-potential to exploit. The

[1] The British merchants collected into a Company and obtained royal permission to trade with India for 15 years from Queen Elizabeth I; they tried it out with insignificant success, while it was Sir Thomas Roe, royal ambassador from James I, who obtained from the Mughal emperor formans in the second decade of the next century — by 1618. See, for instance, R.C. Majumdar, *An Advanced History of India* (Delhi, Macmillan 4th edition, 1978), pp. 628-29.

Vedas and the Upanishads and the Vedic India lay far behind and beyond.

Quelling rival European powers, the most formidable and persistent of them, the French, took another hundred years. The battle of Plassey (1757) marked a decisive point in the process of repressing native resistance and bringing to a close the pre-European phase in India. Sir William Jones arrived as puisne judge, Supreme Court of Bengal, in March, 1783. On 15 January 1784 he established the Asiatic Society and opened to the West doors to the antique lores. This unveiled to the European powers another domain, a domain lost far behind the prevailing situation, the world of "pre-history", to discover, to conquer, to appropriate, to take over.

The event caused a cultural turbulence of tremendous implications. Its surface signification was eloquently acknowledged, while much of the deeper meaning came to constitute a sub-surface with unobtrusive yet compulsive dicta. The Judeo-Christian tradition, with the pre-Christian Greco-Roman as a bed-rock beneath, had acquired a synonymity with human civilization; it now confronted waves of thought and experience stored in a modality alien, essentially different from, the West's rational discursive mode. The Enlightenment legacy, as Gayatri Chakravorty Spivak[2] notes, processed through Hegel and Kant (and later on Marx), had grown into "*the episteme*". This intellectual identity, joined to the praxis of aggression and annexation, had been leading the West in its stride from shore to shore, from conquest to conquest, establishing colonies, building invincible empires — geo-extensive as well as cultural-epistemic.

---

[2] *A Critique of Post-Colonial Reason,* pp. 110-11.

How to relate to the unfamiliar, unexpected phenomenon of the thoughts of ancient India? How to accommodate it in the West's crusade against primitive heathenism, against ignorance and unreason, against all the dark forces combined in the dense miasma supposed to engulf the befuddled east? The situation in India, Edward Said notes, was distinct from the West's encounter with the "near East", easier to recognize within Judeo-Christian parameters.[3] Vedic India was a distant locus.

The need was to appropriate the variant, the "other", which in this instance, claimed the venerability of a hoary past and unexpected levels of perceptual maturity. The need was to claim it within the orbit of the dominant discourse.

The colonizing effort involves negotiating and re-negotiating the colonizer's identity. The need of the moment under consideration, as Chakravorty Spivak notes, had been to develop the narrative, a "grand narrative" indeed, of the "proto-archetypal identity"[4], the idea of an assured Euro-centric origin, a seed-bed of civilization. In 1786 William Jones published *The Sanscrit Language,* tracing common roots of Greek, Latin and Sanskrit, in a "proto-Indo-European" ancestry of languages. After spending decades in the mammoth effort of editing the Rig-veda Sanhita, Max Müller in the Cambridge Lectures of 1882 on "India, What Can it Teach Us?" assured the West,

---

3 *Orientalism*, pp. 57-58; also see: Chakravorty Spivak, *A Critique of Post-Colonial Reason*, p. 8ff.; Bill Ashcroft, Gareth, Griffiths and Helen Tiffin, *The Empire Writes Back*, p. 155ff.

4 *A Critique of Post-Colonial Reason*, p. 8. Chakravorty Spivak appreciates the role of the "meticulous scholarship" of German origin in establishing "the vocabulary" of this ancestral bonding in the "nascent discourses of comparative philology, comparative religion, even comparative literature".

> India is not, as you may imagine, a distant, strange or, at the very utmost, a curious country. India for the future belongs to Europe. It has its place in the Indo-European world, it has its place in our own history, and in what is the very life of history, the history of the human mind.[5]

The common origin, it was argued, had generated outflows. Some of these streams, those spreading into the East and the South, it was assumed, had taken on exotic accents under different climatic conditions, as a result of mixing with indigenous elements, getting into a land-locked position of close insularity, sinking into a rut over hundreds and hundreds of years. The kinship newly discovered promised to be of enormous importance. In the Preface to the third volume of the Rig-veda Sanhita (1856) Max Müller said,

> the study of Sanscrit owes its permanent interest chiefly to the fact that the ancient language of India had been proved to be most intimately connected with the classical languages of Europe and that in it has been found the key to the most secret archives of the history of language in general. The Veda would never have engaged the serious attention of a large class of scholars if this ancient literary relic had not been found to shed the most unexpected light on the darkest periods in the history of the most prominent nations of antiquity.[6]

William Jones's observation of similarities among languages, strongly supported and elaborated in Max Müller's study of language as an index to human civilization, gave rise to the science of comparative philology, which promoted the idea of a common cultural ancestry with wide branchings out.[7] Thus grew the grand narrative, shaping a schema widely

[5] New edition, (London, Longmans Green & Co. 1892), p. 14.

[6] P. V.

[7] The difference Chakravorty Spivak notes between German scholarship and the British, engaged in establishing "the vocabulary of proto-archetypal identity, or kinship (*Post Colonial Reason*, p. 8) deserves separate attention.

accepted, a schema equipped to grapple with the challenge of confrontations in the West's imperial journey ahead.

The formidable construct of the "history of ancient times", or the "the pre-history of civilization", as it came to be designated, easily acquired acceptability as it suited the interest of Occidental supremacy. The Orientalist construction of the "history" of the eastern part of the planet indeed best illustrates Foucault's perceptual determinative at work. History is as the perceiver observes the process. Chakravorty Spivak explores archival material, notes among the base accounts varied impressions recorded by stray young army officers of the East India Company roaming on horseback through the unfamiliar terrain; she appreciates how the "effect", the impression, built up the image —

> It is possible to say that this was the construction of a fiction whose task was to produce a whole collection of "effects of the real" and that the "misreadings" of this "fiction" produced the proper name India.[8]

Gradually, yet steadily, the construct thus assembled, attained textbook infallibility, the narrative came to be incorporated into handbooks, school texts on world history, encyclopaedias of diverse dimensions.

---

[8] *A Critique of Post-Colonial Reason*, p. 8ff.
Neeladri Bhattacharya in "Remaking Custom : the Discourse and Practice of Colonial Codification" narrates the illustrative process of preparing more formal accounts, the "ethnographic texts", which "reveal as much, or rather a bit less, about Indian custom as about the official observers — their minds the conventions of their language, the assumptions implicit in their questions and their conclusions" *Tradition, Dissent and Ideology* (New Delhi, OUP 1996), p. 21. Mrinal Pande in "The Ghadar of 1857: Native Narratives" (Surendra Paul Lecture 2014), presents the "native view" of the mutiny experience recorded in oral recitals close to the soil in Maharashtra, in Awadh. *Bulletin*, February 2016, Ramakrishna Mission Institute of Culture, Calcutta.

What facilitated the process of epistemic prevalence, Chakravorty Spivak calls it "changeover of the episteme", was the fact that scholarship on the native soil of India at that point of time had been on the decline. Since the early days of Yaska and the Vedangas[9], Vedic scholarship had remained engaged in specialized, exclusive, close textual studies. The focus had been on the linguistic, phonetic, semantic and grammatical subtleties and the nuances they introduce, on the distinctive specialities of the numerous recensions of the Veda texts and their multiple exfoliations. The entire engagement remained insular to an ancient tradition which, after the early days of wider trade relations, had been keeping to itself, not venturing out, not imposing on others, hence little known in the outside world. Stray translations and adaptations of texts in Persian during the Turko-Moghul centuries, like Dara Shuko's adaptation of the Isopanishad, for instance, travelled not beyond the continent of Asia.

Again, by the time the Europeans came to discover and to conquer, India had largely lost contact with its own past[10], had mostly fallen off from the peak of her early achievement. On the one hand these parts of the ancient world, sunken into a form of insular inbreeding, had remained cut off from the outer world, particularly from the modern West; on the other, largely under the effect of relocation under geo-climatic

---

[9] The six Vedangas were : grammar (*vyakaranam*), metrics (*chandas*), phonetics (*siksha*), etymology (*nirukta*), intentionality (*kalpa*) and astronomy (*jyotisha*).

[10] Max Müller recollects how in the 1840's when Western Vedicists planned publication of the Rig-veda for the modern world they wanted to know if the work could be done on native soil, the report was that Vedic scholarship had so much declined in Bengal, that "there were no Brahmans there who knew whole of the Rig-veda by heart" and that it was not feasible to undertake the task there. *My Autobiography, A fragment*, p. 193. Of this later on, in Appendix B.

changes, the community had moved away from its habitat in the flourishing phase of its own history and had been sinking into exclusivist rigour of ritualistic paraphernalia. Mehergarh, the Saraswati valley, the ports of Lothal and Dholavira, had all receded into oblivion. There had been a long stretch of ritualistic rigour, of Sastric orthodoxy and priestcraft, a phase of decadent shrinkage.

The stretch of Islamic domination had slowly come to breed a sense of insecurity and complex sets of inhibitions and exclusivist orthodoxy; it further contributed to the state of self-exile. The ancient Indian culture, enfeebled through the phase of political instability after the Gupta era, had been effectively pushed into the position of the colonized subject during the centuries of Islamic rule, into the "interstitial position" Homi K. Bhabha studies in *The Location of Culture.*

II

European scholars started a rescue operation excavating a past which the inheritors of the tradition themselves had left far behind. "Orientalism"assumed the prestigious importance of an archaeological discipline delving into the past of the conquered people for their own benefit as well as for the benefit of the conquering West. The discovery of the past, in terms of cultural-linguistic family kinship newly formulated, promised to reveal invaluable truths about the infancy of the human race in general and, most importantly, of the races inhabiting modern Europe.

The long stretch of the Vedic age in India had generated and developed a rich tradition of Veda exegesis in an idiom alien to the early European scholars. The vast literature known as the Vedangas, the Yaska phase of exegesis close to the Veda texts and to the Veda style of existence, not entirely unknown to scholars like Max Müller who occasionally refer to these, were in general too specialized, too intricate, too remote to the Western researchers. To them the convenient commentary on the Vedas was Sayana Acharya's *Bhasyas*, exegesis composed in much nearer times, thirteenth and fourteenth centuries CE. These presented a simpler reading. Also, the Sayana interpretation better fitted into the Occidental pattern of response. Working under the pressure of his own time[11], Sayana had interpreted the Vedas mostly at the literal level, holding the ancient texts as close as possible to the ritualistic practice prevailing in his own time. To the Western scholars this interpretation, in more accessible Sanskrit, actually presented a profile closer to the picture around on the soil of the colony, a picture of abject impoverishment in more than one sense — a profile easier to recognize. Sayana's interpretation, presenting a thought-pattern elemental, primitive and simplistic, fitted into the emerging picture in the Western perception, a picture of the infancy of human civilization. The state of infancy, the Occident came to believe, had been in a state of retardation in this part of the world, outside of the culture ambit of the adult civilized West.

Conveniently enough, supportive endorsement could be derived from other factors. There were the Dharma Sastras, the corpus of social edicts, which, composed in much earlier times, in times of rising orthodoxy — the Vedic culture then in decadence – recorded ritualistic preoccupation. These texts had been edited and explicated with renewed interest around Sayana's own time. Madhavacharya, brother of Sayana, for instance, had been engaged on royal commission of the Bukka monarch in the 14th century CE, to bring out

[11] Of this later on, in Chapter 4 in the present discourse.

annotated edition of the Parasara Smriti; he effectively applied his enormous erudition to project a rigid ritualistic emphasis, more rigid than in the Sastra itself, almost an uncompromising orthodoxy. The Dharma Sastras by Manu, Parasara and others, interpreted with orthodox zeal by commentators like Madhava and Sayana, defined the do's and the do-not's in everyday life—the emphasis invariably on ritualistic details, propitiatory aspirations and conformist rigour. Sayana, the younger brother of Madhava, interpreting the Veda text, deliberately opted for a ritualistic reading; and the Veda in his reading simply prescribed how to perform the sacrifices to appease the elemental powers in Nature and seek protection in the perilous journey of life. It prescribed ways to pray for prosperity in the form of expanding families, growing herds of cattle and bumper crops.

The absence of written historical documentation had been a big obstacle; the dynamics of historical growth in the ancient period remained obscure to the Westerners. This encouraged in Indology discourse the denial of growth/change in "ancient" times in the East, keeping the entire segment, as Hegel had advised in the case of Africa[12], outside of history. To the nineteenth-century Western scholars centuries outside of chronicled history could easily collapse and the time gap between the Veda texts and Sayana's Bhasyas[13] did not mean much.

To the young administrative personnel of the East India Company whose reports provided substantial basis for the construction of the image of India, the spectacle around, the daily life of the people they had been sent to rule,

---

[12] Cited, *The Empire Writes Back,* 157.

[13] Max Müller occasionally mentions the gap, but does not take serious note of it.

demonstrated a live continuation of the primitive tradition. The swarming population, dark-skinned, ill-clad, impoverished, steeped in superstitions, engaged in alien modes of worship of idols in diverse shapes and poses, yoked to unquestioning allegiance to a powerful priestocracy, the humid heat, the torrential monsoon rains, the dust and grime of the tropical region—it all presented at the geo-cultural level, a primitive profile of humanity left behind. All this, as Edward Said mentions, had presented a show of the "obvious decrepitude and political impotence of the modern Oriental."[14] Elaborate regalia and its gaudy splendour provided examples of exploitative autocracy. Western scholars discovered an archaic module and engaged in the historical venture of deciphering a section of the "oriental" mode — stagnating, almost frozen, persisting over millennia.

Ritualism in this pattern of life from the time of the Vedas to the arrival of the Europeans came to constitute in the interpretive discourse of Comparative Mythology of later

---

[14] *Orientalism,* p. 79. Max Müller in a Westminster lecture (December 3, 1873) noted, "it is true there are millions of children, women and men in India who fall down before the stone image of Vishnu, with his four arms, riding on a creature half bird, half man, or sleeping on the serpent; who worship Siva, a monster with three eyes, riding naked on bull with a necklace of skulls for his ornament. ... Nay, it is true that in the broad daylight of the nineteenth century, the figure of the goddess Kali is carried through the streets of her own city, Calcutta, her wild dishevelled hair reaching to her feet, with a necklace of human heads, her tongue protruded from her mouth, her girdle stained with blood. All this is true; but ask any Hindu who can read and write and think, whether these are the gods he believes in, and he will smile at your credulity. How long this living death of national religion in India may last, no one can tell; for our purposes, however, for gaining an idea of the issue of the great religious struggle of the future, that religion too is dead and gone."

See, Nirad C Chaudhuri, *Scholar Extraordinary*, pp. 304-05.

times, in the studies by Jung, Mircea Eliade, Joseph Campbell et al, a major instance of the "archaic" mode of existence, the repetitive, cyclic, non-linear experience of time, contrasted with the linear, the progressive, the modern, scientific perception. Thus grew the myth of the "a-historical" and the "historical" as cultural binaries. History constituting the major cognitive category in the Enlightenment discourse, the non-European was simply kept out of the historical ambit; with Hegel's Africa it all remained "outside history". India, Ronald Inden notes, could be "kept eternally ancient."[15]

To the Westerner's bewilderment confronting the alien mode of life and thought was added the compulsive need to shorten the time-span of the archaic, particularly when, as in the case of India, it happened not to be dead, but preserved a live continuity with the contemporary. As Rene Guenon noted in 1945, it had to be ensured that no civilized past extended behind the magic moment of the genesis locus of the Greek way of living :

> Because their own civilization hardly goes any further back than the Greco-Roman period and derives for the most part from it, Westerners are led to believe that it must have been the same in every other case and they have difficulty in conceiving of the existence of entirely different and far more ancient civilizations; it might be said that they are mentally incapable of crossing the Mediterranian.[16]

III

The period of consolidation of British power in India, extending over a century after the battle of Plassey (1757) to

---

15 *Imagining India*, p. 1.

16 *Introduction to the Study of Hindu Doctrines* (London, Luzac, 1945), p. 38. See, also, Bankim Chandra Chatterjee, "Krishna Charitra" (1886-1892), *Rachanavali* II, (Calcutta, Sahitya Samsad, 1977), pp. 409-10.

the formal annexation of the territory bringing it under the Crown (1858), had been the germinal period of the Orientalist discourse known as Indology. This period, we know, witnessed complex interactions of social-political-cultural forces both in England and in India. History is a composite of movements in diverse directions; crucial times of transition often record histories of antithetical aspirations.

The success of the British against the Nawab in the battle of Plassey facilitated the process of slow but steady acquisition of power in the hands of the East India Company. This process started with gaining command of larger trade facilities and steadily extended to the assertion of governmental authority over the region of operation. The 1764 war against Mir Kashim, at the level of immediate objective, was for preferential privilege claimed by the British trade company – the privilege of trading in Bengal without paying transit dues. After the battle it was arranged that the Deputy Shubhadar of the region would henceforth be nominated by the British – the control over the administration thus passing into the hands of the British trade company. Robert Clive through a clever treaty obtained a *forman* from the enfeebled Emperor, Shah Alam (1765), a *forman* which granted to the East India Company the *Dewani* of Bengal, Bihar and Orissa. The scheme of trade expansion continued to be fortified by acquisition of administrative control. This scheme, which in Edmund Burke's phrasing began with commerce and ended in empire, proved enormously effective.[17] The trade establishment offered martial assistance to native rulers and ruling dynasties endemically involved in in-fighting, in the north and in the south, in the east and in the west. The

17 Elizabeth D. Samet, "A Prosecutor and a Gentleman: Edmund Burke's idiom of impeachment", ELH 68, no. 2 (2001), p. 402.

Company formed political alliances, signed treaties friendly to their own trade interest, and in the process spread out its tentacles over the entire subcontinent. Eventually, plainly following the logic of the expansionist desire of the hour, the traders laid the basis of the vast empire.

Throughout the period the 1750's to the 1840's the East India Company spread out over the Indian peninsula, gaining control , with varying degrees of visibility. The protracted effort at bringing to subjugation the Marhattas, the Sikhs, the Rajputs, the decades of conflict with the rulers of Oudh, Benares, Mysore and, subsequently, the battles of annexation of Burma and Assam in the east, of Afganistan and the North-Western frontier region, pursued not so much the liberal ideas expounded at the time in the Parliamentary discourse in London, but an emergent aspiration of imperial control over vast territories, outshining rival European powers. The victory against Napoleon's forces a confidence booster, England had emerged as a power to reckon with, a power posed for newer conquests, geo-political as well as cultural-epistemic. The antithetical aspirations mentioned above worked in many ways. Pro-people political ethics and a developed sense of justice were in co-existence with colonial expansionism. Colonization shaped the colonizer. Sir Henry Maine in his Rede Lecture on "the Effects of Observation of India on Modern European thought" (Cambridge 1875), made the comment,

> As has been truly said, the British rulers of India are like men bound to keep time in two longitudes at once. Nevertheless, the paradoxical position must be accepted in the most extra-ordinary experiment, the British Government of India, the virtually despotic government of a dependency by a free people.[18]

[18] Cited, Bhabha, *Location*, p. 184.

Way back in 1784 the House of Commons had resolved that

> To pursue schemes of conquest and extension of dominion in India is contrary to the wish, the honour, and policy of the British nation.[19]

Not approving the expansionist policies of Lord Cornwallis and Lord Wellesley, the Court of Directors, East India Company had reiterated the resolve :

> The territories which we have lately acquired ... are of so vast and extensive a nature that we cannot take a view of our situation without being seriously impressed with the wisdom and necessity of that solemn declaration of the legislature.[20]

Yet, history records the switching over to the path of aggressive annexation in the case of several executive personalities sent by the East India Company as Governors-General to India. These had been the administrators but for whose succumbing to the pragmatics of domination on the soil of the colony, the building of the Indian Empire would have been at the least, a much slower process.

The Marquess of Hastings, appointed Governor-General, arrived convinced of the wisdom in the policy of peace and non-aggression. He himself mentioned in retrospect that in his original plan of action

> There had not been the expectation or the wish of adding a rood to the dominions of the Honourable Company.[21]

---

[19] History records that discomfiture in some of the ventures had aroused strong public opinion against expansionist designs; Pitt had strongly condemned and Welleslie had resigned. See, for instance, R. C Majumder, *Advanced History of India*, p. 698.

[20] Sir Edwin Arnold, *The Marquis of Dalhousie's administration of British India,* (London), cited, R.C. Majumder, *History and Culture of the Indian People*, (Mumbai, Bharatiya Vidya Bhawan, 2002), Vol. ix, p. 11.

[21] Cited, Ibid., p. 12. G. D. Oswell, *Sketches of Rulers of India*, Vol. III, pp. 92-93.

A few years in India, the administrator Hastings turned to expansionist strategies which he now came to explain and defend to himself, and to posterity, as it were, in his personal diary,

> Our object ought to be to render the British Government paramount in effect, if not declaredly so. We should hold the other States as vassals, in substance though not in name; not precisely as they stood in the Moghul Government, but possessed of perfect internal sovereignty, and only bound to repay the guarantee and protection of their possessions by the British Government with the pledge of the two great feudal duties. First, they should support it with all their forces on any call. Secondly they should submit their mutual differences to the head of the confederacy, without attacking each other's territories.

The Governor-General noted how he had been carefully keeping the annexationist agenda at a low key, aiming at a smooth shifting of control from the native rulers to the British authority:

> I have endeavoured to improve the juncture by courteous and conciliatory language to the native Powers; and I do hope I may remove considerable soreness.[22]

Historian R. C. Majumder narrates how successors to the Marquess, Lord Ellenborough, Sir Henry Hardinge, Lord Dalhousie, followed the same path. Each had come as a liberal-minded administrator committed to the no-aggression policy; on the soil of the colony, each got involved in bloody wars, even in shady deals[23] in the race of acquisition of

---

[22] Cited, Ibid., pp. 10-11. The *Private Journal of the Marquess* of Hastings, pp. 30-31.

[23] In his *Private Journal* the Marquess of Hastings candidly noted, "In our treaties with them we recognize them as independent sovereigns. Then we send a Resident to their courts. Instead of acting in the

authority. The "mutiny" of 1857, had behind it regional gestures of resistance in earlier years, even as it anticipated, in a sense initiated, the gesture of revolt, the movement to get away from the "enlightened" grip of the colonizer.

The impact of the event and the threat potential did not go under-rated; the trade corporation was dissolved and the empire was formally "annexed" and brought under direct control of the British Crown.

With India under the direct rule of the British monarch, England attained a position to celebrate victory in its prolonged combative rivalry with other European powers. The annexation took the nineteenth-century success story to new heights, it marked a moment of crowning glory in the wake of the industrial revolution. In a larger context it was a moment of the West engaging itself in the East more extensively and more deeply than ever before.

2.

History indeed records the simultaneous operation of different trends. The opposition and the divergence might later be seen to resolve at some deeper level of a hidden historical compulsion, hidden even to those through whom the forces operate. On the surface, at the level of chronological contemporaneity, the opposition and the divergence are

---

character of ambassadors, he assumes the functions of a dictator; interferes in all their private concerns, countenances refractory subjects against them; and makes the most ostentatious exhibition of this exercise of authority. To secure to himself the support of our Government, he urges some interest which, under the colour thrown upon it by him, is strenuously taken up by our Council; and the Government identifies itself with the resident not only on the single point but on the whole tenor of his conduct." *Private Journal*, pp. 26-27, cited ibid, p. 12ff.

startling in the intensity each unfolds. The decades of imperial expansion, of bitter wars of aggression fought on the Indian soil, we noted, happened to be the decades during which the West came so close to the East, and the ventures of Orientalist scholarship, of studies in Indology, were undertaken with great zeal, on a competitive eagerness shared with other metropoles in Europe. These new cognitive ventures, in Max Müller's favourite metaphor, marked a new "renaissance" in the expanding cognitive sphere.

Earlier efforts at deciphering the ancient lore in Sanskrit texts were all dwarfed in the face of the phenomenal growth of "orientalist" studies, studies in the culture of ancient India under the patronage of the East India Company in its final phase, the 1840's onward, and the intellectual leadership of Max Müller in Oxford. The publication of the first volume of the *Rig-veda Sanhita with Sayana Bhasya* in 1849, a feat of triumphant pioneership in itself[24], marked a significant step towards opening up several major fields of enquiry: Comparative Philology, Comparative Mythology, Comparative Religion.

The growth of Comparative Philology was an academic event of radical importance in the nineteenth century. Scholars note how William Jones's papers researching family kinship between different languages and Max Müller's eloquent pleadings for an expansion of Orientalist studies and the study of languages as the biography of different groups of people, had a liberating effect on the scholastic world. It marked a significant departure from the older idea that Hebrew "was the matrix of all languages".[25] Max Müller in

[24] See, Max Müller, *My Autobiography* on the competitive zeal among European powers in the matter.

[25] Said, *Orientalism*, p. 22ff; *In search of the cradle*, pp. 48-49.

the Introduction to *The Science of Religion*, four lectures given at the Royal Institute, February and May 1870, noted,

> The introduction of Greek into the universities of Europe in the fifteenth century could hardly have caused a greater revolution than the discovery of Sanskrit and the study of Comparative Philology in the nineteenth.....A few hundred years ago, the idea that Hebrew was the original language of mankind was accepted as a matter of course, even as a matter of faith ...[26]

The discovery of the Orient had changed it all. It had generated new knowledge in more than one field and, as the German scholar never tired pointing out, the cognitive conquest had inaugurated another "renaissance" in the history of cultural-epistemic expansion.

IV

In India the nineteenth century was the age of a new awakening, and this too had been a complex event recording trends and counter-trends, gestures and counter-gestures. Colonization conditions the colonizer; it affects the colonized at much deeper levels. The "fore-closure", Chakravorty Spivak tells us, is the experience in which the external onslaught operates as a force that enters the consciousness of the target group, the colonized people, brings about alterations, and leaves traces behind—traces that persist in the colonized natives, the newly constructed "native informant", ever after, beyond the termination point of the political event.

True, the orthodox schools of thought in India in the nineteenth century tried to preserve themselves in traditional grooves, but the "awakening" itself, here too designated a

[26] Indian reprint, Bharat Manisha (Varanasi, India,1972), p. 3; p. 10.

"renaissance" in the eastern part of India, generated opposite trends. Exposure to new learning was extended through educational institutions working at many levels and in increasing numbers. This introduced new disciplines, new modules, new paradigms in the domain of intellectual enquiry, even as the West's interest in India's ancient past quickened in the mind of the "enlightened" Indians a new awareness of the abiding worth of their own cultural heritage. The recognition by modern Europe was highly appreciated, hailed with deep gratification, after the stretch of colonial subjugation under Islam. Thus proceeded the parallel growth of contrary trends: that of Westernization, Indians welcoming — much as Macaulay had wished — the legacy of European Enlightenment, and a growing sense of culture identity, now presented as something valued and important in the history of the human race. The process at work played a dual role: on the one hand it transformed the character of the colonized, de-nationalized them, made the original native a "lost object" and shaped the colonial construct of the "native informant"[27]; and, on the other, it bred a new sense of Indian value which gradually would prove of germinal importance to the growth of a sense of national identity in India.[28]

---

[27] Chakravorty Spivak, *Postcolonial Reason*, pp. 5-6. Ngugi wa Thiongo analysing the process in his volume on de-colonizing the mind, speaks of the moulding impact of English education.

[28] Nirad C Chaudhuri cites part of a letter by Max Müller to the Duke of Argyll, Secretary of States for India 1868:
"India can never be Anglicized, but it can be reinvigorated. By encouraging a study of their own ancient literature, as part of their education, a national feeling of pride and self-respect will be re-awakened among those who influence large masses of the people. A new national literature may spring up, impregnated with Western ideas, yet retaining its native spirit and character." *Scholar Extraordinary*, p. 199.

The two impulses blending together in one of the strange alchemies wrought by cultural interpenetration in history, would lead to hybridization of sorts, even as eventually it would go a long way toward shaping the "freedom movement" on the subcontinent.[29]

That of course would be a faraway prospect. In the immediate context, to the British rulers, promoting English education in India had been a pragmatic need, a need for establishing better control over the subject people; to the Indians, the educated progressive sections, it was welcome as a liberating force. English education was perceived as a gateway to the modern world.[30] Decades before the arrival of Macaulay on the scene, the ground had been prepared for effective implementation of a new system of education, a system which would yield different sets of benefit to the different stakeholders. To the colonized natives it would open entry into the enlightened world of Western culture; for the

---

[29] Bhabha comments on this : "The absurd extravagance of Macaulay's 'Minute' ... deeply influenced by Charles Grant's 'Observations' — makes a mockery of Oriental learning until faced with the challenge of conceiving of a 'reformed' colonial subject."
He adds, "At the intersection of European learning and colonial power, Macaulay can conceive of nothing other than 'a class of interpreters...'" who would be a group of 'mimic man' produced "through our English School, as a missionary educationist wrote in 1819." *Location,* p. 125.

[30] Gauri Viswanathan analyses the compulsions behind the valorization of the study of English literature in the colonial situation— "The beginnings of English literary study in British India", *Oxford Literary Review*, 9, nos. 1 & 2. The attitudinal difference in the response to Western influences of the Muslims, directly and immediately dispossessed by the British, and the Hindus, striving to get out of a century-old Muslim domination, constitutes an area yet to be adequately studied.

ruling power, Max Müller never tired of emphasizing the point, it would facilitate closer communication with the subject people and ensure easier allegiance of the ruled.

In the eastern part of the land, in Calcutta where the headquarters of the East India Company was then situated, the Calcutta School Book Society and the Hindu College had been established in 1817 mostly under Indian initiative.[31] The Calcutta School Society was formed in 1818 with Raja Radhakanta Dev as the Indian Secretary jointly to work with David Hare. Raja Rammohan Roy voiced the growing aspiration of the progressive "native" community when he pleaded with the British governors in favour of Western education. In his letter to Lord Amherst, 11 December 1823, Rammohan placed before the Governor General in Council the expectation and the need of the people of India,

> When this Seminary of learning was proposed, we understood that the Government in England had ordered a considerable sum of money to be annually devoted to the instruction of its Indian Subjects. We were filled with sanguine hopes, that this sum would be laid out in employing European Gentlemen of talents and education, to instruct the Natives of India, in Mathematics, Natural Philosophy, Chemistry, Anatomy and other useful Sciences which the Nations of Europe have carried to a degree of perfection, that have raised them above the inhabitants of the other parts of the world.
>
> While we looked forward with pleasing hopes to the dawn of knowledge thus promised to the rising generation, our hearts

[31] R. C. Majumder cites Alexander Duff's comment in his article on the "State of Education In Bengal and Bihar" (*Calcutta Review* 1844) : "The excitement for Western education continued unabated. They pursued us along the streets; they threw open the doors of our palankeens; they poured in their supplications with a pitiful earnestness of countenance which might have softened a heart of stone." *British Paramountcy and Indian Renaissance,* part II (2007), p. 33.

> were filled with mingled feelings of delight and gratitude; we already offered up thanks to Providence, for inspiring the most generous and enlightened of the Nations of the West with the glorious ambition of planting in Asia, the Arts and Sciences of modern Europe.

The British rulers' intention of establishing a "Sanskrit School under Hindu Pandits", instead, had come as a disappointment — as learners in such an institution would go on cultivating only "what was known "two thousand years ago" and gain nothing new. Studying the Sanskrit grammar or the speculations in Vedanta, efforts at strengthening the base of Sanskrit education, Rammohan felt, would simply keep the country "in darkness". There could be no doubt on the need for modern disciplines in educating the Indians, the Raja reiterated,

> But as the improvement of the native Population is the object of the Government, it will consequently promote a more liberal and enlightened system of instruction embracing Mathematics, Natural Philosophy, Chemistry and Anatomy with other useful sciences which may be accomplished with the Sum proposed by employing a few Gentlemen of talents and learning educated in Europe and providing a College furnished with the necessary Books, instruments and other apparatus.[32]

By the 1830's the spread of Western education had come to be widely appreciated; the Bengali periodical *Sambad Kaumudi* in its 7 August, 1830 issue noted,

---

[32] D. K. Biswas (ed), the *Correspondence of Raja Rammohan Roy*, vol. I (Calcutta, Saraswat Library, 1992), pp. 191-95.
Reginald Heber, Lord Bishop of Calcutta, to whom Rammohan had sent the letter with a request to place it "before the Right Hon'ble the Governor General in Council", found it a surprising document, noting in his *Journal* that "for its good English, good sense, and forcible arguments", the letter was "a real curiosity as coming from an Asiatic". Ibid., pp. 196-97.

> It is true that formerly, i.e., both during Hindu and Muslim rule, there was cultivation of learning in this country, but the organisation for the spread of useful knowledge among the people in general, such as we find during the British rule, was unknown before. There is as wide a difference between the old and present state of things in this respect as between heaven and the nether world. The number of students in Calcutta and its suburbs alone exceeds ten thousand and the provision of cheap text books for their use is a sure means of spreading this education.

The forties and the fifties of the nineteenth century witnessed the spread of English education along paths more clearly perceived both by the givers and the takers. When in 1853 Isvarchandra Vidyasagar pressed for reform measures to update and invigorate the Sanskrit College, he included the request for re-introducing a separate section for teaching English to the learners. In his letter to the Secretary, Council of Education, Isvarchandra assured,

> Leave me to teach Sanskrit for the leading purpose of thoroughly mastering the vernacular and let me super-add to it the acquisition of sound knowledge through the medium of the English and you may rest assured that before a few years are over I shall be enabled, if supported and encouraged by the Council, to furnish you with a body of young men who will be better qualified by their writings and teaching to disseminate widely among the people sound information than it has hitherto been possible to accomplish through the instrumentality of the educated classes of any of your Colleges whether English or Oriental.[33]

Proposing revised curriculum in his "Notes on the Sanskrit College" (12 April 1852) Isvarchandra had argued in favour of a liberal spirit of enquiry; he had noted,

---

[33] Cited, Indramitra, *Karunasagar Vidyasagar* (Kolkata, Ananda Publishers, second edn. 1992), p. 14.

> True it is that most part of the Hindu system of Philosophy do not tally with the advanced ideas of modern times, yet it is undeniable that to a good Sanskrit scholar their knowledge is absolutely required. By the time that the students come to the Darshana and Philosophy class their acquirements in English will enable them to study the modern Philosophy of Europe.

Again, in a letter (7 September 1853) to Dr Mouat, Secretary, Council of education, he wrote,

> That Vedanta and Sankhya are false systems of Philosophy is no more a matter of dispute. ... Whilst teaching these in the Sanskrit course we should oppose them by sound Philosophy in the English course to counter-act their influence.[34]

The events and the trends obviously were being viewed from different angles. The Christian missionaries considered English education an effective means for conversion of Indian natives to Christianity. Macaulay, claiming "no knowledge of Sanskrit or Arabic", could confidently note in his 1835 minute on education in India that

> A single shelf of a good European library was worth the whole native literature of India and Arabia.

Famously he aimed at forming through English education "a class of persons, Indian in blood and colour, but English in tastes, in opinions, and in morals and in intellect".

Educated Indians, the modernizers, the reformers, the educators, pleaded for wider spread of English education, welcomed ampler exposure to the Western thoughts and culture which to them promised an entry to the modern enlightened world. A collaborative venture was shaped; the spread of the new system, promoting essentially opposing interests, proceeded along its destined path.

---

[34] Cited, Manik Mukhopadhyay (ed.), *The Golden Book of Vidyasagar* (Calcutta 1993), pp. 70-71.

Intellectuals, theorists and administrators on the rulers' side, had their doubts about the possible impact of the Westernization of the natives in India and they debated. M. Trevelyan hoped that the spread of education would bridge the gap between the rulers and the ruled, it would better reconcile the subjects to the rule of a superior culture. In 1853 in his statement before the Select Committee of the House of Commons, he commented,

> Familiarly acquainted with us by means of our literature the Indian youth almost cease to regard us as foreigners....As long as the natives are left to brood over their former independence, their sole specific for improving their condition is the immediate and total expulsion of the English....It is only by the infusion of European ideas that a new direction can be given to national views. The young men brought up in our seminaries turn with contempt from the barbarous despotism under which their ancestors groaned to the prospect of improving their national institutions on the English model.[35]

Statesmen with political foresight looked further beyond; Macaulay knew, as he spelt it out in his speech in the House of Commons,

> having become instructed in European language they (Indians) may, in some future age, demand European institutions.

Imbued with the colonizer's spirit of transforming the colonized, at that point he extended unhesitating rhetorical welcome to such notional eventuality. "Whenever it comes, it will be the proudest day in English history", he assured.

The white man's burden had been shouldered. Major-General Lionel Smith, an administrator at a more pragmatic level, had warned the Select Committee that Western education would

[35] Cited, R.C. Majumder, *British Paramountcy*, vol. II, p. 37.

make the natives "feel the value of governing themselves", and that the effect "will be to turn us out".[36] That, however, would be a slow growth, not a smooth one at that. The moment seemed fraught with uncertain possibilities. In a letter July, 1899 Lord Curzon communicated his observations to Max Müller,

> There is no doubt that a sort of quasi-religious, quasi-metaphysical ferment is going on in India, strongly conservative and even reactionary in its general tendency. The ancient philosophies are being re-exploited, and their modern scribes and professors are increasing in number and fame.
>
> What is to come out of this strange amalgam of superstition, transcendentalism, mental exaltation, and intellectual obscurity–with European ideas thrown as an outside ingredient into the crucible–who can say?[37]

In the meanwhile the ruling power, with a few exceptional administrators — as Warren Hastings had been— preferring to rule India, as far as practicable, in terms of its own laws and customs, mainly demonstrated the Macaulay brand of discriminatory attitude. It was a ruthless imperialistic determination to liquidate the cultural identity of the colonized, and to bring them under control. This was the process of what Chakravorty Spivak describes as "the epistemic violence of the worlding of worlds", the typical white man's self-gratulatory zeal for civilizing the non-white on the planet operative all the way.

The debased spectacle of life of the times, the oppression of the lower "castes" in the society and of women, lack of education, firm grip of superstitions, the vested interests of cunning priests and calculating land-holders, poverty and the

---

[36] Ibid., p. 37.

[37] Cited, *Scholar Extraordinary*, p. 302.

destitution of the masses — all these presented to the British rulers the illustrative instance of a land of barbarous savagery. It was a condition which called for a civilized administration and rule of the law. Vigorous, near total, engagement was indicated.

Administrators were deputed to organize the sprawling territory into an ordered kingdom, to give it good "governance", the model inevitably the Western one, and to make good use of this gold mine of inexhaustible yield, the brightest jewel in the British crown. Young officers of the East India Company reported back the dismal spectacle around. Competent white rulers, the Governors and the Governors-General, sent reports recommending measures to impose firmer hold on the colony. Effective strategies were planned with theorists like Mill, Macaulay, Max Müller as counsellors, wise and endowed with foresight. Macaulay wrote his minute in 1835; in 1868 Max Müller wrote to the Duke of Argyll , newly appointed Secretary of State for India,

> India has been conquered once, but India must be conquered again, and that second conquest should be a conquest by education. Much has been done for education of late, but if the funds were tripled and quadrupled, that would hardly be enough.[38]

In 1909 Lord Curzon argued in favour of opening a School of Oriental Studies in England on the ground that

> our familiarity, not merely with the languages of the people of the East but with their customs, their feelings, their traditions, their history and religion, our capacity to understand what may be called the genius of the East, is the sole basis upon which we are likely to be able to maintain in the future the position we have won.[39]

---

[38] Cited, Ibid., p. 199.

[39] Cited, Said, *Orientalism*, p. 214.

Five years later he commented that the founding of a School with this intention was a great obligation,

> In my view the creation of a school like this in London is part of the necessary furniture in Europe.[40]

V

The realm of territorial expansion, the pragmatics of "conquest", pragmatics related to "empire", "territory", provided recurring metaphors in the Orientalist discourse. Max Müller presenting his Cambridge Lectures (December 1882) published as *India, What Can it Teach Us* wrote a dedicatory epistle to E.B. Cowell, "Professor of Sanskrit and Fellow of the Corpus Christie College in the University of Cambridge". In this letter he made ample use of these metaphors:

> You know that at present and for some time to come Sanskrit scholarship means discovery and conquest ... you know also how small a strip has yet been explored of the vast continent of Sanskrit literature, and how much still remains *terra incognita.* ... If some of the young candidates for the Indian Civil Service...if a few of them at least determined to follow in the footsteps of Sir William Jones, and show to the world that Englishmen who have been able to achieve by pluck, by perseverance, and by real political genius the material conquest of India, do not mean to leave the laurels of its intellectual conquest entirely to other countries, then I shall indeed rejoice.

Conquest and conquest, the epistemic domination supports the imperial; the territorial empire and an empire of the mind stand in an alliance of mutual support, sustenance, even of redemption.

---

40 Ibid.

Over decades Max Müller made untiring effort at impressing upon the British Parliament the need for the expansion of Oriental Studies. In all this effort he readily, and of course, strategically foregrounded in his arguments the interest of the Empire. After the Mutiny of 1857 the scholar published a letter in *The Times* (30 December 1857) bearing the caption: "On the Neglect of the study of the Indian Languages as a cause of the Indian Rebellion".

Remedial measures were taken. Administrators arriving from England began learning regional languages in schools established for this purpose, even as natives of the soil were given opportunities of Western schooling. Education proved the most effective channel of cultural infiltration on both sides.

The Asiatic Society operated as a research centre of invaluable importance and it also proved a major source of inside information deriving from closer interaction with the alien community.[41] Chakravorty Spivak focuses on the role of the research centre in "taxonomisimg Sanskrit and thinking alterity of language/culture" and mentions the immense work undertaken by scholars like Arthur Macdonnell and Arthur Berriedale Keith, both administrators and "organizers of the matter of Sanskrit". The impact of it all, she notes, was authoritative,

> From their confident utilitarian – hegemonic plans for students and scholars of Sanskrit, it is impossible to guess at either the aggressive repression of Sanskrit in the general educational framework, or the increasing 'feudalization' of the performative use of Sanskrit in the everyday life of the Brahmanical-hegemonic India. A version of history was gradually established

[41] See, Amalendu De, *Introduction to the Early Correspondence of the Asiatic Society*, (Calcutta, The Asiatic Society, 2003), p. 6.

> in which the Brahmin was shown to have the same intention toward the Hindu code as the codifying British.[42]

Adventures of the mind, encounters in the field of the intellect, worked as global events of historical importance, even as better communication at the pragmatic level served the immediate interest of owning and enjoying an empire. The "owning" adventure, both territorial and cultural, provided the inclusive framework of a total experience of appropriation.

An ambience was thus prepared in which the West provided the perspective and the homology in terms of which enlightened Indians would view themselves and the world. Max Müller felt satisfied that his edition of the Rig-veda would render a great service to the Indians themselves. In 1864 he wrote to his wife,

> I feel convinced, though I shall not live to see, that this edition of mine and the translation of the Veda will hereafter tell to a great extent on the fate of India and on the growth of millions of souls in that country. It is the root of their religion, and to show what that root is, is, I feel sure, the only way of uprooting all that has sprung from it during the last 3,000 years.[43]

Edward Said's famous comment reads,

> What the Europeans took from the classical Oriental past was a vision (and thousands of facts and artefacts) which only he could employ to the best of advantage, to the modern Oriental he gave facilitation and amelioration – and, too, the benefit of his judgment as to what was best for the Orient.[44]

Episteme change-over makes the native see himself as the West sees, as the "other".

---

[42] *Postcolonial Reason*, pp. 229-30.

[43] Cited, *Scholar Extra-ordinary*, p. 92.

[44] *Orientalism*, p. 79.

A few dissenting voices in the late nineteenth century and the early twentieth, voices like those of Bala Gangadhara Tilak, Bankimchandra Chatterjee, Dayananda Saraswati, Sri Aurobindo, tried to make themselves heard. Without immediately entering into the question whether the native colonial ever survives the colonization experience and can assume a critical voice[45], it is to be noted that these dissenting voices, themselves definitely bearing the impress of a westernizing education and cultural hybridization, in their own time could easily be dubbed as effervescence of patriotic self-glorification, chauvinistic distortion of facts.

Reason worked and reality resided as and where the colonizer wished and descried. Cognitive conquest intertwined with territorial-hegemonic expansion and built up an invincible power-structure. The Sovereign in Buckingham Palace reigned over the empire across the oceans, an expanse over which the sun never set.

[45] Arthur Philips talks about cultural subservience, "cultural cringe", under colonial domination; Ashcroft, Griffiths & Tiffin expect subsequent emergence of an indigenous sense of identity. *The Empire Writes Back*, pp. 11-12.

Two

The mission of a life — Max Müller and his effort

The Rig-veda is the most ancient book of the Aryan world. Every hymn, every verse, every word, that can be deciphered in it is a gain.

I had either to collate my own copy, which was very tedious, or invent some new process. This new process I discovered by using transparent paper, and thus tracing every letter. ... this had the great advantage that nothing was left out. ... it was even less fatiguing to the eyes than the constant looking from the MSS. to the copy, and from the copy to the MSS.

Ten years of my life are gone, and I know not whether I shall have sufficient time left to finish a work which once I undertook perhaps with too much confidence.

Max Müller

In the third lecture delivered at Cambridge University in 1882 on what India can teach the West, Max Müller noted,

> It was a real misfortune that Sanskrit literature became first known to the learned public in Europe through specimens belonging to the second, or, what I called the Renaissance period.[1]

By an irony of history, the scholar regretted, the West's meeting with the mind of India did not start from the beginning with the Vedas, but with the products of a much later period.

[1] London, Longmans, Green & Co., New edition, 1892, p. 90.

Much earlier, in 1651 Abraham Roger had translated Bhartrihari into Dutch. As Governor General of India Warren Hastings had a digest on the Indian legal authorities including Dharma Sastra texts prepared by Brahmin Pandits; these texts were first translated in Persian, then in English; Hastings had them published in 1776. Charles Wilkins, trained in Benares under the initiative of Warren Hastings, translated the Bhagavadgita – "The Song of the Adorable One" — in 1785 and the Hitopadesha— "Friendly Advice"— in 1787. The Asiatic Society was established in 1784 and William Jones's translations of Sanskrit texts, mostly of the "classical period", we know, came out between 1789 and 1792.

While the West was savouring these and such other texts of the later phases in the history of Sanskrit literature, the Rig-veda, the earliest text in ancient India, the oldest "book" in human history, remained a faraway signal. In his auto-biography Max Müller recollects,

> The name of Veda had no doubt been known and there was a halo of mystery about it, as the oldest book of the world. But what it was and where it was to be found no one could tell.[2]

Henry Thomas Colebrook's *Essays on the Veda*, first published in the *Asiatic Researches* in 1801, came out in 1805; Frederick Rosen's edition of the first eighth (*astaka*) of the Rig-veda in 1838. Eugene Barnouf in Paris preparing his lectures on the Veda could rely only on these early works.

Interest in the Upanishads had been aroused earlier; the transcendental metaphysic probably had gained easy access to the mind of Europe then responding to the Romantic impulse[3]. In the first Gifford Lecture at the University of

---

[2] *Autobiography*, p. 191.

[3] See, *The Scholar Extra-ordinary*, p. 123ff.

Glasgow (1888) Max Müller had glanced back to his years before leaving Germany and recorded his early contact with Schelling for whom he had translated some of the Upanishads, and his meeting with Schopenhauer, who found in the Upanishads the solace of his life and solace of his death, while the Vedas and the rest of the Vedic texts, in his estimate, were mere matter of priest-craft.[4]

The Rig-veda remained a distant name until, in the 1840's, the persevering explorations by Sanskritic scholars like Colebrook, Wilson, Bunsen began to attract scholars in England, Italy, Germany, France, Russia. The nineteenth-century spirit of expansion, triumphant annexation of the far-away and the hitherto unexplored, reached out to the Orient and its secrets. Max Müller recounts the keen interest in the Veda MSS in Paris at that time and at St. Petersburg. The growing interest had almost generated a competitive eagerness for first publishing an edition of the Rigveda with its native interpretation, the commentary by Sayana Acharya. To the young German scholar, Max Müller tells us, it had been a moment of critical choice when the reputed Sanskritist, Boethlink at the Imperial Russian Academy invited him to come over to St. Petersburg and join him in the work of bringing out the first complete edition of the Rig-veda. The proposal was for young Max Müller to bring all his work over to St. Petersburg where, taking on loan the Rig-veda MSS from the East India Company Library in London, they would do the work — the Imperial Academy financing the project.[5]

---

[4] *Natural Religion* (London, NY, 1889, Longmans Green & Co.), p. 18.

[5] On the unobtrusive hegemonic design operative at the time in the management of Sanskritic studies see, Gayatri Chakravorty Spivak, *A Critique of Postcolonial Reason*, pp. 229-230.

That young Max Müller's efforts ultimately ensured what Nirad C Chowdhuri mentions as the "primacy of England in Sanskritic studies in the Western world", had been the result of a conjunction of several external forces at the moment.

Barnouf and Goldstucker had cautioned the young scholar from Germany against trustful surrender to Boethlink at St. Petersburg, and, as no stable official assignment was forthcoming, the young scholar with scanty financial resources stayed on in Paris – as he had been advised by mentor Barnouf[6]. He came to London to copy and collate certain MSS at the library of the East India Company; and the arrival in London decided it all. Here, Max Müller tells us in his autobiography, he "found the long-sought-for benefactors who were to enable (him) to carry out the work of (his) life".[7] The benefactors included H. W. Wilson, Baron Bunsen, Prussian Minister and a Sanskritist interested in editing the Rig-veda. They were eminent specialists and their recommendation persuaded the Board of Directors of the East India Company.[8] In the first Gifford Lecture 1888 already mentioned, more than four decades after the crucial point of the decision, Max Müller glanced back to this time of uncertainty and un-foretold coincidences,

> However, encouraged and helped by Barnouf, I persevered, and when I was ready to begin the printing of the first volume, I came to England, as I thought, for a few weeks only, to collate some MSS. at the East India House in Leaden Hall Street, and to make the acquaintance of Professor Wilson, at the time the Nestor of real Sanskrit scholars in Europe.

---

[6] Boethlink, Max Müller reminisces, "seems never to have forgiven me, and he and several of his friends were highly displeased at my ultimate success in securing a publisher for the Rig-veda in England". *Autobiography*, p. 183.

[7] Pp. 183-84.

[8] *Autobiography*, pp. 201-02.

> New clouds, however, were then gathering on my horizon. The Imperial Academy of St. Petersburg, even at that time deeply interested in Indian literature, had voted large funds for bringing out an edition of the Rig-veda with Sayana's commentary, and had asked the East India Company for the loan of those very MSS. which I had come to London to copy and collate.... All my plans seemed thus to collapse ....Suffice it to say that .... the Directors of the late East India Company thought it unfair that the MSS. of the Rig-veda should be sent to the Imperial Academy at St. Petersburg at the very time when I had come to London to make use of them; and that, on the recommendation of my old friend, Professor Wilson, the East India Company entrusted me with the publication of the Rig-veda at their expense.[9]

The recommendations must have carried all the weight of the new scholarship in Indology and powerfully pressed the need for its expansion. A better understanding of the culture of the colonized, a deeper interaction with the "Indian subjects", must have presented a persuasive logic. It convinced the Directors of the merchant body who agreed to make a generous grant for printing "an old book" which, the scholar notes, "none of them could understand and many of them had perhaps never even heard of".

Max Müller gratefully mentions Professor Wilson's recommendation of the project, in the Preface to the first volume of his Rig-veda 1849 and, with the gratitude of a life's mission on its way to fulfilment, cites the decision taken by the Board of Directors which reads,

> The Court consider that the publication of so important and interesting a work to which your proposals refer, is in a peculiar manner deserving of the patronage of the East-India-Company, connected as it is with the early religion, history, and language of the great body of their Indian subjects.

---

[9] *Natural Religion*, pp. 19-20.

Thus began the process of the publication of the ancient Indian text for the benefit of the rulers of the "Indian subjects", for the modern West, and, as Max Müller felt, also for the benefit of the Indians of the time and of time to come.

II

Scholars like Bankim Chandra Chatterjee and Sri Aurobindo in colonial India had noted and scholars in the post-colonial era, since Edward Said, note, that in the sphere of Orientalist scholarship Euro-centrism had been operative as a collective drive. Postcolonial studies point out how it had acted as a desire and a will in the West's encounter with the East and in its triumphant conquests, how it had been a conviction shared among European countries on the un-spelt yet firmly assumed basis of a sense of intellectual supremacy of one hemisphere over the other.

The contribution of individual scholars, we note, proved a factor of enormous importance. Dedicated scholars shouldered the work of intense exploration, and interpretive presentation. Orientalist discourse grew through a close inter-weaving of the collective spirit of Occidental superiority, the imperialist ideology, and deep personal commitment on the part of eminent intellectuals. Personal commitment, persevering untiring labour of enthusiastic Sanskritist scholars, built up the discipline of Indology — research in a field where ancient texts speak in another tongue. To readers today, the mammoth quantum of reading and annotating, the labour of "editing" the ancient texts with the help of the modern critical apparatus, the concentrated intellective application by the Western scholars in the face of all hazards, unfolds the spectacle of an amazing feat. In retrospect, the engrossed attention of an individual scholar like Max Müller in this lifelong engagement, appears to rival nothing short of the life-hazarding endeavours of explorers of earlier times, their archetypes portrayed, for instance, in the novels of Conrad. The explorers, committed, dedicated, unsparing, had proceeded along their paths, almost, as they felt, destined for them. The acquisitive thirst at the level of imperial expansion had inspired them as a missionary zeal.

In Max Müller's recollection of the toiling time spent in deciphering the ancient texts of India, we perceive the instance of a near-complete immersion of the individual intellect in the collective endeavour. The editing of the two texts, the Rig-veda and the copious commentary by Sayana, had been a mammoth effort against odds beyond recount. It had been an effort which the deepest commitment, not merely to the work in hand, but to a cause much larger, could inspire. A cause of broadening the ken of human knowledge, of redefining the history of human civilization — as Max Müller kept explaining in his lectures and Prefaces all his life — alone could have sustained it. It illustrates how the Enlightenment inheritance of intellectual domination had almost come to constitute a new kind of religious fervour, loaded with a sense of the historically inevitable — at times almost on the verge of the occult.

Max Müller tells us how even in the early years in Germany, he had grown instinctively aware of the importance of the Veda as the source of, the bedrock beneath, the Upanishadic ideas then much appreciated all around. In the first Gifford Lecture he narrates,

> I soon came to see, however, that these Upanishads were only the latest outcome of Vedic literature, and that in order to know their antecedents, in order to be able to appreciate the historical

> growth of the Indian mind during the Vedic age, we must study the ancient hymns of the Veda. I remember having a most interesting discussion on the relative importance of the Vedic hymns and the Upanishads with Schopenhauer at Frankfort. He considered that the Upanishads were the only portion of the Veda which deserved our study, and that all the rest was priestly rubbish.[10]

In Paris Eugene Barnouf had given a decisive direction and put the searcher on the track. Barnouf's advice was clear and categorical; Max Müller recollects:

> I never can adequately express my debt of gratitude to him. He was of the greatest assistance to me in clearing my thoughts and directing them into one channel. "Either one thing or the other", he said. "Either study Indian philosophy and begin with the Upanishads and Sankara's commentary, or study Indian religion and keep to the Rig-veda, and copy the hymns and Sayana's commentary, and then you will be our great benefactor."[11]

And the commentary of Sayana, the mentor had insisted, must be presented in full:

> "Don't publish extracts from the commentary only", he said; "if you do, you will publish what is easy to read, and leave out what is difficult." I certainly thought that extracts would be sufficient, but I soon found out that here also Barnouf was right.[12]

The enormous labour the effort entailed was truly baffling. In times when the manual process was the only way of copying MSS, the very attempt at copying out the Sanskrit MSS and preparing a full text for his own study and editorial application, presented insurmountable difficulties. The young scholar struggled on with inevitable mistakes and, he records in the *Autobiography*, how he had improvised:

---

[10] Ibid., p. 18.

[11] *Autobiography*, p. 178.

[12] Ibid., p. 179.

> I had either to collate my own copy, which was very tedious, or invent some new process. This new process I discovered by using transparent paper and thus tracing every letter. I had certain excellent *papier vegetal* made for me, and instead of copying, traced the whole Sanskrit MS. ... At first, I confess my work was slow, but soon it went as copying and it was even less fatiguing to the eyes than the constant looking from the MS. to the copy and from the copy to the MS. But the most important advantage was, that I could thus feel quite certain that nothing was left out, so that even now, after more than fifty years, these tracings are as useful to me as the MS. itself.[13]

The meticulous care of years, working out and explaining the ancient scheme in an alien culture, had been a great achievement. To keep plodding through the *pada-patha* and the *samhita-patha*, the *pratisakhyas*, the many recensions, the texts of grammar and rhetoric and lexical exegeses mentioned in the Sayana commentary, presenting it all in the critical edition of the first volume in 1849 — it had been an amazing feat of colossal scholarly effort and a spirit of dedication, an event for all time to wonder at.

III

In the Preface to the first volume of his *Rig-veda with Sayana Bhasya* Max Müller states the objective with which he had embarked on the venture. The aim had been to give "a correct text of the Rig-veda and to restore from the MSS. a readable and authentic text of Sayana's commentary." He had assigned to himself an enormous task, much more daunting, as he did gradually come to realise, than he knew at the beginning. Glancing back to the pioneering effort, in March 1869 composing his Preface to *The Sacred Books of the East*, the

[13] Ibid., pp. 179-180. The formidable difficulties are recalled in the Preface to the first edition of *The Sacred Books of the East.*

scholar presents in a clear outline the principles he had followed in preparing the authentic text:

> The text as deduced from the best MSS. of the Sanhita text, can be controlled by four independent checks. The first is, of course, a collation of the best MSS. of the Sanhita text. The second check to be applied to the Sanhita text is a comparison with the Pada text, of which, again, I possessed at least one excellent MSS. and several more modern copies. The third check was a comparison of this text with Sayana's commentary, or rather with the text which is presupposed by that commentary. In the few cases where the Pada text seemed to differ from the Sanhita text, a note was added to that effect, in the various readings of my edition; and the same was done, at least in all important cases, where Sayana followed a text at variance with our own. The fourth check was a comparison of any doubtful passage with the numerous passages quoted in the Pratisakhya. ...I believe I may say that the text as printed by me is more correct than any MSS. now accessible, more trustworthy than the text followed by Sayana, and in all important points identically the same with that text which the Pratisakhya followed in their critical researches in the fifth or sixth century before our era. I believe that starting from that date our text of the Veda is better authenticated, and supported by a more perfect *apparatus criticus* than the text of any Greek or Latin author.[14]

The meticulous scholarship had been at work in a situation fraught with the inherent problematics of reading an alien culture, an exotic idiom. Comprehending an alien text like the Rig-veda obviously involves a process of internal translation. The other modality of perception is first translated inwardly in one's own idiom of perception and then in one's own linguistic order. This poses a severe set of challenges which the scholar openly admits. In the Preface to the third volume of the *Rig-veda Sanhita*, he had candidly confessed,

> We may collect all the passages where an obscure word occurs, we may compare them and look for a meaning which would be

[14] Pp. xliv-xlv.

> appropriate to all; but the difficulty lies in finding a sense which we can appropriate and transfer by analogy into our own language and thought. We must be able to translate our feelings and ideas into their language at the same time that we translate their poems and prayers into our own.[15]

In the Preface to the first edition of *The Sacred Books*, presenting translation of part of the Rig-veda, he talks about the nature of the deeper challenge,

> It is difficult to explain to those who have not themselves worked at the Veda how it is that, though we may understand almost every word, yet we find it so difficult to lay hold of a whole chain of connected thought, and to discover expressions that will not throw a wrong shade on the original features of the ancient words of the Veda. We have on the one hand, to avoid giving to our translations too modern a character, or paraphrasing instead of translating; while on the other, one cannot retain expressions which, if literally rendered in English or any modern tongue, would have an air of quaintness or absurdity totally foreign to the intention of the ancient poets. There are, as all Vedic scholars know, whole verses which, as yet, yield no sense whatever. There are words the meaning of which we can only guess.[16]

The intellect engages in grappling not merely with words and phrases, but with an unfamiliar modality of perception. Comprehension involves interior acts of translation, understanding presupposes establishing passageways, channels of communication, at deeper levels, between one modality and another.

2

The help of native interpretation, such as Sayana's, does not always satisfy and the Sayana Bhasya, the scholar notes on many occasions, had posed its own problems. True, a

---

15 P. VIII.

16 P. xxxii.

commentary composed in the recent past, the fourteenth century CE, Sayana Bhasya had offered easier access to the Westerners. However, coming towards the end of a long tradition, the Bhasya happens to proceed relating to ancestral voices, indulging in cryptic allusions to the work of earlier Veda scholars, grammarians, linguists. While it had projected a familiar interpretive profile in the native intellectual ambience of its own time, the commentary, however, was no familiar ground to an outsider. At times it truly proved baffling to the Western enquirers. In his autobiography and elsewhere Max Müller affirms that editing the copious Commentary had presented a challenge many times more tough than editing the Veda text — a text where the MSS were very organized and systematic. He narrates his encounter with the Bhasya,

> Sayana quotes a number of Sanskrit works which ... had not yet been edited. Such were the Nirukta, the glossary of the Rig-veda, the Aitareya-Brahmana, a very old explanation of the Vedic sacrifice, the Asvalayana Sutras, on the ceremonial; and sundry works of the same character. Sayana generally alludes very briefly only to these works and presupposes that they are known to us, so that a short reference would suffice for his purposes. To find such references and to understand them required, however, not only that I should copy these works, which I did, but that I should make indices and thus be able to find the place of the passages to which he alluded. This I did also, but over and over again was I stopped by some short enigmatical reference to Panini's grammar or Yaska's glossary, which I could not identify. All these references are now added to my edition, and those who would look them up in the originals, will see what kind of work it was which I had to do before a single line of my edition could be printed. How often was I in perfect despair because there was some allusion in Sayana which I could not make out, and which no other Sanskrit scholar, not even Barnouf or Wilson, could help me to clear up. It often took me whole days, nay, weeks, before I saw light.[17]

[17] *Autobiography*, pp. 203-04.

A scholar meticulously conscientious, Max Müller consults the Brahmanas on occasions where Sayana's "quotations from these are full of mistakes"; he accepts the other readings and notes that the Sayana Bhasya bears the "wear and tear" of many centuries. Yet, on the whole, he admits in every context, he had to go by the Sayana exegesis; and that had been a formidable grapple.

IV

Eugene Barnouf had felt that presenting to the modern world the ancient Rig-veda text along with its native interpretation would be the right thing; it would, as it were, allow the newly discovered antique culture to speak in its own tongue. Again, knowledge, we know, is endorsement; knowing the natives, to the wiser policy-makers in ruling England, had been part of the strategy for gaining better control over the colonial expanse. The Board of Directors of the East India Company, we noted, had agreed to sponsor publication of the Rig-veda with the Sayana commentary, in consideration of the fact that the ancient text reveals so much about "the religion, history and language of the great body of the Indian subjects". To the scholar's reliance on the traditional native reading in the case of the unfamiliar text, had been added the ruler's interest in forming closer ties with the ruled, knowing them better and ensuring firmer control over them. Academic insistence on intellectual authenticity had gained imperial valorization, and the expense proposal had justified itself to the Board of Directors.

Chakravorty Spivak speaks of the way Sanskritic scholarship had been strategically organized ever since the time of the establishment of the Asiatic Society of Bengal; she notes how institutionalized studies imposed on the ancient system had been part of a "planned epistemic violence in the fields of education and law".[18] Actually, the Occidental power-policy had developed a sophisticated mechanism, an urbane modality, apparently intending closer relation with the colonized and, in its subtext, seeking deeper penetration – political as much as cognitive. Western rulers, the more culture-sensitive among them, had been aware of the advantages of interacting with an alien culture under domination in its own idiom. Entry into the unfamiliar ambience along channels of native endorsement, they had known, could be one way to ensure the "consent" of the natives.

Efforts were being made in diverse spheres of relation. Warren Hastings, had been interested in governing India as far as possible in terms of her traditional laws and customs, rules and legal postulates. To this intent, we know, he had appointed a number of Brahmin Pandits to prepare handbooks of native legal postulates; he had sent British officials to Benares to learn Sanskrit. In later years, even when the Indian territory had come under firmer British rule, the British Government showed reluctance and hesitancy in interfering with the age-old intricate social customs in the sprawling Indian society. Rammohan Roy's appeal for establishing institutes promoting the study of modern science instead of Sanskrit schools or colleges, or for legislation against widow-burning (the suttee)[19] and Iswarchandra Vidyasagar's plea for legalizing the remarriage of widows had to come to the British rulers as a demand from within the native community. The appeal had to be supported by the collective voice of the contemporary Indian society, particularly the elite: the eminent Pandits, the

[18] *A Critique of Postcolonial Reason*, p. 268.

[19] *The Correspondence of Raja Rammohan Roy.*

enlightened Rajas — leading citizens interested in social reforms, natives, whose consent mattered.[20]

Max Müller in his lecture on what India can teach the West addressed young Britishers preparing to join the Indian Civil Service. In these lectures, designed as part of the orientation course for the beginners, the scholar made a moving appeal to the would-be administrators waiting to sail for distant India. He emphatically explained to them the need for a close cultural relation between the governors and the governed – particularly when the people governed had a strong culture of their own. The eminent Sanskritist assured the novitiate that the study of Sanskrit literature would be "the best means of making any young man who has to spend five and twenty years of his life in India feel at home among the Indians, as a fellow-worker among fellow-workers, and not as an alien among aliens."

The lectures were published in 1883; in the dedicatory letter to E. B. Cowell noted earlier, the scholar brought out the point. He explained the need in the situation and put on record his expectation that the young administrators, at least some of them, "would follow in the footsteps of Sir William Jones" and would show that the material conquest of India by the British was not left unsupported by "intellectual conquest":

> If some of the young candidates for Indian Civil Service ... if a few of them at least, determined to follow in the footsteps of Sir William Jones and to show to the world that Englishmen who have been able to achieve by pluck, by perseverance, and by real

[20] Iswar Chandra's letter to W. Morgan Esqu., clerk to the Hon'ble the Legislative Council of India, dated 4 October 1855 forwarded the "Petition of Certain Hindoo Inhabitants of the Province of Bengal", seeking legislation in favour of widow remarriage, bearing 986 signatures, the last one by Iswarchandra Vidyasagar. See, Indramitra, *Karunasagar Vidyasagar*, p. 260.

> political genius the material conquest of India, do not mean to leave the laurels of its intellectual conquest entirely to other countries, then I shall indeed rejoice.

"Intellectual conquest" as a cognitive event is effectively consolidated when it appropriates the voice of the "other" and is attentive to it. Presenting Sayana's compendious commentary along with the Veda text, the Sanskritists of the earlier generation too had believed, could facilitate the process.

In the Preface to the First edition of the *Sacred Books of the East* (March 1869) Max Müller mentioned that at the time he had undertaken the massive enterprise, Sayana's commentary was the one reliable guide,

> Those who recollect the history of Vedic scholarship during the last five and twenty years, know best that with all its faults and weaknesses, Sayana's commentary was a *sin qua non* for a scholar-like study of the Rig-veda.

Efforts at editing and presenting "a readable and authentic text of Sayana's commentary", tedious as the task proved to be, he felt sure, were very important :

> I do not regret in the least the time which I have devolved to the somewhat tedious work of editing the Commentary of Sayana, and editing it according to the strictest rules of critical scholarship. The Veda, I feel convinced, will occupy scholars for centuries to come, and will take and maintain for ever its position as the most ancient of books in the library of mankind. Such a book, and the commentary of such a book, should be edited once and for all; and unless some unexpected discovery is made of a more ancient MSS., I do not anticipate that any future Bekker or Dindorf will find much to glean for a new edition of Sayana or that the text as restored by me from a collation of the best MSS. accessible in Europe, will ever be materially shaken.[21]

[21] P. XXXI.

The different translations of the commentary attempted by European scholars like Wilson, Langlois, Benfey, Max Müller affirmed, did not reflect due respect to the Sayana Bhasya which "represents the tradition of India"; as such the Bhasya was a text which must be presented and preserved in translation in its original character. In his Auto-biography and elsewhere, we know, Max Müller kept recounting the toil involved in editing Sayana, toil much greater, as he repeatedly mentioned, than editing the Veda text. All this labour he had undertaken in order to preserve and to present the traditional Indian reading of the Rig-veda.[22]

Not that Max Müller followed Sayana unquestioningly; he found deficiencies in Sayana's interpretation and noted that Sayana could offer guidance at an elementary stage, and in broad outline, not at each stage, nor all the way. In the Preface to the First Volume of the *Rig-veda Sanhita* (1849) the scholar noted,

> In many instances I have derived great help from original MSS. of the Brahmanas, particularly as Sayana's quotations from these works are generally full of mistakes, arising from the old Vaidik forms which transcribers did not know and understand.[23]

In the Preface to the Third Volume of the *Sanhita* (1856), where he felt happy to note that scholars have been coming to appreciate the importance of the Sayana commentary, he hastened to add

> It would have been equally wrong, however, to consider Sayana's Commentary as an infallible authority with regard to the interpretation of the Veda. Sayana gives the traditional, but not the original, sense of the Vaidik hymns.[24]

[22] See, for instance, *Auto-biography*, pp. 203-04.

[23] Pp. XXVII–XXVIII.

[24] P. VII.

Aware of the distance in time between Sayana and the original composers of the Riks, Max Müller formulated the idea of what he considered "corruption" of ancient utterances — the "wear and tear" centuries bring in. He noted how in the case of a "tradition", "growth" happens to involve "decay",[25]

> Sayana gives the traditional, but not the original sense of the Vaidik hymns. These hymns—originally popular songs, short prayers and thanks-giving, sometimes true, genuine and even sublime, but frequently childish, vulgar and obscure — were invested by the Brahmans with the character of an inspired revelation and made the basis of a complete system of dogmatic theology. If therefore we wish to know how the Brahmans, from the time of the composition of the first Brahmana to the present day, understood and interpreted the hymns of their ancient Rishis, we ought to translate them in strict accordance with Sayana gloss.... By far the greater part of these hymns is so simple and straightforward, that there can be no doubt that their original meaning was exactly the same as their traditional interpretation. But no religion, no poetry, no law no language, can resist the wear and tear of thirty centuries; and in the Veda, as in other works, handed down to us from a very remote antiquity, the sharp edges of primitive thought, the delicate features of a young language, the fresh hue of unconscious poetry, have been washed away by the successive works of what we call *tradition*, whether we look upon it as a principle of growth or decay.

Years later, in the Preface to *The Sacred Books of the East*, Max Müller confirmed,

> I do not withdraw an opinion which I expressed many years ago, and for which I was much blamed at the time, that Sayana in many ways teaches us how the Veda ought not to be, rather than how it ought to be understood.[26]

He mentioned how, in a specific situation, in the index at the end of the fourth volume of the *Rig-veda Sanhita*, he happened

---

[25] Volume III, p. VII.

[26] P. XXX.

to disagree with Sayana, and accepted another interpretation:

> As Sayana does not speak authoritatively on the subject, I followed the authority of Sadgurushishya.[27]

Citing texts, he offered an account of the point in question and the reason in support of his deviation from the Sayana line.

....

To prepare a critical edition of the entire corpus of the Sanhita text and the Bhasya called for a giant effort, continued over decades. Naturally it brought moments of exhaustion when the scholar occasionally lifted his gaze to behold how the most productive phase of his life was being spent in this all-consuming engagement, the total plan still extending far ahead. In the Preface to the third volume of the *Rig-veda Sanhita* (1856) he noted,

> When I began this edition, I thought the whole of it would be completed in three or four volumes, and now I find that the first three volumes contain hardly more than half of the whole work. I must confess that I could have wished that the ancient poets of the Veda and their Indian commentators had been less diffuse; for though I believe that no edition of any author in Sanskrit or any other language, for which manuscripts had first to be copied, others to be collated, innumerable references to be verified, and an index to be made of every word, has ever been brought out so rapidly as this edition of the Rig-veda, yet I feel that ten years of my life are gone, and I know not whether I shall have sufficient time left to finish a work which I once undertook perhaps with too much confidence.[28]

The scholar in 1856 was around 32 years of age, and of course he would have a lease of another four and half decades to

---

[27] P. Lxviii.

[28] P. XIII.

complete this project, begin many others and truly to initiate a new phase in all these new branches of scholarship that might later on be brought under the umbrella-spread of "culture studies". The moments of despondency, though, had been authentic. Nothing less than a zealous dedication, a passionate involvement in what he later recalled as the work of his life, a striving for a "cause", nothing less than the excitement of new discoveries which had made him feel for years and decades on the verge of unveiling the unsuspected, could have sustained the pioneering venture.

ऋग्वेदसंहिता

सायणाचार्यविरचितमाधवीयवेदार्थप्रकाशनामभाष्यसहिता

जार्मण्यदेशोत्पन्नेनेंगलण्डदेशनिवासिना भट्टमोक्षमूलरेण संशोधिता

श्रीमद्भारतवर्षाधिपतीनामनुमत्याच

उक्षतरणाभिधाननगरे

विद्यामंदिरसंस्थानमुद्रायंत्रालये मुद्रिता

संवत् १९०६ वर्षे

॥ प्रथमाष्टकः ॥

Sanskrit title page, Max Müller (ed.) *Rig-veda Sanhita* vol. 1

Three

Contrary pulls

But where we can inspire those early relics of thought and devotion with new life, we shall have before us more real antiquity than in all the inscriptions of Egypt and Nineveh

To my mind that question is far more important than all its answers. It is in that question, in the power of asking that question, that the true nerve of the cosmological argument lies.

India, however, is not Greece, and though we may trace the germs and roots of Greek words and Greek ideas to the rich soil of India, the full flower of Aryan Language, of Aryan poetry and mythology belongs to Hellas, where Plato has told us what Eros is and where Sophocles sang.

Max Müller

The white man's eyes break up the black man's body and in that act of epistemic violence its own frame of reference is transgressed, its field of vision disturbed.

H.K. Bhabha

Colonization, already noted in the present discourse, happens to be a conditioning experience for the colonizer too. If colonial experience inducts a "fore-closure" in people colonized, a conditioning never to completely work off, if, once to have been colonized leaves a trace for ever there to tinge subsequent perceptions, so, in a sense, does the experience of colonization in the case of those who colonize. To dominate, to bring to subservience, to keep in service for long stretches of time, hordes of alien humanity, is a cognitive-cultural challenge to the colonizing power, as demanding on the intellectual level as on the material plane of day to day administration. In the case of the colonizing West the experience had expanded and accumulated, significantly conditioning its enlightened self. The process of "worlding of worlds", of dominating and re-defining the colonized section through the imposition of imperial-epistemic control, continues to date, beyond the chronological points of political de-colonization. The gradational ranking of sections of the world into the "first" to the "third" is worlding of worlds under newer nomenclature and altered emphasis.

In the nineteenth-century situation, the heyday of colonial expansion, this process, the double impact of the colonizing experience, on the material level and on the intellective, had mostly operated in the colonizing West's pattern of engagement with the epistemic modalities of the colonized. Euro-centrism is an intellectual, although "positional" compulsion; it generates opposing pulls: the purely cognitive and the crudely colonial. The response of the greater power to the existing system in the conquered community develops complex strategies. The duality and the dynamism in the colonizers' experience ought to figure as no less significant a factor in post-colonial culture studies than the more widely analysed subjugation experience of the colonized.

And here the Western scholars' reading of the ancient culture of India ought to figure as a major illustrative instance. An important episode in the story of the West's colonial adventure, this is an episode truly revealing in each of its many folds, loaded in its accents. The colonizer-colonized engagement in most other parts of the world, in Australia, in sub-Saharan Africa, for instance, easily fall into the pattern Joseph Conrad studies in his novels. The white man's burden of civilizing the coloured on the earth, the enlightened West's commitment to rationalize, to modernize, are well-known credos; — the developed world's responsibility today to democratize the rest is but an updated extension of the older strategy, a newer version of imperial expansion-intervention.

The encounter with India, however, has been an event of a more complex nature. It is a layered, sophisticated account; in a way it tells a richer tale. The eventual "change-over" Chakravorty Spivak talks about, the definitive docketing of the colonial, obviously affects the perception of India. The other aspect of the historical situation (and this awaits probing analysis) reveals the fact that it also induces deep-rooted ambivalences, unresolved inner contradiction in the response of the Western reader-interpreter, the Orientalist intellectual.[1] Homi K. Bhabha notes the "two contradictory and independent attitudes" that "inhabit the *same place*" in colonial discourse: one recognizes reality, "the other is under the influence of instincts which detach the ego from reality", he comments. Multiple and contradictory beliefs are born, contradictory yet coeval statements are articulated, and prove equally authentic. The pressure is enormous. Bhabha mentions the "enslaved master, the unmastered slave."[2]

Max Müller struggling on with the ancient Rig-veda, later on with the other religious texts of the East, had experienced this cognitive dilemma, a genuine "a-poria" Bhabha mentions. In the Veda he had faced a culture, an epistemic modality, not

---

[1] Amartya Sen mentions "contrasting and conflicting Western approaches" and the "variety of Western conceptions of India". *The Argumentative Indian,* p. 139ff.

[2] *Location*, pp. 187-88.

of aboriginal naïve simplicity[3], yet something archaic, alien, unexpected, un-prepared for. Chronicling his life-long adventure the scholar mentions how studying the Rig-veda had proved a much more difficult task than what Europe in its initial eagerness had anticipated or bargained for. He notes that way back, when his mentor Barnouf used to insist that the Rig-veda is a

> fortress that must be besieged and taken, it cannot be left in our rear, he did not know how challenging, baffling the attempt would prove, he little knew how much time it would take to approach it, to surround it, and at last to take it.

Did Western scholarship manage to "take" the fortress? At the end of the long travail the scholar announces

> It (the Rig-veda) has not been surrendered even now, and will not be in any time.[4]

The perplexity, the puzzlement, the situation of what Bhabha describes as "incomplete translation", had baffled the enquiring mind and, at times, it called for skilled efforts at circumnavigating.

Indology grew into a text and a sub-text. The dexterous interweaving of the two demonstrates ingenuity and resilience of the intellective process which forms and re-forms itself, as it adjusts to the colonizing experience. The text relates to the nineteenth-century spirit of conquest, of emancipatory expansion, of arriving at new space, while the sub-text records the compulsions of cultural supremacy, the assertive egotism of the Occident, the intellect's surrender to cultural allegiance.

First the text.

---

[3] The native female figure, dark, heavily ornamented and fierce, in *The Heart of Darkness*, placed by the side of the profile of Maitreyi in the *Brihadaranyaka Upanishad*, for instance, provides a telling contrast.

[4] *Autobiography*, p. 201.

I

In mid-nineteenth century Tennyson had voiced the desire and the aspiration of his time,

> Let knowledge grow from more to more …

In 1888, beginning his Gifford Lectures on Natural Religion, Max Müller, very much a man of the moment, reminded his audience,

> Our nineteenth century, which will soon have passed away, has been described as a century of progress and enlightenment in all branches of human knowledge.

In times of receding frontiers and of new light flooding all areas of human interest, Max Müller argued, religion too ought to be re-explored. He regretted that religion still remained mostly in the fold of a conservative mode, a mode of thought which proudly claimed a stable, "stationary" position in the field of religion; in the face of change and progress in every other sphere, the conservatives proudly claimed a stable position in matters of religious faith. He questioned, "Why should that be so?" The requirement of the hour, on the other hand was, he boldly asserted,

> as in every other pursuit, so in religion also, we want less and less of darkness, more and more of light; we want, call it life or growth, or development, or progress; we do not want mere rest, mere stagnation, mere death.

The century's giant effort had been pushing back frontiers, widening the ken. Knowing generates a cognitive claim, expands areas of control, lends support to the act of building empires of the mind. The comparative approach Max Müller had enthusiastically endorsed in his 1856 essay, effectively opened up over the decades relations and relations; the cognitive zeal, authentic and unsparingly invasive, makes no exception — not even in the case of religion. Max Müller in 1888 makes the bold assertion that the idea that

> Religion rests on a divine and miraculous revelation, and therefore cannot be improved, is neither true, nor honest.[5]

Religion too, he claims, is amenable to scientific study in a historical perspective. The approach in its time did not go unchallenged; Churchmen found the ideas sacrilegious.[6]

However, the century of expansive adventures drawing to its close, conservative criticism did not much affect Max Müller's reputation.

New ideas face resistance. Max Müller in his Cambridge lecture "India, What Can it Teach Us?" glances back to the earlier phases of resistance and notes, "when this new light first dawned on the world",

> they would not have it, they would not believe that there could be any community of origin between the people of Athens and

---

[5] *Natural Religion*, pp. 7-10.

[6] Conservative Churchmen found these ideas "anti-Christian". In a meeting of the Established Presbytery of Glasgow Mr. Thomson, Minister of Ladywell, moved a motion declaring Max Müller's teaching as "subversive of the Christian faith and fitted to spread pantheistic and infidel views amongst the students and others" and questioned Max Müller's appointment as Gifford Lecturer. Monsignor Alexander Munro, Officer of the Roman Catholic Church in Scotland and Provost of the Catholic Cathedral of Glasgow, found the lectures to be "nothing less than a crusade against Divine Revelation, against Jesus Christ, and against Christianity".
See, Nirad C Chaudhuri, *Scholar Extraordinary,* pp. 340-41. Reaction in tune had been operative earlier in 1860 behind the scholar's exclusion from selection to the Boden Chair in Sanskrit in favour of the conservative Monier Monier-Williams.

> Rome, and the so-called Niggers of India. ... I myself still remember the time, when I was a student at Leipzig and began to study Sanskrit, with what contempt any remarks on comparative grammar were treated by my teachers.

Time since then has changed, assures the scholar; closer acquaintance with the East, with India in particular, had been integrated into cognition that defines.

> The concept of the European man has been changed and widely extended by our acquaintance with India, and we know now that we are something different from what we thought we were.[7]

Sanskritic studies had effected a total revision of ideas in the field of philological studies. Close association with the Veda tradition had lent a broader perspective. In the first of the four lectures delivered at the Royal Institution, 19 February, 1870, (later published as *Introduction to the Science of Religion*), Max Müller had mentioned the discovery of Sanskrit and the beginning of the study of Comparative Philology as a revolutionary event as important, as decisive, as the "introduction of Greek into the universities of Europe".[8] He described the change,

> A few hundred years ago, the idea that Hebrew was the original language of mankind was accepted as a matter of course, even as a matter of faith, the only problem being to find out by what process the Greek or Latin, or any other language could have been developed out of Hebrew.[9]

It was the "discovery of Sanskrit" that led towards a solution and initiated a newer perception. The discovery of the ancient religion of the East, closer acquaintance with the Rig-veda, the "oldest book" and the religious experience stored in it —

---

[7] London, Longmans, Green & Co. new edition 1892, pp. 28-29.

[8] Bharat Manisha (Varanasi Indian reprint, 1972), p. 3.

[9] Ibid., p. 10.

different, alien — not only extends the cognitive range, it opens up gateways to newer ways of thinking, newer perceptions. In the lecture on what India can teach the West, as in many other contexts, the scholar assures that the study of Sanskrit language and of the ancient religion in India

> had imparted to the whole ancient history of man a reality which it never possessed before.[10]

In the Introduction to his Autobiography he joyfully recalls how things had happily conspired, almost miraculously, to make the Veda studies possible, studies that, apart from all other aspects consequent, proved to be of historical importance in so far as

> It helps us to learn what we really are ourselves, and how we came to be what we are.[11]

In discovering the mind of India Europe comes to perceive the world a-new; and, in this altered perspective, re-discovers itself. In the process of defining the "other", Europe re-defines itself. It is new space altogether. The experience of colonization, particularly in a faraway territory like India with its ancient history stretching into the hoary past and a millennia-old tradition, affects the West's act of self-reflexivity, alters its self-perception.

II

The study of religion now expands beyond denominational frontiers; the experience of relating to the non-Abrahamic brings conceptual release from orthodoxy. In the closing paragraph of his Preface to the Fourth Volume of *Rig-veda*

---

[10] P. 30.

[11] P. 14.

Sanhita (1862) Max Müller had noted his perception of unsuspected interfaces between religions—"revealed" or "natural". Re-exploration of religion from a rational-historical point of view had started. In the lectures on what India can teach he makes a clear distinction between spiritual aspiration and denominational religions, specific structures of faith. The essential spiritual sensibility he designates "religion", the denominational faith he calls "a religion". The latter derives from the former; the first condition is a matter of sensibility. The scholar feels convinced that spirituality begins in a man who

> once at least in his life has looked beyond the horizon of this world and carried away in his mind an impression of the Infinite, which will never leave him again.

"A being satisfied with the world of sense, unconscious of its finite nature," he notes, would be incapable of any religious concepts."[12] In the Gifford Lecture XX he calls the sacred books of the East "the Bibles of the whole human race"[13]; these are the testaments of the profound truth that man's aspiration to rise above the material level is co-eternal with his existence on earth:

> The whole world in its wonderful history, has passed through that struggle for life, the struggle for eternal life; and every one of us, ... has had to pass through the same struggle; for without it no religion, whatever its sacred books may be, will find in any human heart that soil in which alone it can grow and bear fruit.[14]

Max Müller feels convinced that "anything that lifts a man above the realities of the material life is religion."[15]

---

[12] Pp. 106-07.

[13] P. 540.

[14] P. 569.

[15] P. 568.

Denominational demarcations recede and the scholar discovers, as it were, a shared bedrock from which rises the transcendental aspirations of all mankind, mortal man's common yearning that reaches out to immortality. This aspiration, this essentially spiritual inclination in man— diverse formulations as it may develop, diverse iconicities as it may happen to assume — records a continuous process of growth, aspirational and spiritual. This had acted as the first principle in his "historical" approach to religion and, as we know, Max Müller builds on this premise the foundation of the new science, the comparative study of religion and of myths.

In the prefatory lecture to the series on Anthropological Religion (1892) he mentions how, through his historical investigations into these other religions beyond the "revealed", he had discovered and is determined to preach the truth, that "belief in God, in the immortality of the soul and a future retribution can be gained … and has been gained by the right exercise of human reason alone, without the assistance of what has been called a special revelation." He tells us that in his probing study of the sacred books of the East he had seen how

> What St. Paul, what the Fathers of the Church, what medieval theologians and what some of the most learned modern Divines have asserted again and again was most strikingly confirmed by the records of all non-Christian religions which have lately become accessible to us by the patient researches of Oriental scholars, more particularly by the students of the ancient literature of India.[16]

In Gifford Lecture 8 the scholar had announced,

> However strange it may seem to us, if we simply follow the evidence placed before us, there can be little doubt that the

[16] Asean Educational Series, second reprint, 1986, pp. V–VII.

> perception of the Unknown or the Infinite was with many races as ancient as the perception of the Known or the Finite, that the two were inseparable.[17]

One such race, he knows, had populated India in ancient times. While the close study of the Veda had revealed to the scholar what he later comes to enunciate as a historical growth of religious sensibilities, it had also brought to his notice a distinctive trait in the temperament of this alien group of humanity: he had assured the young audience at Cambridge that

> With them (people in India) … religion was not only one interest by the side of many. It was the all-absorbing interest; it embraced not only worship and prayer, but what we call philosophy, morality, law and government — all was pervaded by religion. Their whole life was, as it were, a mere concession made to the ephemeral requirements of this life.[18]

In this series of lectures he had come to the verge of admitting and acknowledging equal validity, almost a deeper validity indeed, of this "other" modality of perception; and had presented an appreciative apology for its difference:

> Why should they have accumulated wealth? Why should they have built palaces? Why should they have toiled day and night? After having provided from day to day for the small necessities of the body, they thought they had the right, it may be the duty, to look round upon this strange exile, to look inward upon themselves, upward to something not themselves, and to see whether they could not understand a little of the true purport of that mystery we call life on earth. Of course *we* should call such notions of life dreamy, unreal, unpractical, but may not *they* look upon our notions of life as short-sighted, fussy, and, most unpractical, because involving a sacrifice of life for the sake of life?[19]

---

[17] See, pp. 192-220.

[18] *India, What Can it Teach Us?*, pp. 107-108.

[19] Ibid., p. 101.

Of course, we would see, there would be on the part of the scholar occasions of cautious drawing back; yet the perspective emerging here, on an honest reckoning, reads almost as an anticipation of the twentieth-century poet T.S. Eliot's regrets on the modern West losing "life" in the "living".[20]

III

The "historical approach" opens up an emancipatory cross-cultural perspective, almost a global one. Max Müller's work of the reading and the editing of the Rig-veda and the Bhasya by Sayana Acharya, acquires enormous authenticity as, plodding through the alien terrain of the alien ancient texts, Max Müller readily perceives the basic points in the situation, points that may be readily glanced over.

1.

He notes the process of distortion, what he calls "corruption", of the simple meaning of the Veda hymns in the elaborate interpretive corpus of commentaries. In the Preface to the third volume of his *Rig-veda Sanhita* he talks of the "gradual corruption of simple truth into hierarchical dogmatism and philosophical hallucination" in the Sayana Bhasya; all these, he assures, are marks of the inevitable "wear and tear" of many centuries.

A direct approach to the Veda text only, the scholar clearly sees, can lead one to the original signification; following the text, the articulation of the ancient composers, cautiously, he

20 "Where is the Life we have lost in living? / Where is the wisdom we have lost in Knowledge? ..." Choruses from "The Rock", I, ll 14-18.

feels sure: “we shall find that with some effort we are still able to walk in their footsteps”. There would be stumbling blocks and success would not be easy; there would be occasions, he admits, on which “words, verses, nay, whole hymns in the Rig-veda, will and must remain to us a dead letter”. Yet, the discovery of the meaning, when it comes, would unveil wonders,

> Where we can inspire those early relics of thought and devotion with new life we shall have before us more real antiquity than in all the inscriptions of Egypt or Nineveh; not only old names and dates, and kingdoms and battles, but old thoughts, old hopes, old faith, and old errors, the old “Man” altogether — old now, but then young and fresh, and simple and real in his prayers and in his praises.[21]

2.

The sheer antiquity of the Veda text, the scholar appreciates, gives it an exclusivity; the text cannot be, must not be, subjected to editorial manipulation — not even if errors are obvious. Emendations may at best be recommended, in a parenthesis. In the Preface to the First Edition of *The Sacred Books* he notes,

> Considering the startling antiquity which we can claim for every letter and accent of our MSS, … I should deem it reckless to alter one single letter or one single accent in an edition of the hymns of the Rig-veda. As the text has been handed down to us so it should remain; and whatever alterations and corrections we, the critical Mlekkhas of the nineteenth century, have to propose, should be kept distinct from that time-hallowed inheritance. … no scholar of any historical tact or critical taste would venture to foist into it a conjectural reading, however plausible, nay, however undeniable.[22]

---

[21] P. IX.

[22] P. LXXII.

3.

Way back in Germany Schopenhauer had assured the young Max Müller that the Upanishads were the real treasures, the only portion deserving close study, and that the rest, including the Veda, was "priestly rubbish". Max Müller's own impression even in that early phase had been different. It had almost been an intuitive grasp years before he had come to France and consulted Eugene Barnouf. In the Gifford Lectures he states how he had from the very beginning assumed continuity between the Veda texts and the Upanishads; engagement with the texts in succeeding years and decades only confirmed.

> I soon came to see… that these Upanishads were only the latest outcome of Vedic literature… to me it seemed that an historical study of the Vedic religion ought to begin with the hymns of the Rig-veda, as containing in thought and language the antecedents of the Upanishads.[23]

In the lectures on the Science of Religion he notes how in the Veda "there stand side by side the most transparent natural polytheism in the hymns …. and the most subtle theosophy in Upanishads… co-existing and united".[24] The unity and continuity, the scholar knows, is authentic and behind all that appears as "priestly rubbish", "unmeaning ritualism", looms the questioning mind. The question raised by an anonymous ancient voice in the Rig-veda asks—Who (*Kah)*? and Whence (*Kasmaat*)? — Whence came it all? Who knows? In the Gifford Lecture X Max Müller points out,

> To my mind that question is far more important than all its answers. It is in that question, in the power of asking that question, that the true nerve of the cosmological argument lies.

---

[23] Lecture 1, p. 18.

[24] Pp. 36-37.

Speculations on the possible answers in the text, all "guesses at truth", he assures, do flow from the essential spirituality in man's quest,

> from the same conviction that the phenomenal world is not the real world or ... that behind what we see and know there is something which we do not see and which we do not know, that there is something real behind the contingent.[25]

The authentic utterance of spiritual aspiration deeply impresses him. He enjoins philosophers of religion in the future to be less prejudiced and less dogmatic in their approach to Eastern — other — religions than so far they, not excluding Schelling and Hegel, had been.[26]

4.

As to the many gods invoked and prayed to in the Rig-veda, Max Müller clearly perceives two points : (a) although the Veda extols the One whom the sages call by many names, the many gods are there; side by side with monistic thoughts which are perfectly in tune with the spirit of the Upanishads, curiously enough there is the host of gods and goddesses crowding the Vedic pantheon; (b) apparently polytheistic, the Veda cult of worshipping many gods, however, is essentially different from polytheism in the Greco-Roman culture. Max Müller explains to the would-be administrators of India the "lesson of the Veda" and points out the radical difference. The Greco-Roman polytheism, he points out, projects one leading figure, Zeus, or Jupiter, for instance, under whom the many gods and goddesses reign over definite areas of control; the

---

25 Pp. 244; 249.

26 *Introduction to The Science of Religion*, (Indian reprint, Varanasi, Bharat Manisha 1972) Lecture IV, p. 147.

Olympian empire is a structured unit. The Vedas, on the other hand, assign no hierarchic authority-range to any of the gods.[27] Any of them, at the moment of worship, is hailed as the supreme.

> In the Veda... the gods worshipped as supreme ... stand side by side. No one is first always, no one is last always. Even gods of a decidedly inferior and limited character assume occasionally in the eyes of a devoted poet a supreme place above all other gods.[28]

To this strange cult of worshipping "single gods each occupying for a time a supreme position", the scholar assigns a different nomenclature : "kakenotheism", "that is a worship of one god after another", or "henotheism", "the worship of single gods."[29]

5.

The perception of the purport of the ancient relics, in the face of all obstacles, is authenticated by a reverential attitude the scholar brings to bear on his toil. The enormous task assumes the sanctity of a pioneer's effort at unearthing the unknown

---

[27] "It is the peculiar character of that phase of religious thought ... in it Divine is conceived and represented as manifold, and that many functions are shared in common by various gods, no attempt having yet been made at organizing the whole body of the gods, sharply separating one from the other, and subordinating all of them to several or, in the end, to one supreme head." *India, What Can it Teach Us*? P. 149.

[28] Ibid., p. 146.

[29] Ibid., pp. 146-47. Bankimchandra Chatterjee finds the search for terminology a hilarious situation (*Rachanavali*, II, p.816); it had actually been an honest search for a distinctive designation in the case of this un-Hellenic pattern on the part of the Western scholar, keenly aware of the tonal difference between polytheism and polytheism.

and the unexpected, of rescuing an invaluable treasure. The work, as already noted, proves the mission of a life; the zeal and the absorption not only designate Max Müller a giant leader in the West's discovery of the East, but make him a savant figure to the Indians, a friend of India, a *Bharatabandhu*.

In his autobiography he asserts that "the Veda remained and always will remain the oldest of real books, that has been preserved to us in an almost miraculous way". He points out that a "book" in its organized structure marks a far more advanced culture-stage than elementary inscriptions. The Veda, the scholar unconditionally affirms, meets all the requirements of the status of a "book", and happens to be the oldest specimen.[30]

In the Introduction to *The Science of Religion*, he mentions with regret that although perceptive scholars like the French philosopher Cousin had "declared that India contained the whole history of philosophy in a nut-shell", the West in general remained negligent towards it all and "continue to write… as if Kapila and Kanada had never existed". In the Cambridge lectures the scholar cautions the prospective young civil servants in India about the discriminatory attitude operative in the West and exhorts them not to be affected :

> Why should a study of Greek and Latin,— of the poetry, the philosophy, the laws and the art of Greece and Italy,— seem congenial to us, why should it excite even a certain enthusiasm, and command general respect, while a study of Sanskrit, and of the ancient poetry, the philosophy, the laws, and the art of India is looked upon, in the best case, as curious, but is considered by most people as useless, tedious, if not absurd?[31]

---

[30] *Autobiography*, p. 195.

[31] *India, What it Can Teach Us*? Pp. 3-4.

6.

The exclusivity in the West's attitude, the tendency to marginalize, minimize and keep at a distance all that falls outside of its own cultural orbit, had been decisive forces even in the academia; Max Müller is sensitive to the impact. Entering the discussion as to how ancient the Vedas are, with utmost caution Max Müller keeps to the safer side and puts the possible date of the Veda at the shortest distance. He quotes Wilson's criticism in favour of an estimate he himself would have liked to forward, but deliberately, diplomatically, stops short of. In the Preface to volume IV of the *Rig-veda* where he explores in detail the question of the date of the text, he admits that he has been deliberately keeping to the moderate side in arriving "at about 1200 B.C. as the latest date at which … the Vedic bards settled in Northern regions of the Indian continent". He cites the views on this he had recorded in his *History of Ancient Sanskrit Literature* and also Wilson's views proposing earlier dates of origin in the case of the ancient Veda.[32]

In his autobiography Max Müller affords to be less cautious; here he mentions the marks of the prolonged period of growth the ancient text bears. The Veda text, the scholar says, "like an old oak tree, shows hundreds and thousands of circles within circles". He winds up in a way the entire dispute over date and time, noting,

> If we were to place it at 5000 B.C., I doubt whether anybody could refute such a date, while if we go back beyond the Veda, and come to measure the time required for the formation of Sanskrit and of the Proto-Aryan language, I doubt very much whether even 5000 years would suffice for that. There is an unfathomable depth in language, layer following after layer, long

---

[32] P. IX.

> before we arrive at roots, and what a time and what an effort must have been required for their elaboration, and for the elaboration of the ideas expressed in them.[33]

This is the reverential awe the scholar experiences in his lucid perception, in his intellectual engagement when uninhibited, to an optimum extent, by compulsions of situational-positional logic.

And when he recounts his personal experience, glancing over decades of toil, drudgery and patient probing into the alien and the far-away, he speaks in accents of ecstatic fulfilment; the celebrated assertion reads

> If I were to look over the whole world to find out the country most richly endowed with all the wealth, power and beauty that nature can bestow…I should point to India. If I were asked under what sky the human mind has most fully developed some of its choicest gifts, has most deeply pondered on the greatest problems of life and has found solutions of some of them which well deserved the attention even of those who have studied Plato and Kant — I should point to India. And if I were to ask myself from what literature we, here in Europe, we who have been nurtured almost exclusively on the thoughts of Greeks and Romans, and of one Semitic race, the Jewish, may draw that corrective which is most wanted in order to make our inner life more perfect, more comprehensive, more universal, in fact more truly human, a life not for this life only, but a transfigured and eternal life— again I should point to India.[34]

IV

Is the experience then like a pilgrimage to a shrine far away and newly discovered? Could be; and in a sense perhaps it

---

[33] Pp. 194; 200.

[34] *India, What Can it Teach Us*? P. 6.

was; but it does not happen to be that simple. The problematic are what the *sub-text* reveals.

Colonization is a large event, complex and multi-faceted; the experience interferes with and complicates the primary and the spontaneous. Harking back to points noted earlier in the present discourse, we might recall Homi K. Bhabha's comments on the process of the "doubling over" inherent in the colonizer-colonized axis, the process that affects the response on both sides. He notes that "the discourse of post-Enlightenment English colonialism often speaks in a tongue that is forked, not false."[35] Without entering into the post-modernist, post-colonial analytics, the Derrida-esque dismissives and/or Lacanian mappings out of sites of desire, mimicry and identification that figure in chapters of postcolonial discourse, one might simply take note of the contrariety in the Westerners' pattern of response and the complex forces of compulsion behind. In the case of a giant intellect like Max Müller, the contrariety is sharp and the interplay truly revealing.

Europe's interest in the Veda, we noted, the competitive zeal among different European metropolises for first publishing it, Max Müller repeatedly assures, had been so keen because "the Veda was expected to give us a picture of what man was in his most primitive state .... Everybody interested in the origin and the first development of language, thought, religion and social institutions, looked forward to the Veda."[36] The discovery of Sanskrit, he often reminds, had "added a new period to our historical consciousness and revived the

---

[35] See, for instance, Bhabha on the texture of "colonial discourse", *Location*, pp. 95ff.

[36] *Autobiography*, p. 191.

recollection of our childhood, which seemed to have vanished for ever".[37] In the Preface to the third volume of the *Rig-veda* Max Müller had emphasised the point that the Veda literature happens to be of deep interest to scholars because the ancient text sheds "the most unexpected light on the darkest periods in the history of the most prominent nations of antiquity."[38]

The "prominence" provides the perspective. The Veda text is primitive; "the popular songs, short prayers and thanks-giving", "sometimes true, genuine, and even sublime", are "frequently childish, vulgar and obscure"; the hymns, he assures in the Preface to volume IV of the *Sanhita*, "represent the lowest stature in the growth of the human mind". Yet it is so important to decipher and to analyse this because these primitive utterances are documents of an anterior phase in the history of the prominent people of the present.

In the Preface to volume III of the *Rig-veda Sanhita* Max Müller says that as the geologist probes into the "petrified" layers of the "primeval" formations, the historian in the study of the Veda fruitfully engages in an attempt at "gathering-up the threads of the most primitive thoughts of man". He learns to "make the best of rags and tatters" surviving from the primitive past. In the essay on comparative mythology published the same year (1856), he bases the entire argument on the anteriority of the Veda culture, the forgotten infancy of human civilization, fortunately discovered and effectively habilitated, in the historical scheme.

Later, when in 1883 he presented a copy of his Cambridge lectures, *India, What Can it Teach Us?,* to Gladstone, in his letter (dated 18 January), he wrote,

---

37 *India, What Can it Teach Us*? Pp. 29-30.

38 P. V.

> I must confess I have long wished for an opportunity of engaging your interest in behalf of India; I do not mean the mere surface India, with its grotesque religion, its pretty poetry, and its fabulous antiquity, but the real India that is only slowly emerging before our eyes; a whole, almost forgotten act in the great drama of humanity, very different from Greece, from Rome, from modern Europe, yet not so different that in studying it we cannot feel that *mutato nomine de nobis fabula narratur*.[39] The discovery of that new intellectual hemisphere, is to my mind, a far greater discovery than that of Vasco da Gama.[40]

The uncovering of the infancy of human civilization by modern Europe marks the first firm step towards the intellectual conquest of what had long remained "terra incognita", veiled and unknown, not so much in terms of the geo-contour of the land, but as the forgotten earliest phase of the West's own history of evolution. In the dedicatory letter to this volume addressed to the Sanskritist E. B. Cowell, mentioned earlier, he had explained that even if a few of the British administrators proceeding to rule India "follow in the footsteps of Sir William Jones", and move toward achieving the intellectual conquest of India in support of the material conquest, then the scholar would truly rejoice.[41]

To discover, to grapple with, to understand, to codify and to label and docket, is the way to intellectual conquest, the unfailing method of processing the "other". Paul Valery uses

---

[39] "Change the name, and it is about you, that story". — Horace, *Satires*, No. I, Book I, Epistle I, line 69.

[40] Cited, N. C. Chaudhuri, *Scholar Extraordinary*, p. 133.

[41] He added in that letter that his enormous toil, then, at the personal level too, would bring to him a deep sense of gratification, as he could then feel "that I have paid back, in however small a degree, the large debt of gratitude which I owe to my adopted country and to some of its greatest statesmen who have given me the opportunity which I would have found nowhere else." Pp. VII–VIII.

the term "digest"; and the power to digest, Valery knows, makes the West what it is.[42]

V

The awakening of interest in the ancient lore scripted in Sanskrit, in England, primarily arose out of the pragmatics of the immediate imperial experience — the actual task of ruling a far-away unfamiliar territory. Early Indologists had been Britishers entrusted with administrative assignments at different levels and engaged in the act of administering the sprawling colony, harbouring creeds and convictions alien and obscure.

Charles Wilkins (Sir) had joined the service of the East India Company and had come to India in 1770 as a printer. He quickly learnt Persian and Bengali, helped design the first lithographic type for printing Bengali and proved the "Caxton of India". In 1781 he was appointed translator of Persian and Bengali to the Commissioner of Revenue and then Superintendent of the East India Company's Press.

Warren Hastings, the first Governor General in India (1773 – 84), we have been noting, acted as a patron figure in the effort at cultural interaction with the subjects in the colony. Nathaniel Brassey Halhead arrived as a "Writer" in the Company service;

---

42 "From the cultural point of view, I do not think that we have much to fear *now* from the Oriental influences. It is not unknown to us .... The real question in such matters is to *digest*. But that has always been ... the great specialty of the European mind through the ages. Our role is therefore to maintain this power of choice, of universal comprehension, of the transformation of everything into our substance, powers which have made us what we are." *Oeuvres*, ed. Jean Hytier (Paris, Gallimard, 1960), 2: 1556–7, cited, Said, *Orientalism*, p. 250.

he translated the Hindu legal code, prepared from a Persian version of the Sastras in Sanskrit *A Code of Gentoo Laws,* published in 1776.

Henry Thomas Colebrook also came as a "Writer"; he was placed in the Board of Accounts. Posted in Purneah, he studied the resources of the region, published *Remarks on the Husbandry and Commerce of Bengal* in 1795. Lord Wellesley appointed him Professor of Hindu Law and Sanskrit at the College of Fort William.

William Jones (Sir) arrived as puisne Judge, Supreme Court of Bengal in 1783; in January 1784 he founded the Asiatic Society. In 1786 came out his work on the common roots of languages: Greek, Latin, Sanskrit ....

Horace Hayman Wilson, Librarian, East India Company, Indologist of repute, Vedicist benefactor of Max Müller in his Veda venture, had come to India in 1808 as an Assistant Surgeon. His knowledge of metallurgy brought him to be associated with the Mint in Calcutta. He acted as Secretary to the Committee of Public Instruction and superintended the functioning of the Sanskrit College in Calcutta.

This is to name a few. Max Müller notes in his auto-biography that the forces which, way back, had conjoined and made the Veda venture possible, all happened to relate to the political-administrative situation involving the empire at that point of time. He then was a young scholar in London, working on the Veda MSS in the East India Company's Library; the time was

> when the fate of the Company hung in the balance, and when Bunsen, the Prussian Minister, made himself *persona grata* by delivering a speech at a public dinner in the City, setting forth in eloquent words the undeniable merits of the Old Company and the wonderful work they had achieved.

"The same Bunsen, His Excellency Baron Bunsen, the Prussian Minister in London", Max Müller recounts, next moved on to pleading with the Company Chairman for lending sponsorship to the Veda venture. He

> on his own accord went afterwards to see the Chairman and the Directors of the East India Company, and explained to them what the Rig-veda was, and that it would be a real disgrace if such a work were published in Germany; and they agreed to vote a sum of money such as they had never voted before for any literary undertaking.[43]

Almost by a freak of chance, the historical effort at recovering and editing the Rig-veda for the modern world came to obtain endorsement of the ruling trade Company; the endeavour enjoyed the benefit of a moment of crisis and a moment of transition in political power alignment. Max Müller notes,

> It was the change threatening the Government of India, a mighty change it was, that gave me the chance of publishing the Veda ... [44]

The scholar, late in his life, wistfully glances back to the past, to the inevitable closure of the Company after the Mutiny, and notes with gratification that he had been able at least to dedicate the first volume of his edition of the Rig-veda "to the Chairman and the Directors of the much abused East India Company".

The epoch-making colossal cognitive encounter which was to prove a second Renaissance in the West, had mostly emerged out of England's imperial experience — the logic and the logistics of the primary pragmatic threshold remaining determinative and harnessed down the way. Obviously it

---

[43] Pp. 13-14.

[44] P. 14.

would not have been easy for the cognitive venture to have a smooth run without the motivating support of the pragmatics in the situation. James Mill in his sundry dismissal of the cultural elevation of ancient India and the Orient, found it "unfortunate that a mind so pure, so warm in the pursuit of truth, and so devoted to oriental learning, as that of Sir William Jones, should have adopted the hypothesis of a high state of civilization in the principal countries of Asia."[45] Macaulay could accommodate on a single library shelf "the whole native literature of India and Arabia". Against such overt Occidental uppishness the German scholar Max Müller[46] tried to uphold the urgency of the study of ancient Sanskrit language in search of the roots of human civilization. The logic operative at the ground level of ruling a vast empire remained incontrovertible; the scholarly venture sought and derived vital support from the same.

The alliance between the cognitive enquiry and the imperial interest gained wider acceptance and deeper validity. The Crimean war broke out in 1853, and an urgent need was felt for the British army's close acquaintance with the languages of the area. Sir Charles Trevelyan consulted Max Müller about the languages which defence personnel should be acquainted with. Nirad C. Chaudhuri notes,

> Max Müller at once wrote a long pamphlet on *Languages of the Seat of War.* The corner of Europe from north Italy to the Danube, he said, was a real rookery, in which all the lost daughters of the European family of languages had taken refuge. This book needed a second edition in a year.[47]

---

45 Cited, *Scholar Extraordinary*, p. 133.

46 Nirad C Chaudhuri adds a note on the deeper strains of attitudinal difference between the Britishers' engagement in India and in issues Indological, and that of the German. *Scholar Extraordinatory*, p. 127ff.

47 Ibid., p. 175.

In this pamphlet Max Müller had pointed out a parallel situation in England's engagement in India and the imperative need for promoting the study of oriental languages, for opening schools of Oriental Studies. He had taken the opportunity of bringing to notice once again that "It is high time that something should be done to encourage the study of Oriental languages in England." Organized efforts had been made and Seminaries of Oriental Studies had been established in Russia, in France, in Prussia, in Vienna; yet England, the scholar pointed out, happened to lag behind.

> In England alone where the most vital interests are involved in a free intercourse with the East, hardly anything is done to foster Oriental Studies.[48]

Within a few years the 1857 Mutiny in India demonstrated break in communication between the ruler and the ruled and brought to surface the pressing need for closer interaction between England and the land of her largest political investment. The publication of the volumes of the Veda in progress, Max Müller under the assumed name of Philindus published several letters in the *Times*.[49] In these he argued how it was easy to see that "in order to govern a people, and to gain the confidence and goodwill of a conquered race, it is necessary to know their language." Once again he made the strong plea,

> It ought to be, and no doubt will be, one of the first things for Parliament to declare that a study of the native dialects shall be obligatory on every candidate for the Indian civil and military services ... it will ... be the duty of Government to provide

---

[48] Ibid., p. 176.

[49] Among the participants in the debate were Sir Charles Trevelyan, Monier-Williams, Professor Syed Abdoolah from India. See, *Scholar Extraordinary*, p. 176.

> candidates with the means of learning the Indian languages in this country, by establishing an Oriental College.[50]

The opening of schools of Oriental Studies, with all the urgency the scholar pressed on, was getting delayed. More than three decades later when the School of Modern Oriental Studies was started by the Imperial Institute in collaboration with the University College and King's College, London, Max Müller delivered the inaugural address (January 14, 1896); the Prince of Wales was in the chair and Max Müller, Nirad C Chaudhuri recounts, expressed the conviction that "when imperial interests were at stake, the country had a right to expect imperial, … concentrated action".[51]

Again, colonization brings good to the colonized, the superior power brings light, at more than one level. If at the cognitive level, presenting the modern edition of the Rig-veda with Sayana Bhasya, as Max Müller knew, had been a great service to the Indians revealing to them the roots of their culture, at another level the effort at giving good administration itself had been an enormous good done to the natives. The erudite scholar appreciates how it reflects well in the annals of the empire. The Veda scholar shared the confidence with many other leading intellectuals of the century of expansion. It had actually been, they all agreed, a wonderful feat, an amazing one in the dexterity and the concentrated effort it demonstrated every day. Max Müller in reminiscent moods found this a performance, a spectacle, calling for loud approbation.

> The Government of India by a mere handful of Englishmen is, indeed an achievement unparalleled in the whole history of the

---

[50] Ibid., p. 176.

[51] See, Ibid., p. 177.
An interesting account of the Queen listening to Max Müller's lecture on language in Osborne House on the Isle of Wight, much earlier, is given, pp. 178-79.

> world. The suppression of the Indian Mutiny shows what stuff English soldiers and statesmen are made of. If people say that ours is not an age for Epic poetry, let them read Lord Roberts's *Forty-one Years in India*. When I see in a circus a man standing with outstretched legs on two or three horses and two men standing on his shoulders and other man standing on theirs, and a little child at the top of all, while the horses are running full gallop round the arena, I feel what I feel when watching the Government of India.[52]

The empire, the rule, the administrative hold, the political craftsmanship it called for — all these indubitably constitute the ground reality, the ground for the basic bonding between the colonizer and the colonized, the base on which structures of speculative theorizing grows. Intellectuals, giant figures as they were, remained committed to the primary cause. It was the cause of conquest, of expansion, territorial and cognitive, aligned in an axis of mutual support.

VI

In the area of "new knowledge", obviously the political experience of invasive colonization, annexation, appropriation, domination at the level of imperial engagement came to be subsumed under and absorbed in the larger design of the newly opening culture studies. These in the nineteenth century proceeded along three major lines of investigation : (a) studies in the growth of language, (b) in the growth of mythology and (c) in the growth of religion. The "historical" approach eloquently endorsed by Max Müller vigorously engaged in tracing linear growth pattern in all three areas. The new modality of "comparative" studies acknowledged no plurality

---

[52] Cited, Ibid., p. 321.

on an even floor; it built an evolutionary perspective[53] and projected the spectacle of a vertical ascent— events anywhere on earth at any point of the past leading to and culminating in the emergence of the European culture.

Beginning the series of Gifford Lectures fairly late in his life (1888) Max Müller assured his audience that in all his efforts he had wanted to show "how the road which leads from the Science of Language to the Science of Mythology and to the Science of Thought, is the only safe road on which to approach the Science of Religion."[54] This is the road followed by the "historical school" he defended all his life. In the fifth lecture, we noted, he claimed that what the new approach has established is the fact "that in religion, as in language, there is continuity", an unbroken continuity from the earliest origin to date. This, he affirmed, calls for a redefinition of religion, a definition taking into account not only what religion is now, but "what religion was in its origin." The perception of unbroken continuity, of ancestral kinship — the laudable tenet of nineteenth-century liberal humanism — provides in the historical discourse the framework within which to claim, to codify, to locate and to appropriate the "other". India, the Orient, the scholar knew and assured, "belongs to Europe".

Max Müller explained how all that so long had appeared to be coincidental parallelism "in the mythologies, the customs of traditions of distant races, distant in space as well as time, unconnected by any relationship … genealogical or linguistic, civilized and uncivilized, ancient and modern", now happened

[53] Max Müller's disagreement with Darwin was on the feasibility of evolutionary growth from the pre- and non- human to the human; within the fold of human existence the Darwinian paradigm prevailed, cogently and coherently.

[54] P. 25.

to fit into a pattern. Threaded in the sequential order, it all now came to reveal a wonderful course of development, logically coherent and graded. Tracing this, he repeatedly assures, had been his objective. In *Contributions to the Science of Mythology*, he affirms that the antiquarian studies had been important as a step in this direction; the study of the Veda, the earliest surviving text, has been a fortunate experience as a preparation for

> a more comprehensive study of the mythology of other nations and languages … and this for the simple reason that we possess in the hymns of the Rig-veda remnants of a period of mythological fermentation such as we find nowhere else.[55]

The difference between the polytheism in the Veda and the polytheism in Greek mythology, he feels sure, measures up as the distance between a less developed phase and a more mature one, the Hellenic perception marking an "advance". In the Greek pantheon the gods are formed into families and hierarchies; the Vedic hymns, the scholar notes, "enable us to go, as it were, behind this well-organized polytheism and to watch the growth" of gods in the thoughts of man in antiquity.

The Greek gods, he points out, had advanced beyond the Vedic ancestors in yet another aspect, "they are … the very perfection of the human type in their visible appearance". The scholar confidently concludes,

> Here again we find the germs only in the Vedas, far removed as yet from the perfection of Greek mythology.[56]

In the concluding Gifford Lecture he notes the stages of growth, of graded enlightenment, as his glance moves from

[55] Oxford, 1897, p. 22.

[56] Ibid., p. 148.

the deities in the Rig-veda to the concept of God the Father. He shows how "the god of the sky, … the god of the storm-wind, assumed gradually a supreme character", how ultimately "there remained in the end the concept of a Supreme Being",

> representing in reality the highest ideal of the Infinite, as a father or as a creator, and as a loving ruler of the universe. What we ourselves call our belief in God the Father, is the last result of this irresistible development of human thought.[57]

The earlier phases form the base on which revealed religion stands. In his lecture on "Anthropological Religion" he pleads for recognition of non-revealed religions, designated "natural religion", on the ground that these

> supply the only ground on which even revealed religions can stand, the only soil where they can strike root, and from which they can receive nourishment and life.

The non-Semitic, the "natural" modalities of sensibility, now harnessed to form a ground-rock beneath, lends vital support to the Semitic structure of faith.

The scholar perceives that the gods in the Veda, the "gods of nature", were not truly kindred to the gods reigning on the Olympus, the Vedic figures were not "restricted to one phenomenon, even to that which may have given birth to them"; he appreciates that Agni, for instance, "was not simply the actual fire deified", but "from the very beginning something over and above the phenomenal manifestations … a something never to be grasped at once, an agent apart from its acts."[58] Yet, he draws a sequential line of development and in the historical order, he places the Veda mythology as a more

---

[57] P. 572.

[58] *Contributions to the Science of Mythology* (Oxford, 1897), p. 132.

primitive stage prior to and aspiring towards the stage of the Greek myths. The logic remains as it did in the 1856 essay on Comparative Mythology, "India, however is not Greece", Greece, where Plato deliberated and Sophocles sang. India must consequently predate.

Max Müller feels convinced that the sacred Books of the East present "the Bibles of the whole human race"; he truly believes that "we must all have our bookless religion". All the while he places it all in an anterior phase of growth and subordinates it to the emergence of the Abrahamic faith, to Christianity, in particular. Revealed religion, the vision of an almighty Father figure, the scholar remains unwavering in his faith, is an experience which comes when man's spiritual sensibility is in full grown maturity. This marks the shore in man's long voyage of spiritual seeking, while all other creeds and convictions belong to a preparatory stage, the "infantia"[59], where the first stirrings begin.

....

These and such like affirmations and assertions bring messages of a safe home coming for the Western intellect — after the toil and travail of sailing on strange seas of thought and exploring alien terrain. Ecstatic sense of gratification, the feeling of a pilgrimage completed, a mission accomplished, the experience of being guided by the pole star through adventures on the high seas, are balanced off by an inner admission of, almost a surrender to, the compulsion of cultural allegiance. The allegiance is in three major folds: to the logic

[59] A term Max Müller uses in *Contributions to the Science of Mythology*, p. 72. Also see, Preface to the collected edition of his works.

of the empire, to the premise of the superiority of the Hellenic culture, to the Christian faith, the one true religion.

The nineteenth century uncovered the antique treasures, confronted the "other", conceptually habilitated it within the Occidental perceptual framework. It all worked attuned to the spirit of professed liberal ideals and acted as boosters to the triumphant self-gratulation of the season of achievement. The first half of the next century would bring out more neatly argued, more scientifically ordered conceptualization in the field of comparative studies, formulating the historical-a-historical, the linear-cyclic, the progressive-archaic binarity.

The location of culture is not definite, nor absolute; events are in place as the perceiver-chronicler, the Occident, at its own point of positioning, ordains.

TO

MAJOR-GENERAL SIR ARCHIBALD GALLOWAY, K.C.B., CHAIRMAN,

JOHN SHEPHERD, ESQ., DEPUTY CHAIRMAN,

SIR ROBERT CAMPBELL, BART.,
JOHN LOCH, ESQ.,
CHARLES MILLS, ESQ.,
JOHN MASTERMAN, ESQ., M.P.,
HENRY ST. GEORGE TUCKER, ESQ.,
HENRY ALEXANDER, ESQ.,
HENRY SHANK, ESQ.,
RUSSELL ELLICE, ESQ.,
SIR RICHARD JENKINS, G.C.B.,
JOHN COTTON, ESQ.
WILLIAM BUTTERWORTH BAYLEY, ESQ.,
FRANCIS WARDEN, ESQ.,
SIR HENRY WILLOCK, K.L.S.,
SIR JAMES WEIR HOGG, BART, M.P.,
WILLIAM HENRY C. PLOWDEN, ESQ., M.P.,
LIEUTENANT-COLONEL WILLIAM H. SYKES,
MAJOR JAMES OLIPHANT,
JOHN CLARMONT WHITEMAN, ESQ.,
THE HONOURABLE WILLIAM H. L. MELVILLE,
ROSS DONNELLY MANGLES, ESQ.,
MAJOR-GENERAL JAMES CAULFEILD, C.B.,
WILLIAM JOSEPH EASTWICK, ESQ.,

DIRECTORS

FOR MANAGING THE AFFAIRS

OF

THE HONOURABLE THE EAST-INDIA-COMPANY,

THIS ORIGINAL RECORD

OF THE EARLY INSTITUTIONS OF THE NATIVES OF INDIA

IS RESPECTFULLY AND GRATEFULLY DEDICATED

BY THEIR OBEDIENT SERVANT,

MAX MÜLLER.

OXFORD,
October 1849.

Dedication, Max Müller (ed.) *Rig-veda Sanhita* vol. 1

Four

The idiom of yore and Sayana the guide

Niṇyā vachāṁsi (4:3/16)
निण्या वचांसि
(articulations/words/messages from the deep)

Kavīyamānah ka iha pravochaddevaṁ
manah kuto adhi prajātam (1:64/18)
कवीयमानः कइहप्रवोचद्देवं मनः कुतो अधि प्रजातम्॥ १८
(Who is this that asks questions? Whence comes this wonderful mind that asks?)

Ye arvānchastān u parācha āhuryeparāncha
stān u arbācha āhuh (1:164/19)
ये अर्वाञ्चस्तॉं उ पराच आहुर्येपराञ्चस्तॉं उ अर्वाच आहुः।
(Those who know call the upward-faring the low and the downward-faring they call high.)

Dyaurme pitā janitā nābhiratra bandhurme
mātā prithivī mahīyam (1:164/33)
द्यौर्मे पिता जनिता नाभिरत्र बन्धुर्मे माता पृथिवीमहीयम्।
(The sky above is my father begetter, the sacrifice yard is my friend, the earth spreading around is my mother.)

Homi K. Bhabha talks about the situation of incomplete translation in the West's meeting with India[1]. The outsiders'

[1] *Location,* p. 185.

grapple with an alien ancient tradition demonstrates the problematics of the inner "translation" of the "other" idiom, the obstacles Max Müller recounts on numerous occasions. The challenge comes to the fore again when Heinrich R. Zimmer and Joseph Campbell, about a hundred years after Max Müller's mammoth efforts in the 1840's, come to examine possible ways of conversing with myths and symbols of the distant past in the East.

In reading the Veda texts the West had primarily missed out the metaphorical-symbolical modality of perception, the non-literal perception, for instance, which eschews the logic of pragmatics and asserts that "when all is taken out of all, all remains unreduced", "*purnasya purnamādāya purname-vāvashishyate*".

Western Vedicists also missed the long and rich tradition of linguistic-semantic enquiry in ancient India. The deep and complex study of the verbal mode of expression which in the ancient discourse simultaneously analyses the physiological process involved in verbal communication and also lends a mystical metaphysical dimension to the metaphorical style, the idiom of symbols, we know, comes to attract the notice of Western scholars only in recent times.

In the Preface to the first edition of *The Sacred Books of the East* Max Müller mentioned how from the very beginning he had never attached much value to the large corpus of traditional Veda exegesis. Here he had pushed aside the large corpus of ancient Veda interpretation coming down from the Brahmanas and the complex system of linguistic enquiry grown out of it. Mostly owing to the antiquated nature of Vedic Sanskrit and the exclusivity of a system of specialized enquiry, this had remained an obscure area difficult to access. All this that Max Müller had readily put aside almost as cumbersome baggage of scholastic hair-splitting, perhaps as part of the "priestly rubbish" Schopenhauer had cautioned him about, actually happens to constitute a large body of Veda interpretation which over centuries had branched out into highly sophisticated linguistic semantic studies of an ancient world. In turning away from it all and coming to depend on the Sayana Bhasya of the fourteenth century CE, the scholar, with his mentors behind, had missed a whole tradition.

In ancient India the Brahmanas and the related ritualistic exegetical literature, naturally obscure to the Westerners, had generated linguistic studies which record mature preoccupation with the complex nature of verbal signification, the power of the word, and its limitations. The rigorous and meticulous systems of semantic analysis had started in the Brahmanas, particularly in the Vedangas, all belonging to times preceding recorded history in India; and the lines of enquiry had acquired on their pathway newer accents. The untiring scrutiny continued through the Buddhist period and the period of classical Sanskrit as a live discourse in linguistic investigations. The tradition displays subtleties of analysis and startling insights into the relation between the cognitive process and linguistic structures. Some of these preoccupations, scholars of modern times come to appreciate, amazingly anticipate a number of vital points in modern and post-modern linguistic-semantic speculation in the West.[2] Rightly responded to at the time of the nineteenth-century Orientalists' reading of the Veda, these would have opened up to them other, deeper levels of communication embedded in the ancient text of the Rig-veda; and that might have altered the history of Indology.

---

[2] See, for instance, H. G. Coward, *The Sphota Theory of Language*, pp. 3, 7, 136-37.

I

H. G. Coward in the Introduction of his volume on *The Sphota Theory of Language* notes,

> In contrast to the relatively recent stress on linguistics and the philosophy of language in the West, linguistic speculations were begun by the Hindus before the advent of recorded history. Beginning with the Vedic hymns, which are at least 3000 years old, the Indian study of language has continued in an unbroken tradition right up to the present day. The Indian approach was never narrow or restricted. Language was examined in relation to consciousness — consciousness not constricted even to human consciousness. All aspect of the world and human experience were thought of as illuminated by language.[3]

The "unbroken tradition" Coward mentions has a checkered history and unfolds a complex pattern of development. Engagement with the issue of the status of language, the engagement in which the elaborate system of linguistic-semantic search originated, had been anchored in the beginning to the reverential, religious effort at decoding the right, the precise meaning of the message of the Veda – the *vedārthavichāra*. The proliferation of exegetical literature in ancient India records a relentless pursuit of the "exact meaning". One tries to be sure; explication is of vital importance in ancient Indian discourse, particularly as Sanskrit is a language loaded with synonyms and near-synonyms, also as the tendency in ancient formulation is towards metaphorical indirection and aphoristic condensation. The prolonged untiring grapple with the semantics of God-speak threw up queries relating to the broader problem of the function and the functional competence of the verbal mode. The ancient mind grew aware of the frontier of verbal communication.

[3] P. 3.

This awareness, as Coward mentions, has been gaining depth and urgency in the Western culture only in recent times.[4]

The Brāhmanas, of earlier origin and enjoying the status of part of the Veda[5], spell out the minute details of ritual sacrifice corresponding to the *mantras*, the text of the Veda[6]; this is ritual reading of the text. From the Brāhmanas to the Priests' manual, *Purohitadarpaṇam* of later times and of current use, we have noted, there runs an unbroken thread in ritual enunciation.

The Vedāngas had split into six areas and extended the interpretive act into the six branches of *Shikshā* (phonetics), *Kalpa* (intentionality), *Vyākaraṇa* (grammar), *Nirukta* (etymology and semantics), *Chandas* (metrics) and *Jyotisha* (astrology). All these are interrelated and hence integrated in the search for meaning/signification. In an unbroken process of growth the linguistic philosophy of ancient India acquired newer subtleties in the exegetical schools of much later times— the *Sphota* theory of Bhartrihari, sixth century CE, the *Mimāṁsā Sāstra* of Kumāril Bhatta, seventh century CE

---

4 The pre-Wittgenstein, pre-Bakhtin trust of the West in the signifier-signified correspondence, on a representational level— the trust in meaning as implicit in the word — that generally prevailed in the nineteenth century, might have operated as an obstacle when Orientalists came to decipher the multi-vocal structure of meaning and the symbolical mode of indirection in the Veda and the Vedic in ancient India.

5 *Mantra Brāhmaṇayor Vedanāmadheyam*, (mantra and Brahmana taken together constitute the Veda) *Āpastambiya Paribhāsā Sutra*, 1: 33.

6 The forty chapters of *Aitareya Brāhmana*, for instance, detail *Soma* sacrifices, the *Taṇdya Mahā Brāhmaṇa* outlines programmes of *Soma* sacrifice completed in one day, *ekāha,* continued over two to twelve days, *ahinā,* spread out over more than twelve days, at times one full year, *satra*, and so on.

and the *Dhwanivāda* of Anandabardhana and Abhinavagupta, ninth century and tenth century CE, for instance.

Vedārtha, the meaning of the Veda message, the message of truth in the *niṇyā vachāṁsi*, the words/voices/messages from the secret deep, remains the focal point in this prolonged pursuit—diligent, untiring and continuous, through the rolling centuries in the life of an ancient civilization.

If the progression in ancient Indian culture had been from intuition to intellection, from inner illumination in the Veda to polemical argumentation in the Upanishads,[7] the development in linguistic-semantic investigations unfolds a similar course of development. It starts in the assumption of the *daivy Vāc*, divine speech. The Vedas, archetypal body of utterances, the primal modus of transmission, are validated as divine speech; God-speak stands validated once for all.

All that man can attempt in the case is

(a) To receive, to accept and to preserve the logos in its pristine purity. Orality calls for correct pronunciation (*Shikshā*), correct chanting (*Chandas*), correct comprehension of the interrelation of words (*Vyākaraṇa*), of the etymology and the principles of the formation of words (*Nirukta*).

(b) To relate it to practice, to the performance of the sacrificial rites, with the right/specific intention (*Kalpa*) and correct calculation of the prescribed timing (Jyotisha) in the seasonal cycle.

It is interesting to note that although executing ritual performance to perfection—with correct pronunciation, correct chanting etc.— remains the primary objective in the Veda

[7] Bankimchandra sketches out the process for the modern reader in his *Prachāra* essay "Devatattwa o Hindu Dharma", *Rachanavali*, II.

exegesis in the Brahmana tradition of ancient times, the linguistic study in the six branches of Vedanga gradually gets self-absorbed, self-reflexive and follows its own logic, each branch in course of time developing into an independent discipline. The orderly modes of grouping, classifying, dividing and sub-dividing demonstrate mature skill in critical taxonomy.

Under *Shikshā*, phonetics, comes the division of the reading of the Veda text into *Padapātha* and *samhitāpātha* systems. The *padapātha* takes note of the *pada*, the word, in its full grammatical form including the suffix and the form of termination, while the *samhitāpātha* takes words together to constitute larger syntactical units. The *pratisākhya* branch, each *pratisākhya* concentrating on its own recension, describes features of the different parts of speech: the noun, the verb, the prefix and the particle in the *padapātha* and in the *samhitāpātha.* The ancient system of phonetics also studies in detail the function of vowels and consonants, vowels expanded and shortened (*udātta* and *anudātta*), formulates principles of syllabification. Scholars in modern times appreciate the sound basis formed in the *Shikshā* discipline which lent support to the Paninian system later on.[8]

Vāc, speech, is sacred, divine, *daivy*; pronunciation, vocalization, however, is a physiological gesture — verbal and pre-verbal. The recognition of the elementary aspects of the mechanism, the purely "phenomenal" aspect of verbality, as modern scholars designate it[9], dates back to the Rig-veda itself

---

[8] For a brief outline, see V. M. Apte, "The Vedangas", *The Cultural Heritage of India*, I (the Ramakrishna Mission Institute of Culture, Calcutta, paperback 2001), pp. 266-275.

[9] See, for instance, Coward, *The Sphota Theory of Language*. p. 3ff.; Coward appreciates the mature vision in the inclusive perspective.

where we are told of the four levels of articulation/expression/verbalization:

Catvāri vāc parimitā padāni tāni vidurbrāhmaṇā ye manīshiṇah
Guhā trīṇi nihitā nengayanti turīyaṁ vāco manushyā vadanti.
(1: 164/45)

चत्वारि वाक्परिमिता पदानि तानि विदुर्ब्राह्मणा ये मनीषिणः
गुहा त्रीणि निहिता नेङ्गयन्ति तुरीयंवाचो मनुष्या वदन्ति ।।४५

(Speech is at four well defined stations; wise thinkers know of them. Three of these positions remain hidden and do not come into notice. The fourth and the highest is the position of human speech.)

Speech here is measured in four parts, steps, or grades; three of them are accepted as secret. Satapatha Brāhmana[10] describes these as *anirukta,* non-verbalized: (a) the hissing of serpents, humming of insects, (b) the notes of birds, (c) the voice of animals[11]. The fourth step in the progressive journey stands for human speech; it is formally verbalized and fully furnished with an ordered schematic design.

The *Nirukta* branch of the Vedanga attempts an exhaustive semantic scrutiny, seeks to bring out all possible shades of meaning in a text, taking into consideration the etymological origins of words. The term *nirukta*, meaning *nihsheshādukta,*

---

[10] Vol. IV. 1.3. 16.

[11] BBC Channel Four programme "The Story of India, the Beginnings" (http: // www.mvgroup.org) shows Michael Wood on his visit to an interior village in Kerala where young learners are taught chanting Veda mantras for a fire sacrifice. The incantation includes "vocal sounds not related to any known language"; the sounds form groups or clusters which have no human meaning. These, the interpreter explains, derive from bird song; these non- and pre-human voices cannot be written down. The oral tradition alone can capture and convey.

what has been exhaustively said, stands for a semantic of complete, exhaustive explication. Yaska, with many *niruktakāras*, etymologists, like Sakatayana, Gargya, Sakapuni, before him, re-asserts the conviction in a long tradition, the conviction that mere chanting of the Veda mantras is not enough, proper comprehension of the meaning alone makes it fruitful. There is the cautioning in the Rig-veda text that mere recitation without full comprehension is "*aphalā*", fruitless and "*apuspā*", without flowers, unproductive, sterile (10: 71 / 5). Yaska explains these plant metaphors in the Veda, relating them also to the two levels of implication — the ritual and the spiritual — both of which must be integrated in effective comprehension[12]. With this conviction Yaska proceeds to map out the full semantic field of the cardinal words enlisted in the lexicon of earlier times, the *Nighaṇtu*[13]. Yaska and his trust in signification are often related to the gnostic trend in the ancient tradition.[14]

Yaska, with mastery over the Vedic lexical field and dexterity in analytical reasoning, raises subtle points of etymology, word formation and signification. He faces the debated question whether all nouns are derived from verbal roots/action words, and makes a broad generic division, between (1) words derived from verbal roots, retaining actional signification, and, consequently, loaded with temporal dimension, and (2) words not derived from verbs, and thus, non-actional, simply denoting states of being, not necessarily time-bound.

[12] "*Yāgnadaivate puspaphale devatādhyātme bā*", (*Nirukta*, 1: 20), the caution applies to the entire range — ritual-theistic-spiritual.

[13] The lexicon is so named, because the words listed come from the Veda. Yaska explains, "*Nighaṇtabah kasmāt, nigamā ime bhabanti*" — why called Nighantu?— for the reason that the words derive from the Veda mantras. (*Nirukta,* 1: 1. 1/4.)

[14] See, for instance, V.S. Agarwala, "Yaska and Panini", The *Cultural History of India* Vol. I, p. 293.

"*Bhābaprādhānyam ākhyātam, sattwapradhānāni nāmāni*", comments the etymologist (*Nirukta*, 1: 1. 1/10). In the structure of a sentence comprising both, Yaska notes, the actional words naturally dominate.

In Sanskrit the same word-forms are often derived from different roots signifying different action-impulses. Yaska demonstrates how the same word (*go*, *āditya*, *prithivī*, *rātri*, and a whole host of them) happens to carry diverse signification coming down from different source roots. The scholar gives the invaluable advice that in the act of interpretation, etymological derivation must be traced and the specific shade of meaning must be deciphered in each specific context.[15] Prioritization of the contextual over the lexical in the sphere of semantic speculation speaks of a highly mature level of experience in handling words and the functioning of words.

The *Vyākaraṇa* (the Sanskrit word literally means the act of analysing) branch begins, in a way, in the *padapātha* practice, and, sustained by the penetrative studies of Yaska, reaches a point of full formulation in the work of Panini. Language and its modalities of signification never ceased to fascinate the ancient mind. *Vāc* is divine, a primal force in the Rig-veda: the rishis reach up to her, attain the power of articulating, bringing forth, what had been in their inner mind/thought, only through devoted effort, performing pious sacrifice

---

[15] Yaska cites diverse meaning of words and notes the vast range of nomenclature and signification — 21 names for *prithivī* (the earth), 26 for *aswa* (horse), 36 for *nadī* (river), 100 for *udaka* (water) for instance, — and he comments: "*Samānakarmāṇi samānanirvachanāni nānākarmāṇi chennānā nirvachanāni yathārthang nirvyactabāniti*" (shared derivation from the root would produce similar meaning, whereas, with divergent etymological sources, words would have divergent meanings; interpretation must be as it suits the context / total pattern of meaning), *Nirukta*, 2: 1. 7/9.

(10: 72 / 3); *Vāc* is the deity of sentience, co-extensive with the entire range of cognition, inspiring all gestures of action in all forms of life (10: 125). The Taittiriya Saṁhita mentions that Indra himself had explained speech, *Vāc*, to the gods. The sixty-four grammarians[16] mentioned in the *Astādhyāyī* by Panini as his predecessors, belong to a long tradition of competent linguistic studies. Yaska had led the long Nirukta (etymology) tradition to a peak point; Panini, coming at a later point in the line of explorations, brings the grammatical tradition to a point of full maturity. Panini's scrutiny of the question whether the word or the sentence should be taken as the stable verbal unit — a question which had engaged the etymologist Yaska in his own time—comes close to our debate on the diachronic and the synchronic reception of words and word-sequences.

Again, speech, at the physiological level, constitutes a temporal sequence; letters, phonemes, words, parts of sentences are progressively left behind, as verbal communication proceeds towards completion. The ancient scholars, leading exponents Yaska and Panini, later, engage in examining whether verbal units left behind are lost; if they are, how does speech deliver the consistent full message? Introducing a subtle distinction between "*vināsha*", annihilation, and "*adarshana*", disappearance, the linguists conclude that verbal units articulated are not absolutely lost, it is not a case of "*vināsha*", but merely of "*adarshana*", passing out of sight, which leaves a trace, a "*purvabhāvanā*", behind. The temporality in verbal sequence, in speech and in hearing, the process of threading together of units in succession and the formation of a continuum as a stable verbal unit — are all studied with clarity of perception and analysis and conclusions are deduced with

[16] Apisali, Kasakritsna, Gargya, Bharadwaj, Sakatayana among the eminent ones.

mature understanding both of the cognitive process and of the physical pragmatics involved.

The Mimamsa school in its early phase accepts the eternality of the verbal mode, the "*sabdapramāṇa*", on the ground of the eternality of the Veda, God-speak; as the enquiry gets self-reflexive and analytical, in its later phases it enters into the intricate question of the idea of the permanence of the word or of the sentence, in the face of the fact that articulation is transitory at the physiological and at the physical level. A greater trust, evolving out of minute reasoning, is placed on the sentence, the *vākya*. The sentence as a unit accommodates intentionality/expectation, "*ākānkshā*", the meaning of individual words, "*yogyatā*", and the syntagmatic positioning of words, "*sannidhi*"; all these, together, constitute a quantum of meaning, complete and autonomous.

Debate on the question as to how the temporality / transience of articulation and audition at the physical level is overcome in the integrity of the intentional semantic order, is of central importance in the discourse and it continues in the post-Buddha phase of *Sphotavāda*.

If earlier speculation had enjoyed a comfortable cushioning in what operated as a first premise in the Brahmanic tradition, the conviction that the Veda articulations stand on absolute validation, that they are "*swatahpramāṇah*", post-Buddha systems face a challenge. Rejecting the idea of the primal validity of the Veda text, the anti-vedic, "*a-vaidika*" school turns to the naturalistic assumption that the relation between words and meaning is only conventional and of a contingent nature. The linguistic polemic now rises to another level of abstraction; Bhartrihari (580 CE), a major exponent of the "*sphota*" theory, for instance, develops the concept of a unitary whole word, "*akhaṇdavākyasphota*". The idea here, as T. R.

V. Murti notes, is that "the several sounds of letters and words uttered by the speaker and heard by the listener, serve merely the purpose of arousing or invoking the Sphota (Whole Sentence Unit), already present in each one of us".[17] The Sphota theory posits two levels on the epistemic plane: that of empirical verbality and of the intended meaning. It distinguishes levels of speech: the "*vaikhari*", overt speech — letters, words, sound ..., the "*madhyamā*", internal speech, "*antarjalpa*", and "*pasyanti*", the intentional, looking forward to expression.

It thus traces the verbal process, the act of speech, from the external to the internal, from the articulated to the intended, from the many to the one. Behind the articulated is the intended; articulation may be a variant, the intention is the determinant. Differences, Bhartrihari knows, presuppose unity: "*avedapurvakah hi vedah*". The analyses develop the idea of "*sabda-Brahma*", the Word as the spirit of the universe.[18]

II

Vāc, speech, in the Rig-veda, already noted (10: 125 / 4; 6), claims to be co-extensive with sentience; as a goddess she is the force behind the inner acts of cognition and the external actional applications at all levels of existence. Naturally, Poetry, a more developed, much higher and purified level of speech, a specialized form, demonstrates more explicitly, and more rigorously too, the mechanism in the process of articulation — expression, figuring forth. In poetry, resembling organic shaping forth, it involves "aesthetic incarnation".

The linguistic semantic enquiry coming down from the time of the Veda extends into the area of aesthetics in the age of Classical Sanskrit literature and literary speculations; it

17 *The Sphota Theory of Language*, p. (X).

18 Cited, Ibid., p. (XII).

reaches newer heights, acquires newer tonal subtleties, for instance, in the *Dhwani* theory of Anandabardhana (ninth century CE) and in *Lochana*, the commentary on it, the *tikā*, by Abhinavagupta (tenth century CE). Language in poetry, we are told, is poly-semantic. Signification operates on several floors: the literal, *vāchya*, the figurative, *lākshaṇik*, the poetical, *vyangya*, *pratiyamāna*.[19]

The poet Kalidasa (fourth to fifth century CE), we recall, in the invocation to his *Kumārasambhavam*, prayed for access to the mystics of semantic efficacy, for mastery over the power of synchronization of speech and meaning. The synchronicity, the poet averred, is as holy and as potent as the union of Parvati and Parameswara, the primal progenitors of the universe.[20]

Kalidasa believes and theoreticians Anandabardhana and Abhinavagupta later argue, that meaning is a complex process resembling the life of an organism. The body is as important as the life and spirit within. Appreciation, understanding, response, in the area of aesthetic experience, involves a journey from the exterior to the interior. The gradational course of aesthetic signification, Dhwani theorists assert, is an inclusive process, transcendental in nature; here the primary level is not rejected, not left behind, not subdued, it is simply assimilated and transcended in the poetical, the projected, *pratiyamāna* meaning.[21] Anandabardhana uses the metaphor of a lamp: the wick burns, it has to be trimmed and cared for,

---

[19] *Dhanyāloka*, *Udyota* 1:2.

[20] "*Vāgarthābibasampriktau, vāgarthapratipattaye // jagatahpitarau bande PārvatiParameswaram*".

[21] The commentator Abhinavagupta, the author of the *Lochana*, was a scholar in Kashmir Saivism and had authored an expository treatise on this philosophy. The influence of the synthesizing transcendentalism in Kashmir Saivism on the Dhwani school of aesthetic speculation awaits fuller exploration.

the light emanates. The literal, the primary meaning in a verbal structure is in the role of the wick; the light is the metaphor for the deeper meaning.[22]

This higher, transcendent meaning, though not exclusive of the literal or the primary signification, is beyond the yield at the level of mere denotation, it is more than an aggregate. The metaphor used to illustrate is that of the charm of a beautiful woman, the *lāvanya* which, not located in any specific part of her physiognomy, is yet an emanation from the whole.[23] The literal and the poetical, the lexical and the metaphorical are synchronized and iconized in the living form of beauty. Speech, *Vāc*, we know, is extolled in the Rig-veda; Sukta 71, Sloka 4, in Mandala 10, uses the metaphor of a loving surrender, an unveiling. A loving wife, we are reminded, reveals her beauty and charm only to the beloved husband.

The word, the verbal form, is used as an efficient vehicle, and it is loaded with meaning (divine message and/or human expression). The speaker transmits, he communicates, while the auditor decodes — the right receptor decoding in the right way. The co-ordination between the transmission and the reception, at the two ends of the communicative action, presented to the Indian mind in antiquity an intriguing process; unraveling the mystique and the mechanism of this kept generations of scholars engaged over thousands of years.[24]

---

[22] "*ālokārthi yathā deepashikhāyān yatnabānjanah // Tadupataya tadbad arthe vāchye tadādritah*". 1:9.

[23] "*Pratiyamānang punaranyadeba vastwasti vānishu mahākavīnām// Yattat prasiddhāvayavātiriktang bivāti lavaṇyamibānganāsu*". Ibid. 1:4.

[24] For a brief sketch of the developments and branching out in semantic speculations after Abhinavagupta and up to the sixteenth century, one might start with Gaurinath Sastri, "Sanskrit Poetics", *The Cultural History of India*, vol. V, pp. 299-302.

Much of this, the deeper levels of engagement and the subtler extensions of the enquiry, that had flourished hundreds of years before Sayana, remained unaccessed in the reading of the early Orientalists — in a situation facing varied obstacles and burdened with complex compulsions operative at numerous levels of the East-West encounter.

III

The true strength of the Vedic text, as both Bankimchandra and Sri Aurobindo noted, lies in the inclusiveness, the integration of the many and different levels of experiential perception into an integral vision. It is not, as the Western Indologists had thought,[25] a collection of unconnected, incoherent "primitive utterances" in the infancy of civilization; it is an embracive, compacted corpus of man's varied perception of his position in the universe, his multi-faceted complex relationship with the forces outside and around. A scrutiny of the tone and the tenor in the hymns, even when taken as stray samples, from the Rig-veda largely unfolds the mystique of this "nature worship" that Max Müller had designated "Henotheism" or "Kakenotheism".[26]

---

[25] This is a perception running, for example, from Max Müller and his contemporaries down to the translator-commentator W. D. O'Flaherty in the Penguin collection of 108 hymns from the Rig-veda,1981, revised edition 2000, pp. 11-12. V. Ganguly's *Vāsanti Bhāsya* published by the Asiatic Society Calcutta in 2004 presents a committed counter-assertion, questioning the Occidental reading; it reads the Rig-veda as a metaphorical spiritual pilgrimage from mortality to immortality. See., pp. XXIV-XXIX.

[26] Bankimchandra's humour, we noted, makes hilarious reading of the erudite scholar's perplexity in the face of the Vedic worship of numerous gods — "Devatattwa O Hindudharma", *Prachār*, 2nd year, *Rachanavali* II (Sahitya Samsad), pp. 815-16.

Agni leads. *Agnimile*, I worship Agni. With this begins the Rig-veda. With paeans to Agni in diverse forms and accents open Mandalas 1 to 7 and again Mandala 10, the last one. Even though the division into the Mandalas, the structuring into Suktas and Riks and the overall designing of the text may be left to the masterly management by Vyasa in later times, the pre-eminence of Agni in the Rig-veda remains incontrovertible. Sri Aurobindo interprets Agni as the divine will operative in man : *kavikratuh*, the spark of energy derived from the prime progenitor, the Creator. B. Ganguly interprets the elaborate enunciation of sacrificial performance in the Rig-veda as "the silent, esoteric, immortalizing sacrifices going on *within*".[27] Agni is the *hotā*, the *purohitah,* positioned in the fore front, in all pious, aspirational activities.

The interesting point here, as in other instances, is that signification extends over a large range. Agni is the energy that ignites (a) at the physical level where it is born of a friction between the two pieces of dry wood, *araṇi* (1 : 31/ 2,4, ...), where its advent is indicated by the mass of spiralling smoke looking like the tail of a meteor (1 : 27/11 ...), it is the blazing flame that consumes everything.

At the same time Agni, at the inner spiritual level (b), is *jātaveda*, all-knowing, *kavi* who creates and expresses eloquently.[28] Here Agni stands for the urge behind creation, the highest cognitive-creative urge, the energy in all human effort and action.

Both ends in the range of signification, with intermediary levels of connectivity, remain operative. Agni who consumes

---

27 *The Rig-veda Saṁhita*. p. xxiv.

28 Sitanath Goswami presents etymological-derivative shades of meaning of the term *kavi*. *Rik Saṁhita* (Calcutta 1974), p. 280.

forests (1 : 66/1, 66/4 ...), Agni who is nurtured with offerings of *havya/ghrita* measured with large feeder spoons, *juhu/darvi* (1 : 12/6 ...), Agni who assumes different forms and operates in different ways on earth as blazing fire and in the heavens above as the sun or as lightning (1 : 68/1; 71/5; 73/2; 79/1, 3; 10 : 45/1...), is definitely the fire that lights up as well as burns; it is the fire, the access to which had been a decisive event in the history of civilization. The pre-fire phase is mentioned as the time of the Rakshasas, the uncivilized primitives, assaults from whom must be prevented; prayers are for the decimation of all such forces (10 : 87/7, for instance). Worship of Agni is a ritual remembrance and a celebration through elaborate sacrifices. This is a ground-level signification with its ready appeal to populace engaged in the primary pursuits of life; and prayers to Agni for good turn of events in life — rich crops, increase in wealth, triumph over enemies — in a way constitute gestures of self-confirmation and self-reliance. Man who had accessed fire and put it to his own use, can and should prove an achiever in every sphere.

The same Agni, however, is the all-knowing creative expressive urge, the spark of the purest essence which, properly nurtured, is capable of purifying, burning up all the dross and illuminating the divine potency in man.

Agni is worshipped in both roles at both levels in the same Sukta, as in Sukta 12 in Mandala 1. Born of dry wood, fed *havya* ladled out as offerings, Agni is *kavi* and *satyadharmā*, the visionary creator and the preserver of Truth, the *pāvakadidiva*, the translucent purifier; in Sukta 36, Agni stands for intellect at its best and also generates spiralling smoke (Sloka 9), Agni is the god of sustenance and protector from all forms of evil and evil impulse (Slokas 12, 14). In Sukta 58 Agni is the roaring forest-fire (Sloka 4) and the repository of wisdom and intellection (Sloka 9). Similar balancing operates in Sukta 1, Mandala 10 as in many other hymns. Prayers to Agni are simultaneously for sustenance — *anna*[29] — wealth, longevity, fame, increase in family and also for unfailing direction of the right path, the path of *ritam*, of ethical discrimination (1 : 32/2, 5-8, 17; 72/1 ...). The ability to know the right from the wrong, the basic moral sensibility, is a precious object of prayer; and keeping away from *pāpa*, reprehensible action, is always prayed for. The blazing fire is a veritable agency of burning-up all impurities (7 : 15). Born knowing all, *jātaveda,* Agni knows everything from the very beginning. *Satyadharmā, prajnāvān, pāvaka, kavi*, are some of the recurring epithets automatically associated with Agni, almost synonymous. The earnest yearning is for imbibing in oneself the knowledge, the cognitive energy, the energy of intellection that sees through illusory appearances and reaches unto Truth. Sri Aurobindo asserts,

> Psychologically, then, we may take Agni to be the divine will perfectly inspired by divine wisdom, and indeed one with it, which is the effective power of the Truth-consciousness.[30]

Indra, the ruler in the heavens, the slayer of the Vrittras and the Panis and evil-doers and obstructors around, releases the waters and wields the thunder. Indra is invoked in the largest number of hymns in the Rig-veda. Bankimchandra had explained in simple terms the etymological meaning of the name, which is an *abhiḍhā*, a designatory term. The root *ind*

---

[29] Mention might be made of the inclusive vision projected in the Upanishads, later in time, the perception that physical sustenance is the primary threshold and here we must not look down upon *anna*, food—*annam na nindyāt* (3 : 7); *annam na parichakshita* (3 : 8). Existence stretches from the corporeal to the spiritual, from the *annamayakosa* to the *ānandamayakosa* — including both.

[30] *The Secret of the Veda*, pp. 65-66.

meaning to shower, to pour down, one who pours down bears the name Indra, derived from the actional root. Bankim reads the term also as a name for the sky in its capacity of pouring down rains, even as the sky is Aditi in its infinite dimensions and Dyau in its capacity of transmitting sunlight.[31] Indra releases waters in showers of rain as well as the waters of life. He is the powerful one. The rishis bring prayers to him for bounty at all levels.

The first eight Suktas, numbers 4 to 11, by the sons of Viswamitra – Madhucchanda and Jetri – in Mandala 1, invite Indra to the sacrifice. They offer him generous shares of *anna* and *soma* and plead with earnest prayers for protection from foes and for the gift of cows, the gift of wealth and the gift of strength and power. May Indra, the powerful one who had destroyed Vrittra, Vala, Panis, Sishna and other evil ones, the enemies and creators of obstruction, Indra who had released waters from the high heavens, Indra the rain giver (1: 32 / 1, 11, 12; 33 / 6, 10; 6: 32 / 3 …), protect us, the rishis pray. The pragmatic validity is of all time and of germinal relevance. Numerous and varied accounts are given of the heroic exploits of Indra, his fight with Vrittra and the Panis, his mighty act of pulling down the citadel, the *pura* of the enemies – the act that had earned him the name Purandara, the demolisher of the city/ citadel of the foes (6: 32; 33). Speculation in modern scholarship abounds as to the racial identities of the hostile groups and the ethnic implications of the conflict.

However, mighty Indra is also the wisest of the wise (1: 4 /3, 4; 5 / 6, 7), the greatest among the gods (1: 5 / 6), the unbeatable genius (1: 4 / 4). Those well-endowed with the gift of knowledge, know his true might (1: 11 /7); the hymns and

---

[31] *Rachanavali* II, pp. 788-89.

paeans composed by such earnest worshippers add to the luminous glory of Indra (1:5 / 8; 10 /1). Verily, Indra is a symbol, an iconic figure of prowess in a symbolical sense; the wealth Indra gifts is of a metaphorical significance – even as the cows, the *gāvah*, are symbols of the glow / light / rays of knowledge in the Rig-veda. The symbolism operated as a live channel of signification to those who naturally spoke the language, those who, starting at the literal level, could access the rest of the semantic field.

Sri Aurobindo interprets Indra as "the master of the luminous mind", the "enlightened intelligence which fashions right or perfect form of thoughts"[32], his gifts are the gifts of light, of inspired thought:

> For this light is in its entire greatness free from limitation, a continent of felicity, this power is that which befriends the human soul and carries it safe through the battle, to the end of its march, to the summit of its aspiration.[33]

Sharing the full spiritual accent in Sri Aurobindo's reading, or not, one discerns a duality, at times multiplicity, of signification in the hymns of the Rig-veda. This is an inclusive vision that extends from the familiar physical to the highest spiritual, from the ritualistic to the metaphysical. Usha, the goddess of dawn, brings a new day, awakens all living beings at the end of a dark night; greetings and prayers to her not only reflect the elemental joy of life at the advent of daylight, but also voice an eagerness to be cleansed anew of all evil impulses (1: 123 / 3), an aspiration toward wisdom and the knowledge of truth (1: 123 / 6). Light at daybreak metaphorically denotes illumination of the inner soul.

---

[32] *The Secret of the Veda*, p. 260, 262.

[33] Ibid., p. 265.

The Aswins, the physician gods, heal bodily ailments. Ghosa, daughter of sage Kakshiban, in Suktas 39-40 in Mandala 10, recounts numerous feats of healing performed by the heavenly healers and prays for eradication of her own disease. The range of healing happens to be more extensive in Mandala 7, for instance, where sage Vasistha on behalf of worshippers recollects how the Aswins had rescued Atri from the dark depths of sin (71/5); prayers to the healing gods are for being lifted out of the darkness of ignorance (73/1).

Vedic worship, in a way, is the expression of a sense of values; things that serve man in any form – natural or manufactured – are appreciated. For instance, the chariot, the *ratha*, and the drum, the *dundubhi*, are invaluable in their utility, adorable objects in life. The prayer or the pious wish is: may the chariot, the *ratha,* made of the strong mature body of the *vanaspati*, the mighty senator of the wood, prove firm, invincible; may it lend us vital support in hours of need, in our battles with the enemy. May the drum, the *dundubhi*, sound powerfully, may its roar strike terror in the mind of the enemy, may it loudly announce our triumph (6: 47 / 26, 27, 29, 30). The attitude of veneration and of pious resolve, called *sraddhā*, is adored as a goddess who sanctifies all action. Generous acts of donation, *dānakarma*, among other good deeds, are acts of piety that ennoble the doer (8: 21 / 16–18; 10: 117). Hymns and paeans adore and celebrate. Bankimchandra brings out the inner spirit in such worshipful formulations in his essay on Devatattwa O Hindu Dharma mentioned.[34]

Indeed, worship in the Rig-veda, in the ancient Indian culture itself, is an attitudinal inclination, a reverential spirit that endows the physical universe with metaphysical qualities and proportions. It endows the forces of nature with aspects of

[34] *Rachanavali* II, pp. 809-10.

divinity, not exactly Henotheistic or Kakenotheistic, as Western scholars would have it, but metaphorical in its essence. The verbal mode of indirection and multi-signification ensures operation on many levels and on an inclusive range.[35]

2

This sacramental vision of the physical universe, the mortal habitat, again, extends to an immensely valuable set of eco-ethics. Sage Dirghatama Ouchathya says, "the Sky above is my father, the sacrificial area is my friend, the great Earth is my mother". The earth and the sky, *dyāvāprithivī*, the father and mother, are holy; they constitute our lovely abode. The recurring prayer is: may this be spacious and well endowed, nourishing and sustaining (1: 160; 6: 32/2; 50/3, 13; 70, for instance), even as loving parents are. Water, *ap*, poured down as rain or surrounding the earth as oceans, dug-up from beneath or flowing as natural streams, is divine in its capacity to germinate, to cleanse and to quench (6: 70/4; 7: 47, 49; 10: 9 ...). May water, the life-sap, always be bountiful to us.[36] Rivers,

---

[35] Heinrich R. Zimmer in his study of the myths and Puranas of ancient India brings out the aesthetic-mystical sensitiveness to the symbolic and the metaphorical in the antique vision. He points out the "intellectual frustration" in the West's attempt at reducing the "unfamiliar to the well-known" which, he notes, satisfies a sense of cultural superiority, but denies live interaction, true conversation, with the modality of indirection, the style of meta-literate symbolism in ancient civilization. See, *The King and the Corpse,* (1948, Indian edition, Motilal Banarasidass, Delhi, 1999), pp. 2-3.

[36] The Dharma Sastras of later times put sharper focus on the ecological impact. Taking care of water resources, recovering water bodies and digging new wells and tanks – *purta karma* – is highly recommended in the *Likhita Saṁhitā* (2:4); again in the *Vishnu Saṁhitā* (61: 1-7) such acts are valued as virtuous deeds equal to the performance of elaborate sacrifices.

life-streams of demographic zones, are holy and divine; the mighty Saraswati and her sister streams, or the Indus, major sources of rain clouds, abode of wealth, are in the role of a caring mother (6: 61; 10: 30 / 12-14; 10: 75).

The advent of the season of rains is welcome and eagerly awaited; frog-voice ushers in the event and frogs are a friendly lot to greet. *Manduka*, the frog, is the *devatā*, the theme, in Sukta 103 in Mandala 7. Rishi Vasistha prays. He lovingly describes the livery of varied shades of colour the frogs are apparelled in – smoke grey, light and deep, and yellow. He appreciates the year-long patient waiting of the frog community for the season of rains, he deeply appreciates the collective jubilant joy of these creatures at the advent of showers, the rejuvenating showers that nourish the innumerable species of healing herbs. Medicinal herbs, *osadhayah*, are heavenly blessings; their motherly touch heals and sustains. May these divine gifts remain abundant, bountiful, caring and curative to the afflicted and the ailing (10: 97). The forests, *aranyāni*, are dense and vast, resonant with voices of numerous forms of life, fragrant like musk and laden with delicious fruits. A forest in which cultivators do not interfere, is a nourishing mother to living beings (10: 146).

The diurnal movement of time measures man's daily existence; all hours are propitious. Even as goddess Usha brings a fresh dawn, the bountiful, compassionate goddess night, *Rātri*, spreads out silence and peaceful rest (10: 127), rest that restores.

Holiness pervades; sacred are the heavens above and the particles of dust below. Things are blessed, *madhumat* — big or small, high or low.

Spiritual sensibility, Bankimchandra noted, grows slowly and marks advancing levels of human civilization. The sacramental sense of being enfolded in a benign scheme, the sense that vibrates in the hymns of the Rig-veda, is indeed unlikely to flourish in the 'infantia' of human civilization, in times of the primitive man's desperate struggle for physical survival. Man awed by the forces of nature, in strife with nature, and man at home in nature, as part of nature, are different profiles.

IV

Speculations about the mystery of Creation in the Rig-veda reach high levels of abstraction and project a mind that – adopting Wordsworth's phrasing, one might say — had thought long and deeply. *Asato sadajāyata* (10: 72 / 2), we are told; the idea of existence evolving out of non-existence is affirmed once again in the *Nāsadiya Sukta* (10: 129). The concept of the ultimate reality in the *Purusha Sukta* (10: 90) as infinite, as the begetter of everything and bound by nothing, as the ultimate beyond time and space, beyond all terms of mortal measure — {सहस्रशीर्षा पुरुषः सहस्राक्षः सहस्रपात्... (a Person with thousand heads, thousand eyes, thousand feet); He covers the entire earth and exceeds by the measure of ten fingers} — directly reach into the transcendental monism in the Upanishads. All this is perception far beyond primitive modalities.

Nor do the transcendental metaphysics figure exclusively in the last Mandala, number 10, supposed to be of later composition and closer in time to the Vedantic perception. Sukta 164 in Mandala 1 is laden with mature philosophical enquiries and speculations. The cyclic movement of time is perceived as an endless process (riks11 to 17). The metaphor of the wheel used here, the wheel with a fixed still centre, *chakranāvi,* and numerous spokes, *ara,* connecting the centre to the outer periphery, the *chakranemi*, denotes the temporal process; this is a recurring metaphor also in the Upanishads.[37] The dual positions of process and stasis, of action and inaction, involvement and non-involvement, are projected in the *dwā suparṇā* sloka (1:164/20) in the metaphor of the two birds, two profiles of one self, one engaged eating a tasty fruit, the other disengaged, a mere observer. This again is a metaphor that recurs later in the Upanishads.[38] Sloka 1:164/45 formulates the four stages of speech we mentioned earlier, three of the stages pre-verbal and unrecognized as speech, and the noblest, most developed one at the human threshold. It all demonstrates an inclusive range of perception, a perception that leaves out nothing and relates to everything.

Queries are posed at basic points, on vital issues: what is the nature of Truth? Where does Creation begin? Who knows? Who had witnessed it? The body and life grow out of the soil, we know; but where does the soul come from? Who asks? What is the nature of the mind that is capable of asking (1:164/4-6)? The questions posed in Mandala 1 relate to the perplexed, anxious query in Mandala 10, Sukta 121 —"which god do I worship with my offerings", *kasmai devāya havishā vidhema*? (कस्मै देवाय हविषा विधेम।।). This question recurs in succession 9 times in the Sukta. The answer is: "the one who makes it all and pervades it all and whom nothing binds, nothing exhausts" (10: 121).

The position of man in relation to the universe was not, in

---

[37] The poet T. S. Eliot had studied ancient Indian culture at Harvard; Eliot makes beautiful use of the wheel image, the still point at the centre of the turning periphery, to signify God's time and terrestrial time, time and eternity, in his *Four Quartets*.

[38] *Swetāswatara*, 4:6; *Mundaka*, 3:1/1.

the pre- and non- Cartesian modality of perception, defined by any principle of "otherness". It was not man *and* the universe; man was himself placed *in* the universe, man was part of a total design, a design manifested in and through and beyond all that constitute and surround.[39]

The Suktas in the Rig-veda, as the ecstatic incantations in the Upanishads, unfold before us this holistic perspective; and this is true to the poly-semantic character of the language itself. The "meaning" spreads out, as it were, in concentric circles of expanding diameters. Heinrich R. Zimmer in *The King and the Corpse* refers to this as the "meaning" the depth of which is never to be reached, never to be exhausted.[40]

This sacramental vision of existence, outside of the Judeo-Christian cult of authoritarian personal God — a Messiah, a Prophet, the Creator apart from creation— totally baffled the nineteenth century Western scholars. While it was easier to recognize the many gods in the Veda pantheon, the forces of nature deified, the quest for the One beyond— whose identity is a matter of perennial puzzlement (*kasmai devāya?*)—mostly went unheeded. That people performing sacrificial rituals and making offerings of food and drink, of *anna* and *soma,* to the gods of air, water, fire, rain and thunder, had all the time been asking deeper questions, that existence for them had been a many-tier experience, escaped the Westerners' notice, or failed to attract them seriously.[41] The Sayana Bhasya, an exclusivist

---

39 Dualist philosophy in the Sankhya system, later in the Bhakti Cult, were all later developments, secondary branching off from the original monistic perspective.

40 P. 5.

41 Max Müller recognized the amazing depth in the query, in the Preface to vol. III, Rig-veda, p. VIII, again, in Lecture X on 'Comparative Study of Religious Problems', *Natural Religion,* pp. 244-45, for instance, yet passed it over.

ritualistic reading, taken apart from the long tradition of ancient *Vedacharchā* on the sub-continent, presented to the Orientalist scholars the primitive man's infantile profile, cowering in the presence of the formidable forces of nature, un-deciphered, uncontrolled and untamed. The human stature was much dwarfed. It all remains a historical document of mis-directed interpretation, the outsider's reading— authentic intellectual engagement under situational-positional compulsions.

On such readings and mis-readings were built-up the huge edifices of Comparative Religion and Comparative Mythology, analytical sciences in later times dexterously probing "racial memory" and "generic consciousness".

V

Sayana the guide.

When Western scholars in Paris, in St. Petersburg, in London considered Sayana Bhasya as the one authentic native interpretation of the ancient Rig-veda, they failed to heed two vital points :

1. That several millennia had elapsed between the composition/compilation of the Rig-veda and the composition of Sayana Acharya's commentary on the same in the fourteenth century CE; and that time had brought changes in the social perspective, in the priority pattern, in the set of positional compulsions, and consequently on the points of emphasis,
2. That Sayana represents, as he had chosen to represent, a particular position in the long and complex history of Veda exegesis; that Sayana had adopted one line of

> interpretation, the *yajnapaksha*, ritualistic reading of the Veda text relating to sacrificial performances. This had been directly coming down from the Brahmana line of reading the *mantras* in terms of ritual practice. In assuming this stand, Sayana had chosen to stand aside from the other exegetical tradition, the *ātmapaksha*, the tradition of metaphysical-spiritual interpretation derived from the Aranyaka-Upanishad way of explication.

The Western scholars failed to appreciate that Sayana's reading did not truly present the entire native tradition of Veda exegesis. The Brahmanas, the Dharma Sastras, the Sayana Bhasya, the Purohitadarpanam, threaded together, constitute one branch of interpretation and adoption in practice; it all acts as one artery in a complex network. Taken out of the larger corpus of Veda interpretation in ancient India, wrenched off the sequential stand preferred by Sayana himself, the Bhasya could not be in a position to do justice either to the Veda *mantras*, or to itself.

True, Max Müller mentions the passage of time, he talks about Sayana's references to other commentators and he is aware of the "wear and tear" the intervening centuries cause. In all this Max Müller actually has in mind the textual problems he had to face handling the Sayana Bhasya; the attitudinal changes time had wrought in the social psyche in India did not come into visibility in his reading.

True, the astute scholar occasionally displays sensitive perception, although a rather hazy one, of temporal succession in matters relating to India — as when he says that

> The Veda, like an old oak tree, shows hundreds and thousands of circles within circles,

or when he acknowledges that

> There is an unfathomable depth in language, layer following after layer, long before we arrive at roots and what a time and what an effort must have been required for their elaboration, and for the elaboration of the ideas expressed in them.[42]

again, as he affirms his perception of a continuity in the Indian culture. Without ever being on the Indian soil, the scholar has the feel of an unbroken line of heritage coming down from the time of the Rig-veda to the India of his own time. This continuity, he mentions in *India, What Can it Teach Us*, may not be so easily perceptible in urban India, in cities like Calcutta, Bombay, Madras, yet it is truly operative in rural India, "in the true India of the Indians."[43]

The continuity, however, — the Western scholars were not in a position fully to appreciate this — is not a simple, straight linear extension, as it might have been in the case of a primitive culture groping along a single track. It had been a much more complex journey in the life of a mature, full grown civilization which had spread out in many directions, had proved amenable to multiple readings, had generated many channels of interpretation and re-interpretation. Here the old oak tree mentioned by Max Müller, or its Indian cousin, the mighty banyan, is a good metaphor.

Time traverses long stretches and the Veda culture passes through phases, assimilates the experience of shifting existential emphases. The journey, an un-chronicled historical process, is yet a vital, shaping influence in the life of this group of humanity; the larger perspective mostly remains out of sight in the Western perception. Gayatri Chakravorty Spivak

---

[42] *Autobiography*, p. 200.

[43] P. 7.

mentions Hegel's idea of an unmoving stagnation, a "stop on the spirit's graphic journey", the name of which is India, The consequent impact, she notes, is a misconception of the historical process in one part of the planet and a mishandling and an unauthorized interference,

> One might say that the epistemic story of imperialism is the story of a series of interruptions, a repeated tearing of time that cannot be sutured.[44]

Homi K. Bhabha notes how to the colonizing West

> India is the perpetual generation of a past-present which is the disturbing, uncertain time of the colonial intervention and the ambivalent truth of an enunciation.

He shows how disruptive intervention in historical sequentiality, which catches the historical "outside the hermeneutic of historicism", operates as "elements of a strategy".[45]

A serious "interruption", a disruption, a "tearing of time", indeed takes place and causes a rupture in the closely woven texture of the millennia-old history of Vedic India, as Sayana Bhasya of the fourteenth century CE is appended to the ancient text of the Rig-veda and the compilation is held up to the world as a total profile — text and exegesis together.

VI

In the field of Veda scholarship in ancient India, we know, the Brahmanas and the Aranyakas marked two pathways, two major channels of interpretation.[46] Designated the *Pūrva*

---

[44] *A Critique of Postcolonial Reason*, pp. 47-8; p. 208.

[45] *The Location*, pp. 186-87.

[46] *Cultural Heritage of India*, vol. 1, p. 311 ff. maps it out for the general reader.

Mimāṁsā (interpretation at the earlier, the primary, stage) and the *Uttara Mimāṁsā* (interpretation at the later/next stage), together the two completed explicating the Veda (a) at the level of sacrificial rites meant for the performing figures of the *Adharyu*, the *Hotri* and priests in other positions, and (b) on the level of spiritual-metaphysical intellection. Those in the group of the *Brahmavādin,* seekers of Truth — rishis like Yajnavalkya, Vachaknavi Gargi, enquiring royalties like king Janaka, for instance— would involve themselves in this. The two lines were complementary, not antithetical or mutually exclusive. The *Pūrva-* and the *Uttara-*, the first and the next, are threaded together — the relative terms each denoting the other.

Graded progression on an ascending order had been in view. Inclusion, rather than exclusion, complementarity, rather than contrariety, had been the mark of the ancient attitude. The rhetoric of indirection, irony and antithesis in the verbal mode effectively functioned in instrumental roles. The archetypal enquiring mind iconized in the boy Nachiketa asks; and he receives exhaustive exhortations on the ultimate truth of existence from Yama, the Lord of Death. Yama best knows, as he commands, the secrets of life, and of death.

While the Aranyakas had grown into the monistic metaphysics in the Upanishads, the Brahmana tradition had produced a large corpus of elaborate ritualistic enunciations in Sutras and Sastras coming to claim in ritual discourse the status of definitive Veda exegesis and Vedic formulations.[47] This line of development, intended from the very beginning to act as directions to priests conducting sacrificial rites, gradually

47 "*mantrabrāhmaṇayorvedanāmadheyam*"— as mentioned earlier, the mantras (Veda texts) and the Brahmaṇas together constitute the Veda—claims the *Ãpastambiya Paribhāsā Sutra*, 1: 33.

engaged in spelling out details of application in the areas of all ritual performance, yoga practice and, in course of time, ritual worship in numerous modes. Rituals and performing schedules have a utility value: they hold together the community. Shared social ethics impose a moral order. Cohesion in community life leans on both; dependence increases as the social structure grows more complex.

2

It is noted that the Vedic cult in India, most of its progress formally un-chronicled, follows a consistent course to the end of the Gupta era, the fifth century CE — the Puranas, the Epics, the Tantra/Agama cult, scholars assure, fully shaped by then. This is a long stretch, of several thousands of years, that covers the growth of diverse trends, even of the discordant discourses — the anti-Vedic, *a-Vaidika,* discourses of Buddhism, Jainism, Carvaca schools of thought. The spectacle, if we strain after visualizing the prolonged process, is one of a philosophy of life, a social ethos and a religious tradition — all integrated into a growing culture.[48] It is a live culture which is continuously and consistently engaged in adjusting itself to the changing needs of the time, explaining itself, defending or justifying itself, relating itself to the evolving life pattern of the community of adherents.

---

[48] The integration in the Indian culture of the rhythm of existence at the pragmatic level and of the ethical-spiritual — the spheres that in the Western scheme of things are kept separate as the secular and the religious — remains a puzzle to the West. Early Indologists regretfully mark "moral weakness" in the Indian character; sections in Max Müller's lectures on what India can teach the West are devoted to consider whether the Indians have any sense of moral discrimination, whether they at all know truthfulness.

The process involves condensation, simplification, popularization — bringing it all within the grasp of the commoner — so that it may reach the growing populace immersed in the increasing complexity and the intricacies of daily existence. The Dharma Sastras, the Smriti Saṁhitas, are re-formulations of the traditional. In the opening sloka in each of them re-formulation is sought for in particular situations at particular points of time in the growth of the community; and the lesson delivered bears the stamp of contemporaneity.[49] In the Santi Parva of the Mahabharata Bhishma offers a detailed, elaborately illustrated discourse of counsel to Yudhisthira. The Mahabharata is designated the fifth and the last Veda; and the discourse of counsel is a document of the accumulated wisdom of the entire Vedic age. Here the grand hero Bhishma, the patriarch presiding over the end of a cycle, recounts in a condensed form the entire ethical-spiritual lore and seeks to bring it offer solace to the much troubled mind of Yudhisthira. The text takes a synoptic/synaptic view and preserves for all time the essentials of an entire culture. The process these texts illustrate is one of glancing back, re-viewing the total situation, taking stock of one's positional identity, and then addressing the needs of the hour.

Sayana Acharya and Madhava Acharya, two brothers centuries later, in the royal court of the Bukka monarchs of the

[49] A group of rishis approaches the great Manu absorbed in meditation, and prays for a fresh formulation suited to the needs of the time (1: 1-3), so begins the Manu Smriti. In the Parasara Smriti Vyasa in meditation on the snow-clad mountain surrounded by tall pines, is approached by rishis with a similar request, particularly in the context of the *Kali yuga*; they all decide to approach the sage Parasara and place the plea before him (*Ā̃chāra Kāṇda* 1: 1-18); sloka 19 onward begins the enunciations by sage Parasara. The focus is precisely on the moment, its character and its needs.

Vijaynagara empire in the fourteenth century CE, belong to this tradition of re-interpreting and re-adapting the age-old ancient system in order to relate it to their own time. The contemporary situation in their case had been a critical moment, a time of threatened survival of the ancient culture in the face of Islamic onslaught. The threat perception had been deep; resistance to the incursive other culture called for all-out efforts, political and social, martial and cultural. Attempts at reviving the ancient Vedic culture formed part of the defence stratagem adopted by the Bukka monarchs. The enormous erudition of the two Acharyas, Sayana and Madhava, had been harnessed to lend academic Sastric support to the defence strategy. The Vedic tradition, much altered in course of time, was by the time of the Bukkas in a phase of decadent ritualism; and revival efforts restored orthodoxy and ritualistic rigour.[50]

"*Desabhedāt kālabhedāt pungbhedād anyathā anyathā// paryavasati sastrārtha iti purvamavādisham*"

(the meaning of the Sastra changes to suit differences in place, in time, in demographic composition and other such factors – our preceptors of earlier times said),

Madhava Acharya noted in the introductory verse, the "*Tikakāropakramaṇikā* to his annotated edition of Parasara Smriti. In the forties of the twentieth century Heinrich R. Zimmer acknowledges with deep conviction the need for consulting the old tradition in every passing age from the sphere of its own anxiety, its own perplexity, its own sense

---

[50] Biswanath Bannerjee in "Veda-study in Medieval India", analyses how the 'Veda-study in medieval India ... had fallen on evil days', how, mostly in the hands of priests and ritualists, it had been interpreted in terms of performative orthodoxy. *Corpus of Indological Studies*, vol I, Sharada Publishing House, New Delhi, 1992.

of urgency. Living through the War years, experiencing the pressure of the political-economic-cultural crisis, as he did, Zimmer knows that "the replies already given cannot be made to serve us"; yet in *The King and the Corpse* he asserts, "the powers (in what he calls "the everlasting oracles of life") have to be consulted again directly — again, again, and again".[51] So stands the need of the hour.

Indeed, coming to Sayana Acharya and his interpretation of the Rig-veda, we have to keep in mind that questions such as: who speaks? when? to whom? — are important. The space-time location largely decides. Is the explicator-speaker one who had composed a text? Is he/she one who studies it at another time, in another ambience, distanced at times by hundreds of years – as in the case of the Sastra texts and their commentators in ancient India? The reader's response is rooted in his own time; the intellect's acts of viewing, re-viewing and relating things, events, ideas, involve the temper of the time, the positioning of the viewer, the "subject" in Foucault's formulation. The interaction of different sets of contemporaneity is of vital import in the cultural history of ancient India. As Madhava Acharya unambiguously states, every age re-defines the ancient tradition and re-adapts to the same. The story of re-addressing, re-consulting, as Zimmer describes, itself is a record of the dynamics of change in the life of a community down the ages.

The West's perception of ancient India left out of consideration the process of this historical growth on the subcontinent. The dynamics of a living community were lost sight of, finer curves were blurred in the perception of it all as a timeless moment of an early primitive past long left to stagnate.

---

[51] *The King and the Corpse*, p. 4.

MSS (18a-1870-71-I) image : Sayana Bhasya, Vedārtha Prakāsha

VII

By the time of Sayana and Madhava, Islam had been the ruling power in the major part of India for more than a hundred years; the Turko-Afgan Sultanate was already disintegrating into smaller kingdoms involved in political rivalry and infighting. The South had been all along putting up bold resistance to the forces of Islamic penetration; the foundation of the Vijaynagara empire had been a major event in this. The empire including Mysore, Kanara, Chingleput, Trichinopoly and Kanchi, and, in the first half of the fifteenth century CE, extending over the whole of south India, coast to coast, had been a massive force engaged in effective self-defence. The Sangama dynasty, the Bukka and Harihara monarchs, pushed back the Islamic powers for a considerable period. Historian R. C. Majumder notes,

> The significance of the Vijaynagara empire in the history of India is that for well-nigh three centuries it stood for the older religion and culture of the country and saved these from being engulfed by the rush of new ideas and forces.[52]

Not merely a political power, the Vijaynagara empire indeed constituted a stronghold for the cultural values of the ancient Vedic tradition in India. Threat perception growing in intensity, the need for defence stratagems gained urgency. The pressure generated compulsive gestures of conservation — of constructing and strengthening ramparts all around. On the surface it was a time of flourishing trade and material prosperity; visitors from outside lauded the spirit of rejuvenation in the field of literature and the fine arts. Beneath it all, and in support, the deeper commitment of the Vijanagara

---

[52] *An Advanced History of India*, p. 360. Envoys from abroad, like Nicolo Conti from Italy, Abdur Razzaque from Persia, left glowing accounts of the city and the empire.

rulers was a careful preservation of the native identity, the tradition of Vedic culture. Rituals in religious practice were forcefully reinstated, an orthodox social ethos, enunciated in the Dharma Sastras, for instance, was revived; most of the Smriti Sastra texts were re-edited during this time under royal commission.

Erudite scholars, Madhava and Sayana, in the court of Bukka I and Harihara II were powerful Ministers at counsel; Sayana Acharya was himself a brave soldier – his valour, his lightning sword-strokes, were eulogized by poet-singers.[53] The two court scholars-cum-Ministers, two brothers, Madhava Acharya and Sayana Acharya, commissioned by the emperor Bukka[54], shouldered considerable part of the assignment — facilitating what came to be considered a revival of Vedic culture in the fourteenth century, a renaissance of the ancient Hindu tradition in the south.

2

Sayana, as he mentions in the introductory text, *Rigveda bhāshyopakramaṇikā,* had already composed his Bhasya of the Yajurveda to facilitate the performance of sacrificial rites

[53] Sayana's *Alankāra Sudhānidhi* records, "*jagadvirasya jāgarti kripāṇah sayaṇaprabhoh // kimityete brithātopagarjanti paripanthinah*" (the mighty sword of the masterly Sayana is awake and alert; what can the opponents do but shout in vain.). Cited, Introduction, *Sayaṇacharyakrita Rig-veda Bhāsyopakramaṇikā* ed, Baladeva Upadhyaya.

[54] "Both brothers mention the Emperor's order. In the prefatory verse to his *Rig-vedabhāasyopakramaṇikā* Sayana mentions that the emperor had ordered, "*Bukkāmahipatiādisana*", his elder brother Madhava to compose a commentary on the Rig-veda; but burdened with other engagements, Madhava had relegated the task to him. Madhava Acharya in his "*Tikākāropakramaṇikā*" (the commentator's preface), verse 3, to the Parasara Smriti, mentions the order of the Bukka emperor, "*Sri-Bukkana-kshmā-patih*".

by the principal group of priests, the *adhyaryu*; and now, as desired by his elder brother Madhava, he engages in preparing a Bhasya of the Rig-veda for the next group of ritual performers, the *hotri*,

"adhvaryavasya yajneshu prādhānyāt vyākritāh purā

Yajurvedo atha hotrārtham rigvedovyākarishyate." (5)

(The Adhvaryus play the dominant role in a sacrifice; in consideration of this, first I composed a commentary on the Yajurveda. Now, for the benefit of the Hotri, I prepare a commentary on the Rig Veda.)

His commentaries, the Bhasyas, are to help the performing priests. This is the "*yajnapaksha*", the position, the level, the side, of performing rituals. Yaska in the *Nirukta*, we noted, mentions three levels of meaning: *yājna*, *daivata* and the *addhyātma*, the ritual meaning, the theological and the spiritual. Sayana engages in explicating the primary level of signification — signification in terms of the sacrificial acts to be performed by priests in different positions — of the *adhvaryu,* of the *hotri* and other groups of priests.

Indeed, Sayana had specialised in the field of interpreting the ritualistic system of practiced religion; he had composed commentaries on numerous Brahmana texts. One of the volumes in his *Sudhānidhi* series is *Yajnatantrasudhānidhi*[55], on the technical details in ritual performance of sacrifices, intended to assist the performing personnel. In agreeing to compose a Bhasya of the Rig-veda Sayana, as he mentions in the *upakramaṇikā*, adds to the list of his instructive texts for priests.

[55] The series includes *Purushārthasudhānidhi*, a collection of verses on *purushārtha*, the objectives in man's life, *Ayurvedasudhānidhi*, a treatise on the Ayurveda science in ancient India, *Alankārasudhānidhi* on Sanskrit rhetoric. Sayana Acharya was a man of the world, a man of action — in the royal court, in the battle-field, in explicating the ancient scriptures.

Sitanath Goswami, in his edition of Rik-Saṁhita notes,

> Sayaṇa, the most celebrated commentator of the Saṁhitas, shows only the sacrificial interpretation since that is easier to grasp for an ordinary person not endowed with the rare qualities of understanding the other difficult interpretations.[56]

Sayana brings out the metaphorical meaning in the first verse in Mandala 1, Sukta 164 and says that he could, as in this case, go on recording interpretations at the spiritual level; but owing to certain factors — one of them is the problem of adding to the volume of the book, the other a temperamental disinclination toward the non-ritualistic, transcendental modes of interpretation — he would refrain from that. He would give symbolical-spiritual interpretations only in cases, like the verse on the two birds, where that happens to be the dominant signification:

Ebamuttaratrāpi adhyātmaparatayā yojayitum sakyam. Tathāpi swaraswatvavābād granthavistārabhayācca na likhyate.

Yatra dwāsuparṇā ityādausphutamādhyātmikohi arthahpratiyate tatratatra pratipādayāmah.

(In this way, I could go on adding spiritual interpretations. But, owing to the fact that my taste does not incline that way, also to the fact that it would add to the bulk of the book, I do not give that interpretation. I would be giving spiritual explanations in cases where, as in the case of the sloka related to the two birds, it is absolutely necessary.)

Explicating the Veda text for practising priests, Sayana focuses on the ritual performance which, he believes, truly brings out the meaning — *arthajnānasya tu yajnānusthānatvāt* — he affirms.[57] One does not actually comprehend the significance of the mantras, unless one performs, executes, he asserts, *Na hi etairmantraih kaschidapi arthābabudhyate.*

[56] Calcutta, 1974, p. 16/VI, f.n. 2.
[57] Baladeva Upadhyaya (ed), *Sayaṇacharyakrita-rigvedabhasyo-pakramanika*, p. 12.

Eteshu anubhaba eba yadā nāsti tatsamyaktvam tadiya sādhanatvang cha durāpetam.

(From the mantras alone one does not realize the meaning. Unless one performs and experiences, the real significance and the purpose (of the mantras) remain unaccessed.)

The priestly performer, the *adhvaryu*, or the *hotri*, realises the whole thing through its execution: *Karmaṇi tu addharyaorartha vivakshā vidyate, bodhascha sambhabati*, Sayana assures.[58]

Reciting Veda mantras without realising the significance is meaningless; one who does this simply bears a burden:

Yastu vedamadhitwāpi arthagnānam na vijānāti sāyangpumān bhāramibaharati.[59]

(One who reads the Veda without getting its real significance is like a person who simply bears a burden or a load.)

Mechanical chanting is unproductive, it leads nowhere — even as dry wood, thrown at a spot where no fire burns, never gets ignited:

yathāgnirahitapradeshe prakshiptang suskang kāsthang na jwalati tadvat.[60]

Sayana explains the function of the six Vedangas used as tools in the explicatory process, the importance of the Mimāṁsa system as a polemical support, and concludes the *Bhasyopakramaṇikā* with the affirmation that his Bhasya would interpret the Rig-veda text following the six Vedangas, within the framework of the Brāhmaṇa tradition:

Tadartham rigvedāsmāvih sharangānusāreṇa vyākshāyate.

---

[58] Ibid., p. 19.

[59] Ibid., p. 44.

[60] Ibid., p. 45.

Erudite traditionalists, Sayana, and Madhava freely draw the support of the vast culture continuum in favour of their own interpretations. Madhava Acharya, editing and annotating the Smriti texts, cites parallel enunciations from other commentator-interpreters, from the Mahabharata and the different Puranas. Sayana, composing his commentary on the Veda text, seeks support in the *Nirukta* and the *Mimāṁsa* systems. All these numerous other texts, including the Sutras of Aswalayana, Max Müller had frequently stumbled against. These constituted a live tradition up to Sayana's time, but were unavailable in the middle of the nineteenth century in modern edited form; naturally frequent references to these texts in Sayana, we remember, had posed serious challenges to Max Müller.

3

Sayana takes his position, adopts the *Yajnapaksha,* with an implicit assurance that this is not in contradiction to, or in rejection of, the Aranyaka-Upanishada line of interpretation. A true insider[61], Sayana knows the two to be complementary. Only the one comes first, the other comes next – perhaps in a graded scale of the powers of reception and of assimilation. He knows, and he endorses the co-valence of the two approaches exploring two aspects of the Veda: *vede pūrbottarakāṇdayoh krameṇa dharmabrāhmaṇovishayah* (in the case of the Veda interpretation, the object of the first and the next, of the purva- and the uttara-, are ritual practice, and ultimate truth respectively).[62] He unambiguously

[61] Bankimchandra makes the early distinction between the roles of the reader as an "insider" and as an "outsider", a new comer. *Rachanavali,* III, p. 164ff. Of this later on, in the next Chapter.

[62] *Rigvedabhāsyopakramaṇika*, p. 47.

acknowledges the complementarity of the two : *tad ubhayajnānang vedasya sākshāt prayojanam,*[63] (hence, the knowledge of both is directly required).

Both are vitally related to the Veda — even as the signifier is to the signified, the *pratipādaka* to the *pratipādya*, as the progenitor is related to the progeny, the *janaka* to the *janya*:

Sambandhastu vedasya dharmabrāhmavyang saha pratipādyapratipādakabhāvah tadiya jnānena saha janyajanakabhābah.[64]

(The relation between the Veda (mantras) and the sacrificial practice is like the relation between the subject and the predicate, with the inner meaning it is as between the begetter and the begotten.)

He knows and he endorses the view that the ritualistic aspect, the *karmakāṇda* he sides with, together with the six *vedāngas,* he is taking recourse to, fall into the category of *aparāvidyā*, the field of a secondary pursuit of knowledge; whereas the pursuit of the ultimate truth, *paramapurushārthajnānam*, in the Upanishads is the *parāvidyā*, the highest metaphysical-spiritual pursuit.[65] Citing the *Taittiriya Āraṇyaka*, Sayana re-iterates the conviction that one who acquires the knowledge of Brahman knows the ultimate, *Brahmavid prāpnoti param*; one who knows Brahman becomes like Brahman, *Brahmaveda Brahmaiva bhavati.*[66]

With such knowledge Sayana takes his stand, chooses his own path and proceeds — not eschewing the other modality, the *ātmapaksha*, but preferring to present the other profile – ritual performance — keeping in view the urgent need of the time.

---

63 Ibid.

64 Ibid., p. 46.

65 Ibid.

66 Ibid., p. 48.

As he avers, he does fall back on the *ātmapaksha*, the metaphysical-spiritual line of interpretation, on occasions, in cases where the symbolical meaning alone makes the point. Sayana's example is the verse (Rig-veda, 1: 164/20) on the two birds, *dwāsuparṇā*, one engaged, the other disengaged.

VIII

When Sri Aurobindo finds Sayana the wrong guide in Veda studies, when he comments,

> Only those whom a strong and unquestioning orthodoxy dispenses from the obligations of the critical spirit, can for a moment imagine that Sayana holds for us the key to their meaning.[67]

he does not actually take into account the historical compulsions on Sayana and his compatriots. The "unquestioning orthodoxy" which had projected Sayana as the great commentator, had indeed been promoted as a survival strategy of the historical moment. The revival of the traditional in Vijaynagara, if a "renaissance" as designated by traditionalists, had been a renaissance of orthodoxy, a revival of exclusivist ritualistic rigour. Marshalling the sacred and the sanctified, the desperate defence gestures look backward, stress the externals and, almost desperately, seek shelter under all this in times of threatened identity.

Viewed in the historical location, Sayana needed neither to be taken as the one unfailing giant figure on whose shoulders one had to stand to get a view of a millennia-old tradition, nor as a wrong guide responsible for the errors of interpreters from the other hemisphere to arrive several centuries later, for the errors in perspective in the nineteenth-century Westerners' reading of ancient India.

---

[67] *Sri Aurobindo Archives and Research*, December 1985, p. 153.

Eugene Barnouf and Max Müller and the other early Indologists from the West met Sayana, found his Sanskrit easier to access. The ritualistic reading in his Bhasya appeared illustrative of a primitive pattern of propitiatory cult; and this happened to be in general conformity with the priest-craft-ridden daily life observed on and reported from the faraway land. All this, at the historical moment, lent itself to the "construction" of the past of India — for the benefit of the wondering West and also of the Indians themselves. The take-off point removed from the origin by several thousands of years, the West met ancient India not in the best of her time, but, unfortunately, in a phase of decline, in a state of desperate shrinkage, of exclusivist decadence.

Plodding through the long toiling decades, Max Müller had felt elated — and this happened to sustain — almost over-awed by the enormity of his responsibility. In a letter to his wife he mentioned in 1864 how he felt convinced that his presentation of the Veda text with Sayana's commentary would "tell to a great extent on the fate of India and on the growth of millions of souls in that country."[68] His understanding was perfect, prophetic. He had shown the natives the "root of their religion"; and Indians, including the section that happens to be inheritors of the Vedic antiquity, have been looking at the roots as the Orientalists had displayed. If the approach had been, as the dissenters argued, a wrong one, the wrong start had determined it all.

Again, interpreting the culture of the colonized for them, as Edward Said points out, is an act laden with historical overtones and shaped by forces of complex compulsions. Westerners uncovered the past of India to the Indians; and this

---

[68] Cited, *Scholar Extraordinary*, p. 92.

remains a celebrated achievement in the operation of what Michel Foucault would designate "enunciative modality"[69] in the handling of history. In Ronald Inden's phrasing this illustrates the working of "hegemonic agency", of discriminating "imperial knowledge."[70]

[69] *The Archaeology of Knowledge* (Routledge Classics, Indian Reprint 2007), pp. 55-61.

[70] *Imagining India*, p. 36.

nāsadīya sūkta

नासदासीन्नो सदासीत्तदानीं नासीद्रजो नो व्योमा परो यत्।
किमावरीवः कुह कस्य शर्मन्नम्भः किमासीद्गहनं गभीरम्॥ १ ॥

nāsad āsīn no sad āsīt tadānīṁ nāsīd rajo no vyomā paro yat |
kim āvarīvah kuha kasya śarmannambhaḥ kim āsīd gahanaṁ gabhīram ||1||

Then even nothingness was not, nor existence,
There was no air then, nor the heavens beyond it.
What covered it? Where was it? In whose keeping
Was there then cosmic water, in depths unfathomed?

न मृत्युरासीदमृतं न तर्हि न रात्र्या अह्न आसीत्प्रकेतः।
आनीदवातं स्वधया तदेकं तस्माद्धान्यन्न परः किञ्चनास॥ २ ॥

na mṛtyur āsīd amṛtaṁ na tarhi na rātryā ahna āsīt praketaḥ|
ānīdavātaṁ svadhayā tad ekaṁ tasmād dhānyanna paraḥ kiṁ canāsa ||2||

Then there was neither death nor immortality
Nor was there then the torch of night and day.
The One breathed windlessly and self-sustaining.
There was that One then, and there was no other.

तम आसीत्तमसा गूहळमग्रे प्रकेतं सलिलं सर्वाऽइदम्।
तुच्छ्येनाभ्वपिहितं यदासीत्तपसस्तन्महिनाजायतैकम्॥ ३ ॥

tama āsīt tamasā gūḷham agre 'praketaṁ salilaṁ sarvam ā idam
tucchyenābhv apihitaṁ yad āsīt tapasas tan mahinājāyataikam ||3||

At first there was only darkness wrapped in darkness.
All this was only unillumined water.
That One which came to be, enclosed in nothing,
arose at last, born of the power of heat.

कामस्तदग्रे समवर्तताधि मनसो रेतः प्रथमं यदासीत्।
सतो बन्धुमसति निरविन्दन्हृदि प्रतीष्या कवयो मनीषा॥ ४ ॥

kāmas tad agre sam avartatādhi manaso retaḥ prathamaṁ yad āsīt |
sato bandhum asati nir avindan hṛdi pratīṣyā kavayo manīṣā ||4||

In the beginning desire descended on it.
That was the primal seed, born of the mind.
The sages who have searched their hearts with wisdom
Know that which is kin to that which is not.

तिरश्चीनो विततो रश्मिरेषामधः स्विदासीदुपरि स्विदासीत्।
रेतोधा आसन्महिमान आसन्त्स्वधा अवस्तात्प्रयतिः परस्तात्॥ ५ ॥

tiraścīno vitato raśmir eṣām adhaḥ svid āsī3d upari svid āsīt |
retodhā āsan mahimāna āsan svadhā avastāt prayatiḥ parastāt ||5||

And they have stretched their cord across the void,
and know what was above, and what below.
Seminal powers made fertile mighty forces.
Below was strength, and over it was impulse.

को अद्धा वेद क इह प्र वोचत्कुत आजाता कुत इयं विसृष्टिः।
अर्वाग्देवा अस्य विसर्जनेनाथा को वेद यत आबभूव॥ ६ ॥

ko addhā veda ka iha pra vocat kuta ājātā kuta iyaṁ visṛṣṭiḥ |
arvāg devā asya visarjanenāthā ko veda yata ābab ||6||

But, after all, who knows, and who can say
Whence it all came, and how creation happened?
The gods themselves are later than creation,
so who knows truly whence it has arisen?

इयं विसृष्टिर्यत आबभूव यदि वा दधे यदि वा न।
यो अस्याध्यक्षः परमे व्योमन्त्सो अङ्ग वेद यदि वा न वेद॥ ७ ॥

iyaṁ visṛṣṭir yata ābabhūva yadi vā dadhe yadi vā na |
yo asyādhyakṣaḥ parame vyoman so aṅga veda yadi vā na veda ||7||

Whence all creation had its origin,
he, whether he fashioned it or whether he did not,
he, who surveys it all from highest heaven
he knows or maybe even he does not know.

Translation, A. L. Basham

Five

Voices of dissent : Bankim, Tilak, Aurobindo

One of the dangers against which I must warn the student of Vedic Literature is the tendency to accept unquestioned the dicta of foreign Orientalists.

The general tendency of European scholars, who have so great an influence on you, is to decry your past history, to call for its virtual erasure from your memory

Bankimchandra Chatterjee

Vedic scholarship has built upon this conjectural science of philology, upon a brilliantly ingenious and attractive but wholly conjectural and unreliable interpretation of the Vedas, a remarkable, minute and captivating picture of an early half-savage Aryan civilization in India. How much value can we attach to these dazzling structures?

We may therefore surmise that our actual Sanhita represents the close of a period, not its commencement, nor even some of its successive stages.

Sri Aurobindo

The native answers display the continual slippage between civil inscription and colonial address.

Homi K. Bhabha

In the International Congress of Orientalists in London (September 14 to 21, 1874) Max Müller, President of the Aryan section of the programme, noted how under the impact of the work of the Orientalist scholars the "religion, the literature, the whole character of the people of India are becoming more and more Indo-European."[1]

[1] Cited, *Scholar Extraordinary*, p. 300.

This is a lucid perception of the process of de-nationalization of the natives in the colony, the process of fore-closure, as Chakravorty Spivak designates; and this is part of the sub-text beneath the account of the nineteenth-century renaissance in India, of the modernizing impact of the exposure to the enlightened West. The interplay between the surface projection, and the subordinated, the sub-text, comes out as Max Müller in the address further notes,

> A new race of men is growing up in India, who have stepped, as it were, over a thousand years, and have entered at once on the intellectual inheritance of Europe .... It is true, that the old school of Sanskrit scholars is dying out, and much will die with it which we shall never recover, but a new and most promising school of Sanskrit students, educated by European professors, is springing up, and they will, nay, to judge from recent controversies, they have already become most formidable rivals to our own scholars.... They work for us, as we work for them.[2]

The colonizer-colonized axis is shaped; the "doubling over" as Homi K. Bhabha perceives, operates at both ends and colonization prevails as a total, inclusive experience. Max Müller once again projects an unerring insight.

Yet, colonial India did speak. De-nationalization had not induced a state of total de-sensitization. True, thankful grateful Indian intellectuals, Raja Radhakanta Dev Bahadur and Swami Vivekananda among them, felt permanently beholden to the European scholars for a restoration of the importance of the ancient Vedic tradition at a time when it had miserably declined on the native soil, true, they came to voice and to shape the mainstream native response[3]. Yet, standing apart,

---

[2] Ibid., p. 300.
The scholar had visualized the shaping of a new India under the impact of Western culture, education and government — although he knew that India can never be fully Anglicized.

[3] Of this later on, in Appendix B.

some of the probing intellects in the nineteenth century and the early twentieth — Bankimchandra Chatterjee, Balagangadhara Tilak, followers of Dayananda Saraswati, Aurobindo Ghosh, — noticed the Euro-centric accent in Orientalist scholarship. They understood the challenges and obstacles in the situation of a cross-cultural confrontation and they had a clear perception of the imperial compulsions at work. The dissent they voiced reflects the major points of emphases in the post-modernist critique of later times.

Themselves exposed to English education and its impact of de-nationalization at the level at which the thinking-knowing mind is shaped, Bankim, Tilak, or Aurobindo, obviously, are not pure "natives", but colonial constructs. They are products of the colonizing process. Yet they are critically aware of their experience; and their major benefit on the experience of colonization is a mastery of the "modern" rational analytics, acquisition of a critical-polemical apparatus, the idiom of Occidental parlance. The perspicacity of their understanding and their assessment of the nature of a meeting of alien cultures – what David Frawley in *The Myth of Aryan Invasion* calls a "clash", given of course a parity of agency—help them largely to overcome colonial constraints. They voice a spirit of questioning which naturally had been pushed back and suppressed[4] in its own time; but it assumes historical

[4] In 1994 Sahitya Akademi published a tome, *Bankimchandra: Essays in Perspective* (ed., Bhabatosh Chatterjee), a collection covering the stretch from Bankim's own time to date. The one article in this anthology on "Bankimchandra and Indological Research" presents Bankim as a Neo-Hindu revivalist and regrets Bankim's failure to accord right appreciation of the Westerners' interest in ancient India, and their laudable achievements.
Fore-closure remains operative long after the event of chronological de-colonization.

significance, almost of a prophetic nature, in the post-colonial ambience of interrogation.

I

Dayananda Saraswati (1824–1883), whom Sarvepalli Radhakrishnan hails as one of the makers of modern India, had dedicated himself to the task of rescuing the true spiritual essence of the Veda, projecting a Vedantic perception of the entire Vedic culture in place of the ritualistic one prevailing. Sri Aurobindo appreciates the historical contribution of Dayananda's effort,

> A nation grows into what it shall be by the force of that which it was in the past and is in the present, and in this growth there come periods of conscious and subconscious stock-taking when the national soul selects, modifies, rejects, keeps out of all that it had or is acquiring whatever it needs as substance and capital for its growth and action in the future: in such a period of stock-taking we are still and Dayananda was one of its great and formative spirits.[5]

Indeed, history turns and returns, without repeating itself in a mechanical way. Sayana in his time under the threat of Islamic penetration, had sought umbrage in the ritualism in the Brahmanic tradition; the Arya Samaj, Brahmo Samaj reform programmes, with different sets of emphases[6], bring the wheel full circle seeking release from ritualistic orthodoxy.

---

[5] *SABCL,* Vol. 17 (Pondicherry Ashrama), p. 336.

[6] Max Müller responds differently to the two reform programmes. To the Brahmos he had been very well-disposed, expecting the reformists finally to embrace the one true religion, the Christian faith. Correspondence with Keshab Chunder Sen and Protap Chander Mozoomdar brings it out. Nirad C Chaudhuri cites Mozoomdar's letter in reply to Max Müller, the letter in which Mozoomdar had to state that a "wholesale acceptance of the Christian name by the Brahmo Samaj is neither possible nor desirable". *Scholar Extraordinary,* p. 315. Dayananda and his reform efforts to Max Müller count among the

If Dayananda Sarswati's *Satyarth Prakash* (1875) breathed of the native soil in the land, Bankim, Tilak, and Aurobindo later on, belonged to the group of colonized "Indo-Europeans" Max Müller had felt happy to welcome. Bankimchandra Chatterjee, born June 1838, had his schooling in the English system of education. At Midnapore in Bengal, where his father was Deputy Collector in the British administration, Bankim learnt English with Mr Tidd and Mr Sinclair; later he studied at Hooghly College and at Presidency College, Calcutta. He came out as one in the first batch of graduates (1858) from the newly established Calcutta University and was immediately appointed Deputy Magistrate and Deputy Collector. A second generation Indian administrative executive in the British Government, Bankim was an insider to the mechanism of nineteenth-century British rule in India.

Exposed to English education when six years of age, Bankim also had the benefit of the traditional system of Sanskrit education at a *Tole* in Bhatpada, a reputed centre of traditional Sanskrit studies. One of the keenest intellects of the century, enjoying the benefits of both systems of education, striding the contemporary social life-scape with an insider's perception of the cross-cultural confrontation, Bankim, in a sense, is an excellent illustration of a Europeanized native. If colonization erases the position of the pre-colonial self, the identity of the authentic native informant, it also opens up interesting studies in cross-cultural moulding and re-moulding, studies in the

dangers in the contemporary situation. In a letter to the Parsee reformer Malabari he mentions two risk points in the Indian response at that point of time: "that of undervaluing or despising the ancient national religion, as is done so often by your half-Europeanized youths, and that of overvaluing it, and interpreting it as it was never meant to be interpreted, of which you may see a painful instance in Dayananda Saraswati's labours on the Veda". Ibid., pp. 314-337.

formation and transformations of modalities of perception among the colonized. Bankim is a case in point.

Satires like "*Ramayan'er Samalochana: konoVilati Samalochak-praneeta*" (A Critical estimate of the Ramayana by a Western critic), and "*Kono Especial'er Patra*" (Letter form a specialist) published in the *Bangadarshan*, expose misreadings of Indian literature by eager Europeans to hilarious effect.

Two long essays serially published in the *Prachar* during the period 1884 to 1886 — one entitled "Krishna Charitra", the other "Devatattwa O Hindu Dharma" — engage in detailed study of the Western scholars' understanding of Indian texts like the Vedas, the Mahabharata, the Bhagvadgita. With unerring precision Bankim, himself a scholar of a rational temperament and an admirer of modern Europe's reliance on reason and science,[7] locates the major points of confusion, misconception and the cultural-political bias operative in the early phase of Indological studies. In "Krishnacharitra" Bankim notes the exclusivist egotism in the Western philosophy of knowledge:

> One of the features of Western scholarship is to assume that the system prevailing in their part of the world is the one system to be expected everywhere, in the life of every community.[8]

If this had been an inhibiting propensity in the Western cognitive philosophy, the egotism, the Euro-centric sense of

---

[7] One remembers the appreciative assessment of British rule in *Anandamath*, also the frank admission in an essay in *Vividha Prabandha,* that the Britishers have played a beneficial role in India, that they have brought new knowledge, new methodology, newer modalities. Two major concepts we owe to them, Bankim had noted, are individualism and nationalism. See, *Rachanavali* II. Pp. 240-41.

[8] Ibid., p. 412. Tr., present author.

cultural privilege, Bankim notes, came to affect their sense of historical perspective too,

> They (Western Sanskrit Scholars) are engaged in discovering principles of the historical process, yet it is impossible for them to accept the idea that the Hindus, defeated and a dependent people today, had ever been civilized, and that their civilization had been a very ancient one. Hence, with one or two exceptions, they generally engage in under-estimating the glory of ancient India... In this effort they proceed with the assumption that all that speak well of India in the ancient Indian texts are baseless or interpolations, all that speaks against the tradition is true and important.[9]

Bankim's detailed study of the Vedas, particularly the Rig-veda in the essay "Devatattwa O Hindu Dharma" had been serialized in the *Prachar* during its first two years (1884–1886) under varying captions; and the work had been mentioned in the first "advertisement" to *Krishnacharitra* published separately in 1886. Yet it remained unpublished in book form and largely unnoticed, during the author's life and long after his death. Jogeshchandra Bagal in his Introduction to the second volume of the collected works of Bankimchandra brought out by Sahitya Samsad, recollects how a casual mention of these articles in a Presidential address by Sajanikanta Das in 1938 — more than four decades after the death of Bankim in 1894 — brought these essays to notice.[10] These *Prachar* articles, taken along with Bankim's 1894 Presidential Addresses to the 'Literary Section of the Society for the Higher Training of Young Men' and the incomplete manuscripts of "Letters on Hinduism" today present the profile of an enlightened nineteenth-century Indian.

---

9 Ibid., pp. 409-10. Tr, present author.

10 P. XXV. Ibid., p. 1032: Bankim's "Advertisement to Krishna Charitra"; Bankim here mentions the work as on the subject of devatattwa; the caption used in the *Rachanavali* was given by Sajanikanta Das.

A modern Indian mind, generously exposed to the Western culture dominating the nineteenth-century era of liberal values, engages in a critical assessment of the European scholars' understanding of ancient India and the hegemonic impact of it on the colonized Indians.[11] Bankim's penetrating insight, the sweep of his historical vision, his grasp of the principles of growth in human civilization — all are far ahead of his time.

Through a vigorous analysis Bankim explores the significance of Vedic terms and the system of Vedic nomenclature. Rectifying common misconceptions in popular thinking, Bankim points out, for instance, that the word "*rishi*" means not necessarily a sage or a savant, but simply one who speaks — *yasyavākyang sa rishi*, or that, as Yaska had assured, the term "*devatā*", etymologically derives from the root "*div*" which "means to shine"[12]; and it refers in the Vedic Suktas not essentially to an iconic god, a deity, but to something which is lustrous, of prime significance, the principal referent, the "subject".

In *Krishna Charitra* Bankim had offered methodologies for placing ancient texts in space and time; in his studies in the Rig-veda he traces meanings and messages encompassing the literal and the spiritual. He acknowledges that the world of nature provides the primary scaffolding to the Vedic precepts,

---

[11] In *Rachanavali* III (Sahitya Samsad, Calcutta, 1969). Jogeschandra Bagal mentions (p. 293) that the "Letters", starting as personal correspondence and trailing into essays divided into chapters", composed a forceful exposition of his response to the core of spirituality in the Indian tradition; these remained incomplete and unpublished and were first published in *Bankim Protiva* edited by Bimalchandra Sinha of the Paikpara raj.

[12] *Rachanavali* II, p. 781. Max Müller recognizes the etymological meaning of this word: *The Sacred Books of the East*, Preface to the first edition, p. XXXVII.

and he argues that this, the firm footing on the first step, and the inclusive vision which ignores nothing, leaves out nothing, together constitute the great strength of the ancient modality of intellection. The many gods in the Veda, he demonstrates, are but the manifestation of the same spirit, the ultimate, the *atman//sat*, in numerous forms or aspects.

•

The whole apparatus of the many gods in the Veda, Bankim in his February 1894 Presidential address to young scholars in higher training notes, differs from the Greek and Roman polytheism; "nor is it monotheistic in the sense in which monotheism is understood in Europe", Bankim notes and adds

> Professor Max Müller finding himself forced to face this difficulty in characterising it, has coined a new word — *henotheism*, and given it that name.[13]

Years back in the *Prachar* article "Devatattwa O Hindu Dharma" Bankim had noted the sense of puzzlement on the part of Max Müller, a perceptive reader bound to his cultural constraints. Bankim felt amused at the erudite scholar's search for nomenclature in Greek dictionaries, and himself solved the problem with an insider's ease. He assured that the worship of different forms under different appellations only indicates the range of aesthetic-spiritual sensibilities of the ancient visionary composers of the Suktas.[14] In the lecture to the young Vedicists Bankim notes,

> To contemplate or to glorify the Powers of Nature was to contemplate His attributes. The Infinite is not realizable to our minds in its Infinity. We can bring our mind into close contact with it only by contemplating those finite portions of Infinite Energy which we can perceive and comprehend. This is what the Vedic poets tried to do.[15]

[13] *Rachanavali* III, p. 158.

[14] *Rachanavali* II, p. 816; pp. 808, 820.

[15] Ibid., III, pp. 158; 239-40; 245-63.

He reminds the young scholars,

> In an age in which the bent of the national mind was to see in the vast forces of nature evidence of the Might of the great Architect of all, to view and to contemplate each of the forces separately as manifestations of His energy, to personify and to adore it, the language of the adorers necessarily assumed a form in which an exterior veil of physiolatry had to be penetrated before the listener could obtain a glimpse of the great Formless and Invisible Shadow of Glory within.[16]

Bankim uses the term "polymorphous monotheism" to describe the exterior-interior alliance, the integration of the surface and the inner core. The recognition of divinity in the many forces of nature, the awareness of one God//spiritual principle, operative behind the universe and the pure spiritual experience recorded in the Upanishads are elevated levels of spiritual sensibility.[17] The vision in its highest reach is non-theistic, it is self-realization, *atmajnāna*.

A rationalist by temperament, Bankim in the 1894 address appeals to the critical intellect in young enquirers. "Think for yourselves", he tells the young audience; thoughtfulness, even if occasionally leading to error, is preferable to "intellectual imbecility". An objective, rational, free spirit of enquiry alone, he points out, can protect the Indian mind against opposing extremes: (a) a blind acceptance of all that appears to be sanctioned by tradition, and (b) the compulsive pressure of the Westerners' reading as the one authoritative interpretation.

---

[16] Ibid., p. 166.

[17] In his essay on Devatattwa Bankim notes the great contribution of St. Paul, the importance of the blending of the ancient Greeks' pagan sensibilities into the Christian faith. In this, Bankim believes, St. Paul, the great formulator of the religion, builds a strong, natural basis for Christianity, a truly formidable scaffolding as it is. *Rachanavali* II, p. 815.

He warns them against the danger in the tendency "to accept unquestioned the dicta of foreign Orientalists" or the views of a Pandit,

> If a great Pandit should tell you that the Vedas are eternal, do not believe him unless you can find reasonable evidence in the Vedas themselves of their eternal existence; and if Professor Max Müller should tell you that the Vedic mythology is nothing but a series of solar myths, never believe him unless you find ... that that is the only rational explanation which it admits of. Never surrender your judgment to authority in matters like these.[18]

In *The Myth of Aryan Invasion* (1994) David Frawley calls for a re-writing of Indian history and points out,

> If Hindu scholars are silent, or passively accept the misinterpretation of their culture, it will undoubtably continue.[19]

One hundred years earlier, in 1894, Bankim in the address under consideration had placed before his young audience, Veda scholars in the making, the responsibilities of Indian scholars and their commitments. He exhorted the young scholars to remember that

> what is excusable in a Weber or a Whitney, as the result of prejudices which critics of a foreign race, unacquainted with the country can never wholly set aside, would be unpardonable in a Hindu.[20]

Bankim is one of the early culture scholars to note the difference between the outsiders' reading of alien culture texts on the one hand and the participatory reading by the insider on the other. He tells his audience that with all honest effort the Western scholars like Professor Max Müller never share

---

[18] *Rachanavali* III, p. 161.

[19] Aditya Prakashan, pp. 57-58.

[20] *Rachanavali* III, p. 164.

the Indian view-point, they never see the Veda in its native perspective[21]; in their reading the Veda utterances are "erroneously misconstrued ... as the utterances of a primitive people hankering after the good things of the world." Intervening centuries, Bankim knows, have distanced generations of Indian scholars too from their past. He believes, only a revival of the loving interest in the tradition can bridge the gap and enable the Hindus to "get glimpses of the profound signification of these grand utterances of our glorious forefathers".[22]

So thinks Bankim, insider to the native culture and a person closely acquainted with the administrative-epistemic modality of colonial intervention. He alerts the young generation regarding the negative impact of Western penetration, the risk involved in cross-culture interference, particularly in the case of a colonized people with a millennia-old tradition of its own. He makes an earnest appeal,

> Do not lose your reverence for the past; it is on the past that you must plant your foot firmly, if you wish to mount high in the future. You are not a race of savages who have no past to remember; you cannot dissever yourselves in a day from the associations and influences of a past which extends over at least five hundred centuries:- you cannot annihilate in a day a past national existence which has survived the annihilation of hundreds of empires, of hundred systems of religion, and which has surveyed unconcerned the downfall and ruin of many kindred civilizations. I have to make my warning so emphatic because

---

[21] Arguing the issue with Hastie in the letters in *The Statesman* (September 23 to November 18, 1882), Bankim effectively makes the point that an insider with less formal education or critical training, better understands the inner spirit of a culture than an outsider, whatever level of critical acumen the latter may command. Ibid., pp. 186-224.

[22] Ibid., pp. 150-157.

> the general tendency of European scholars, who have so great an influence over you, is to decry your past history, to call for its virtual erasure from your memory.[23]

2

In 1892, the year in which Bankim's *Krishna Charitra*, his masterpiece postulating a methodology for re-reading ancient texts, appeared in book form, Balgangadhara Tilak (1856-1920) of Maharastra, a graduate from the Deccan College, Puna, a brilliant mathematician and a dedicated teacher, presented a well-researched paper at the Ninth Oriental Congress held in London. Tilak tried to ascertain the time of the Rig-veda on the basis of astronomical calculations of the position of stars, particularly of the Orion — the equinox in the Orion mentioned many times in the Rig-veda. He argued in the paper that the Rig-veda, the earliest surviving text, records a civilization which must have prevailed at a time "not later than 4000 B.C." — a date much earlier than what modern Western scholars had assumed.

The paper came out in book form the next year (1893); in the Preface Tilak noted with regret that while "the high antiquity of Egyptian civilization is generally admitted", "scholars still hesitate to place the commencement of the Vedic civilization earlier than 2400 B.C." He presented his own findings:

> I have endeavoured to show in the following pages that the traditions recorded in the Rig-veda unmistakably point to a period not later than 4000 B.C. when the vernal equinox was in Orion, or, in other words, when the Dog-star ... commenced the equinoctial year.[24]

---

[23] Ibid., p. 165.

[24] *The Orion*, 1893, (Cosmo Reprint, New Delhi 1984), p. III.

The dating of the ancient text on the basis of astronomical references and calculations, Tilak believes, enjoys a special authenticity, determined as it is by the "unerring clock of the heavens."[25]

With firm conviction and with elegant academic poise, Tilak asserts,

> Some scholars may doubt the possibility of deriving so important and far-reaching conclusions from the data furnished by the hymns of the Rig-veda, and some may think that I am taking the antiquity of the Vedas too far back. But fears like these are out of place in a historical or scientific inquiry, the sole object of which should be to search for and find out the truth.[26]

The presentation, however tentative the tone, is part of the native dissent, the nineteenth-century debate with the colonizers' accounts and estimates. Tilak, grew into a nationalist reformer; as an educationist he founded the Deccan Society with the vision of a system of national education to replace the British system. He had a keen and clear perception of cross-culture anomalies in the colonial situation. His confident grip on astronomical calculations and his courageous assertion in the Orion essay, forwarded from within the colonial framework, reflect both sensitiveness to the resistance factor in the Western response and a scholar's trust in the non-privileging objectivity of intellectual enquiry.

---

[25] Ibid., p. 220.
In the 1862 Preface to the fourth volume of his Rig-veda, Max Müller, we would remember, had raised the question, "Can the age of the Vedic hymns be fixed by astronomical evidence?" He had given considerable space to a detailed exploration, quoted Wilson's views in favour of a greater antiquity of the Veda, and, in his wise decision he had disengaged himself from the debate on the ground that his field of study was "Sanscrit literature", and not "Indian astronomy", p. XV.

[26] *The Orion*, p. V.

II

The most clearly enunciated, most systematically worked out discourse of dissent in colonial India is Sri Aurobindo's reading of the Rig-veda. Engaged in translation and interpretation of the epics and the Upanishads as early as the Baroda days, Sri Aurobindo on his final retreat to Pondicherry in 1910, had turned to a probing study of the Vedas, Upanishads and the Bhagavadgita. He published his readings mostly in the monthly review journal *Arya* over the first two decades of the century. These are texts enormously relevant to, in fact essential in, any effort at shaping a postcolonial critique of the experience of colonization in India, any effort at re-reading at present times not only the Rig-veda, but the entire tradition of ancient India, and reviewing the long history of India's colonial experience.

Aurobindo, we know, was expected to turn out a "modern" Indian shaped by the Western culture, much more deeply Westernized than the Indo-European type Max Müller had welcomed. Aurobindo's father had arranged schooling for his children in England and ensured a cultural distancing from the Indian tradition.[27] At Cambridge young Aurobindo prepared for the Indian Civil Service examination; he was expected to join the administrative service of the British Raj.

On his return to India in 1893, after fourteen years of education in England, young Aurobindo, belying parental expectations, learnt Bengali and Sanskrit in an effective process of better relating to roots. His interpretation of the Rig-veda and the Vedic texts records the response of an Indian who

---

[27] A.B. Purani mentions that during the first five years at home in India Aurobindo did not know Bengali — the language in use in the family being English and Hindusthani. *The Life of Sri Aurobindo* (Pondicherry, Aurobindo Ashram, fourth revised edition, impression 2006), p. 3.

had benefited from the exposure to Western education. He had preserved over the years of schooling abroad respect for the precious heritage of the ancient Indian tradition. On the strength of his exposure to the ways of thinking in the West, the scientific intellectual orientation he had acquired in school, he had developed a truly "modern" perspective in which to review and to re-vision the past of India.

A scholar one generation later than Bankim, Aurobindo is much more sharply sensitive, more directly critical, in his experience of colonization. He is fully aware of the de-nationalizing effect of uncritical imitation of the Western mode which had marked the Indian response in the early phase of exposure to the West. Yet, as in the *Foundations of Indian Culture* and in other contexts, Aurobindo records his trust in a significantly benign effect of the exposure; he believes that Indians can benefit from it, provided they make the proper use of the experience,

> I am thinking of certain influences, ideas, energies, brought forward with a living force by Europe, which can awaken and enrich our own cultural activities and cultural being if we succeed in dealing with them with a victorious power and originality, if we can bring them into our characteristic way of being and transform them by its shaping action.[28]

History permits no moving backward; "we cannot go backward to a past form of our being", he notes, yet we can make a gain of our loss:

> We can go forward to a large repossession of ourselves in which we shall make a better, more living, more real, more self-possessed use of the intervening experience. We can still think in the essential sense of the great spirit and ideals of our past,

[28] "Is India Civilized?" Serialized in the *Arya,* December 1918– February 1919, included in *The Foundations of Indian Culture*, SABCL, vol. 14, p. 387ff.

> but the form of our thinking, our speaking, our development of these has changed by the very fact of new thought and experience; we see them not only in the old, but in new lights, we support them by the added strength of new view-points, even the old words we use acquire for us a modified, more extended and richer significance.[29]

This is an acute observation on the experience of colonial conditioning and its lasting impact, an acknowledgment of the effect of "fore-closure" as it would come to be designated later in postcolonial discourse, and a trust in the scope for transcending the same. Aurobindo glances over stages in the colonial experience: the first phase of blind acceptance and a subsequent phase of "a more subtle assimilation and fusing" in which the response of the colonized "involves no mere return but … hastens a restatement". Aurobindo notes,

> Of this freer dealing with past and present, this preservation by reconstruction, Vivekanada was in his life time the leading exemplar and the most powerful exponent.[30]

This process, he feels, must continue till the restatement is complete. The intention behind the publication of the *Arya*, Aurobindo explains in the Note "*Arya's* Fourth Year", had been "to approach the synthesis from the starting point of the two lines of culture which divide human thought and are now meeting at its apex, the knowledge of the West and the knowledge of the East".[31]

Aurobindo's analysis of the Indian experience of European colonization presents a powerful discourse, an open-eyed critique of the long history, vibrant with "post-colonial" sensibilities anticipated long before the specific approach had made its formal entry.

---

[29] SABCL, 14, pp. 392-93.

[30] Ibid., 17; pp. 414-15.

[31] Ibid., 17; p. 400.

III

His close and extensive study of the Veda texts records an enormous effort at scholastic engagement.[32] The essays serilaized in the *Arya* during the period 1914-1916, together with the notings and drafts made in a number of Note Books and scribbled on loose sheets of paper, published since the 1970's in volumes of *Sri Aurobindo Archives and Research*, bear out the range and the depth of his enquiry. In a short passage, one of these Note Book entries presumably written during the period 1905-1906,[33] Aurobindo formulates what appears to be a basic conviction: he asserts that the fountainhead of the entire Hindu culture is the "small body of speech, the Veda". From this, he affirms, grows all systems of religions, philosophy, ethics. Around 1913 preparing in Pondicherry the study of the Veda to be serialized in the *Arya*, Aurobindo makes the same point, brings out the centrality of the Veda scriptures, tracing an unbroken line of continuity from the thoughts of the Vedic rishis down to Sri Ramakrishna and Vivekananda. He points out, "the Veda was the beginning of our spiritual knowledge; the Veda will remain its end.[34]

In his close study of the Veda texts, particularly the text of the Rig-veda, he had come to recognize the major points of misconstruction in the Westerners' understanding of the ancient pronouncements. Aurobindo, we remember, had studied in depth the works of Bankimchandra. Two kindred points of emphasis in their response to the Indologists'

---

32 The editor in the December 1978 Volume of the *Sri Aurobindo Archives and Research* notes that "Far from being plunged in some incommunicable Absolute for days on end", during this period Aurobindo shouldered "a scholastic toil" of enormous proportions. P. 212.

33 *SA Archives and Research*, April 1977, p. 31.

34 Ibid., December 1985, p. 152.

interpretation are (a) both Bankim and Aurobindo notice in the approach of the European scholars an element of Euro-centric egotism, the cultural imperialism operative on global scale in the aftermath of geographical expeditions and the spread of the modern European culture; (b) both of them focus, each in his own idiom of perception, on the deeper, meta-literal meaning of the Vedic utterances — mostly unnoticed in the Western interpretation.

Unsupported at that point of time by advanced archaeological research, solely guided by the light of what now we may designate his poetical-spiritual prescience and penetrating insight, Aurobindo registers three major points of dissent:

One:

Aurobindo questions the validity of the first premise in Western Indology, the theory of an Aryan invasion, the arrival//intrusion of a different race of Indo-European origin. He raises the question "whether the whole story of an Aryan invasion through the Punjab is not a myth of the philologists."[35] On this issue he notes, again remarkably anticipating modern perception, the inadequacy of comparative philology, one of the sciences Aurobindo finds at that point of time "unhappily still young and still largely conjectural in their methods."[36] In the MSS "Chapter for a work on the Veda"[36a] he had noted,

> The scholars of Europe have constructed for themselves by a study from outside of degenerate humanity at the point of lapsing back into the animal, a fanciful psychology of prehistoric humanity; they have read into this psychology the most ingenious

[35] *The Secret of the Veda*, (Pondicherry Sri Aurobindo Ashram,1956; 1999), p. 6.

[36] Ibid, p. 3.

[36a] *SA Archives And Research*, December 1985.

> Alexandrian conceits possible to the richly stored and rapidly creative modern scholastic imagination, and this compound they have presented to us as the ascertained meaning of the Veda. They base their version on the inchoate sciences ... of Comparative Philology, Comparative Mythology and Archaeology, — branches of conjectural learning ...as yet and in themselves ... so inchoate, so imperfect, so devoid of sure fundamental laws...

Aurobindo perceives the insupportability of the idea of familial bonds of kinship between one language and another which, as modern anthropologists and linguists assert, remain conjectural unless endorsed by archaeological research.

He also rejects the north-south divide — the Aryan-non-Aryan/Dravidian divide — in the linguistic as well as physiognomic features in the demographic distribution on the sub-continent. Soon after his return to India, Aurobindo had planned extensive studies in the growth of languages, jotting down significant points in the pages of his Note Books. The intention, the editors of *Sri Aurobindo Archives and Research* tell us, was to "write a full treatise" on the origins of Aryan speech in which Sri Aurobindo hoped, "the old Arya bhasa from which the Indo-Aryan and Dravidian languages are all derived" would be reconstructed.[37]

In the MSS of "the Origins of Aryan Speech" now included in SABCL 10, we note, Aurobindo sets aside Max Müller's formula of family relations between languages as mostly based on conjecture, attributing undue importance to superficial similarities. He notes the baseless ethnological theories built on the slender basis of guesswork speculation,

> The philologists have ... split up on the strength of linguistic differences the Indian nationality into the northern Aryan race and the southern Dravidian, but sound observation shows a single

[37] *SA Archives And Research*, December 1978, p. 213.

> physical type with minor variations pervading the whole of India from Cape Comorin to Afganistan.

Western scholarship had built a huge structure on this

> brilliantly ingenious and attractive but wholly conjectural and unreliable interpretation of the Vedas, a remarkable, minute and captivating picture of an early half-savage Aryan civilization in India. How much value can we attach to these dazzling structures? None, for they have no assured scientific basis.[38]

Aurobindo's project on linguistic research remained incomplete; the second part of his study in "The Origins of Aryan Speech" was never written out. However, thoughts were shaping in his mind. In *The Secret of the Veda* Aurobindo notes that it was through the study of Tamil, that he came to glimpse the truth. He says, it was through the study of "this Dravidian language that I came first to perceive what seems to me now the true law, origins and, as it were, the etymology of the Aryan tongues". Aurobindo assures us that the "original connection between the Dravidian and Aryan tongues was far closer and more extensive than is usually supposed."

Two:

Aurobindo rejects the premise that the Rig-veda is just a collection of separate clusters of statements, discontinuous – without any coherent philosophy or faith running through and holding them together. He refuses to accept the idea that it is just an assemblage of scattered utterances of the primitive human mind, "helpless" utterances which reflect mortal fear and a sense of insecurity in the face of the forces of nature and record survival-motivated gestures of propitiation. He delves into the deeper symbolism in the Veda Suktas; he brings out the embedded cosmic vision iconized in the many gods

[38] SABCL 10, pp. 553-54.

of the sun, the dawn, fire, water, the winds and the rest, and thus reconstructs a contour of the ancient vision, presents what he believes to have been the Rishis' total, inclusive perception of the essence of human existence on earth. Appreciating the maturity in the verbal form as well as the depth and range of the visionary quality in the Veda text, Aurobindo feels that this "would not easily be possible in the beginnings of thought and psychological experience or even during their early progress and unfolding."[39] Here too, we remember his probing study of the thoughts of Bankimchandra. Bankim, tracing a consistent growth from the Rig-veda to the Upanishads, had elaborated on the essential monistic perception underlying the surface level polytheistic structure. With confidence Aurobindo ventures the "surmise" that "our actual Sanhita represents the close of a period, not its commencement, nor even some of its successive stages."[40] In his close study of the deeper, the meta-literal symbolical signification of the Suktas he traces a coherent purposeful pattern of meaning. This semantic body, he argues, is not only incorporated in the more than one thousand Veda Suktas, but also prepares for and leads up to the Upanishads. The Upanishads, he notes, could not and did not appear "out of a previous void"[41] without a prolonged and sustained preparation.

In the *Arya* essay on the Upanishads, June 1920, Aurobindo focuses on the symbolical idiom in the ancient Veda and in the Upanishads, the metaphorical indirection which had baffled the Westerners,

---

[39] *The Secret of the Veda*, p. 12.

[40] Ibid., p. 12.

[41] Ibid., p. 5.
Bankimchandra in the *Prachar* article "Devatattwa O Hindu Dharma" traces stages in the development of spiritual awareness in the human mind in the history of human civilization. *Rachanavali* II, p. 792.

> It is to a great extent this element (older symbolism) no longer seizable by our way of thinking that has baffled certain Western scholars and made them cry out that these scriptures are a mixture of the sublimest philosophical speculations with the first awkward stammerings of the child mind of humanity.[42]

Referring to the many passages in the Upanishads directly taken from the Veda, Aurobindo emphatically notes,

> These passages cannot be dismissed as childish aberration of the intelligence void of sense or of any discoverable bearing on the higher thought in which they culminate. On the contrary we find that they have a deep enough significance once we can get inside their symbolical meaning.[43]

Three:

Aurobindo naturally moves away, as we noted, from the Sayana line of literal-ritualistic interpretation, the interpretation which the Western scholars had accepted as the authentic, definitive, native reading of the Veda text. Sayana, he believes, had been a wrong guide. Reaching into the deeper symbolic level of interpretation, he makes a bold effort in the *Arya* essays to discover, to bring to light, the idiom of yore. In the essay cited above he notes,

> This Vedic and Vedantic imagery is foreign to our present mentality which does not believe in the living truth of the symbol, because the revealing imagination intimidated by the intellect has no longer the courage to accept, identify itself with and boldly embody a psychic and spiritual vision; but it is certainly very far from being a childish or a primitive and barbarous mysticism;

---

[42] Included in *The Foundations of Indian Culture*, later printed as Introduction to the 1971 collection *The Upanishads*, Pondicherry, Shri Aurobindo Ashram.

[43] *The Upanishads*, pp. 6-7.

> this vivid, living, luminously poetic intuitive language is rather the natural expression of a highly evolved spiritual culture.[44]

Aurobindo starts with a conviction that words and phrases in the language in which the ancient scriptures are composed, convey meaning at multiple levels. This with him is a conviction born as much of a close acquaintance with the semantic designs operative in the ancient texts, as of a poet's intuitive grasp of symbolical valences beyond the merely literal, beyond "the surface meaning of the words and sentences", as he terms it.[45] The close study of the texts of the Upanishads and the Bhagavadgita he had been engaged in since the early Baroda days, had familiarized him with the metaphorical idiom; these texts had unfolded to him the many levels of meaning. Aurobindo uses the term "multi-significance".[46] In the *Arya* essay now figuring as Chapter IV in *The Secret of the Veda*, Aurobindo recounts his journey in search of the meta-literal meaning of key words and basic nomenclature in the Veda. At the primary level *go* is cow and *ghrita* is clarified butter and *yagna* is offerings at a sacrifice. From this Aurobindo reaches what at this point of his argument he designates the "psychological" level of signification. With the rational rigour of a true researcher, Aurobindo narrates in *The Secret of the Veda* the challenging task of decoding the ancient text, the antique idiom. The effort required taking into account the etymological significance of words — as in the case of "*purohita*", "*agni*", "*ghritam*", "*go*" etc. —, together with the contextual as well as the

---

[44] Ibid., p. 8.

[45] Ibid., p. 42.

[46] *The Secret of the Veda*, p. 49. As an example he draws our attention to the fact that the word "*yagna* is used in the Bhagavadgita in the "symbolic sense for all action, whether internal or external, that is consecrated to the gods or to the Supreme". Ibid. p. 41.

associational shades of meaning. Aurobindo places before us the polemically graded queries he had to face and seek answer for, in this quest for the inner structure of thought embedded in these utterances which, on the surface level, convey a message easy to decipher at the level of ritualistic practice. This journey, he tells us, leads him along the path of tracing or re-tracing, "the great passage" discovered by the "ancestors, the ancient Rishis". This is the passage from the material level of existential signification to the visionary realms beyond.[47]

The surface level, the ritualistic one, is at which Sayana Acharya had interpreted the text; this was the level at which the Western Indologists in search for the infancy of human civilization sought and found a comfortable footing. Aurobindo congratulates himself on his "fortunate ignorance of the commentary of Sayana"[48] at the time he came to read the Veda. The Sayana Bhasya, with all its authoritarian erudition and rational schematization so widely admired, Aurobindo comments, had played a decisive role in misguiding the Western scholars as well as many of the Indian Vedicists:

> It is the final and authoritative binding of the Veda to this lowest of all its possible senses that has been the most unfortunate result of Sayana's commentary. The dominance of the ritualistic interpretation had already deprived India of the living use of its greatest scripture and of the true clue to the entire sense of the Upanishads. Sayana's commentary put a seal of finality on the old misunderstanding which could not be broken for many centuries. And its suggestions, when another civilization discovered and set itself to study the Veda, became in the European mind the parent of fresh errors.[49]

[47] Ibid., p. 46.

[48] Ibid., p. 39.

[49] Ibid., p. 23.

Sayana's tendency, Aurobindo notes in his exegetical engagement with the Rig-veda[50], was "to obliterate all fine shades and distinctions between words and to give them their vaguest general significance". Aurobindo attends to the etymology and the contextual cluster of associations; he recollects his exploratory way of decoding:

> What for instance could be made of clarified butter dropping from heaven or dripping from the horses of Indra or dripping from the mind? Obviously this was a grotesque nonsense, ... But I found that "*ghrita*" was constantly used in connection with the thought of the mind, that heaven in the Veda was a symbol of the mind, that Indra represented the illuminated mentality and his two horses double energies of that mentality and even that the Veda sometimes speaks plainly of offering the intellect, "*manishā*" as purified "*ghrita*" to the gods, "*ghritamnaputammanishām*". The word "*ghrita*" counts also among its philological significances the sense of a rich or warm brightness. It was by this concurrence of indications that I felt justified in fixing a certain psychological significance for the figure of the clarified butter.[51]

Were the Rishis in the Rig-veda praying for cows, *go*, horses, *aswa*, and all other physical-material objects? Aurobindo notes his findings,

> The fruits of the offering were in appearance purely material — cows, horses, gold, offspring, men, physical strength, victory in battle. Here the difficulty thickened. But I had already found that the Vedic cow was an exceedingly enigmatic animal and came from no earthly herd. The word *go* means both cow and light and in a number of passages evidently meant light even while putting forward the image of the cow.[52]

---

50 For instance, in the draft interpretation of the Suktas in the first Mandala of the Rig-veda placing his metaphorical reading side by side with Sayana's , *Sri Aurobindo Archives and Research*, (Vol. II., No. 2, Dec. 1978).

51 *The Secret of the Veda*, p. 43.

52 Ibid.

The many gods, Aurobindo perceives, are children of Aditi who, Bankim had assured much earlier, stands for infinity. In the Veda text, Aurobindo notes, the gods are "described as increasing man, bringing him light, pouring on him the fullness of waters, the abundance of the heavens, increasing the truth in him, building up the divine worlds, leading him against all attacks to the great goal, the integral felicity, the perfect bliss." The opposing forces, the demons, he points out,

> are all powers of division and limitation, Coverers, Tearers, Devourers, Confiners, Dualisers, Obstructers, as their names indicate, powers that work against the free and unified integrality of being. These Vrittras, Panis, Atris, Rakshasas, Sambara, Vala, Namuchi, are not Dravidian, non-Aryan kings and gods, as the modern mind with its exaggerated historic sense would like them to be; they represent a more antique idea better suited to the religious and ethical preoccupations of our forefathers. They represent the struggle between the powers of the higher good and the lower desire.[53]

So it proceeds in Aurobindo's exegetical essays and through the innovative translation of selected Suktas of the text, demonstrating the conviction:

> Once the sense of the Vedic symbol is known, the spiritual intention of these legends becomes apparent and inevitable ... their materials have been skilfully welded together by firm hands and any inconsistency in our handling of them shatters the whole fabric of their sense and their coherent thinking. Thus there emerged in my mind, revealing itself as it were out of the ancient verses, a Veda which was throughout the Scripture of a great and antique religion,...a Scripture not confused in thought or primitive in its substance, not a medley of heterogeneous or barbarous elements, but one complete and self-conscious in its purpose and in its purport, veiled indeed by the cover, sometimes thick, sometimes transparent, of another and material sense, but

[53] Ibid., p. 46.

> never losing sight even for a single moment of its high spiritual aim and tendency.[54]

With a penetrating perception of the true rhythm of an ancient culture, Aurobido surmises that the Vedic utterances were aimed at levels of audience: the initiated and the laity. While the elect, the empowered, the initiated could access the higher levels of the visionary ecstasy, the commoners could be held together through daily participation in shared ritualistic practice. To preserve them in an ambience of the spirit of worship and trust in the essential goodness in the scheme of the universe acted as the operative intention at the primary level of solidarity. He notes.

> They (the Rishis) favoured the existence of an outer worship, effective but imperfect, for the profane, an inner discipline for the initiate, and clothed their language in words and images which had, equally, a spiritual sense for the elect, a concrete sense for the mass of ordinary worshippers.[55]

Later in the argument Aurobindo reiterates,

> The hypothesis on which I shall conduct my own enquiry is that the Veda has a double aspect and that the two, though closely related, must be kept apart. The Rishis arranged the substance of their thought in a system of parallelism by which the same deities were at once internal and external powers of universal Nature, and they managed its expression through a system of double values by which the same language served for their worship in both aspects.[56]

IV

Being attuned to the rhythm of valencies, the idiom — verbal as well as experiential — on the part of the reader is an

---

[54] Ibid., pp. 46-47.

[55] Ibid., pp. 7-8.

[56] Ibid., pp. 32-33.

important factor; in the absence of this, meanings appear disjuncted, drifting, elusive. This privilege of the insider to a culture is what Bankimchandra had in mind when in his 1894 address he reminded the younger generation of Indian scholars of their invaluable inheritance and urged them to engage in a fresh, critical, modern, yet empathic approach to the ancient scriptures. Aurobindo almost acts it out.

In an ironical twist away from parental planning, young Aurobindo had re-claimed his Indian ancestry, established kinship with the age-old tradition and earned for himself a deep sense of belonging. Reading the Rig-veda in the early decades of the twentieth century in terms of its deeper symbolical meaning, Aurobindo is a true insider, a participatory reader. In evolving a post-Sayanacharya, post-Orientalist modality of deciphering the symbolical, multi-tier significatory potential of words, phrases and discourses in ancient India, Aurobindo responds from within the native hermeneutic field. He has behind him a long tradition which, we noted, the ancient linguists, the rhetoricians and exegetists had carried on to amazing points of finesse. He had come to relate to this tradition, to own it in the depth of self-realization, identity-assertion; and, history records, in his own system of visionary speculation, he led the ancient tradition to newer reaches of spiritual-metaphysical conceptualization.

Bankimchandra, in service of the Brirish Government in India, inspired the spirit of nationalistic assertion; as Aurobindo notes, he gave the nation a *mantra*, a slogan of worshipping the motherland, and alerted young intellectuals about the de-nationalizing impact of colonial dominance, the epistemic violence implicit in it. Dayananda Saraswati spent his life working out a reform of the Vedic tradition, then mostly in the grip of cunning priest-craft, and planning to re-establish its vital relation with contemporary life. Balagangadhara Tilak, immersed in the study of Vedic astronomy and the ancient culture, grew into a nationalist leader in the field of anti-colonial politics. Aurobindo Indianized himself, opened up to the nationalist upsurge of the early twentieth century, walked the activist way, went back to the scholastic mode, stayed absorbed in the study of the Vedas, the Upanishads, the Bhagavadgita and the related lore, shaped a post-colonial idiom of articulation much ahead of his time, before committing himself totally to the life of a spiritual seeker.

Time since Bankim had been moving fast. The gap, of nearly three decades, between Bankim's *Bangadarshan* and *Prachar* and the *Arya* at Pondicherry, had wrought significant alterations in the cultural-political perspective. Bankim with his open-eyed perception of the Euro-centric compulsions of imperialism in Oriental scholarship, had yet considered British rule in India as something welcome in the situation prevailing — as an event promising liberation from the Islamic rule then in its worst decadence.

Aurobindo had joined the activist squad bent on freeing the motherland from the clutches of alien domination; his response to the imperialist design, in the intellectual field as much as in the political, happened to be uncompromising, relentless and unambiguous. He had come to question the adequacy and the validity of the Western Indologists' interpretation of the culture of ancient India much more acutely, to voice dissent in a sharper tone, with a much more decisive accent and on an actional level. It was a post-colonial dissent before its time. Long before the formulation of categories in today's parlance, long before the emergence of Bachelard's category of "epistemlogical acts and thresholds", long before Foucault's denomination of subjective historiography, Aurobindo had questioned the authority of the Westerners' reading of the past of India — the Hellenic mind's response to an un-Hellenic civilization. In his quest for higher spiritual levels of consciousness, in the vision of a Supermind, he had immersed himself in the contemplation of evolutionary transcendence for Man, trans-nation, global and generic.

What is more important, of greater historical significance in the growth of post-colonial discourse, is that Aurobindo had asserted that the Veda, instead of recording the "infancy" in the history of man, marks the peak point of an ancient civilization in full growth, full maturity. In placing his trust in the historical reality of an earlier civilization different from the later wave, Aurobindo visualizes a multi-linear growth pattern. This in an embryonic form introduces the idea that man's journey of civilizing himself in different parts of the planet need not have followed a uni-linear course; it might have followed different paths at different points of time, reached different peaks and met different ends. The idea of multiple tracks of development in the case of human civilization, of multeity in the pattern of growth and in modalities of maturation — is a premise that awaits prime position in civilization studies. Aurobindo had given a start.*

---

* Also see, the author's 'Introduction', *Sri Aurobindo: a Postcolonial Reader*, (ed. Sati Chatterjee), Centre for Sri Aurobindo Studies, Jadavpur University, 2015.

Six

The comparative engagement : changing tropes and the stable premise

The bridge of thoughts and sights that span the whole history of the Aryan world has its first arch in the Veda, its last in Kant's Critique of Pure Reason

If Hegel calls the discovery of the common origin of Greek and Sanscrit the discovery of a new world, the same may be said with regard to the common origin of Greek and Sanscrit mythology. The discovery is made, the science of comparative mythology will soon rise to the same importance as comparative Philology,

Max Müller

Yet so great is the force of attractive generalisations and widely popularized errors that all the world goes on perpetuating the blunder talking of the Indo-European races, claiming or disclaiming Aryan kinship and building on that basis of falsehood the most far-reaching political, social or pseudo-scientific conclusions.

Sri Aurobindo

We cannot borrow God.

Heinrich Zimmer

The modern hero-deed must be that of questing to bring to light again the lost Atlantis of the co-ordinated soul. Obviously this work cannot be wrought by turning back, or away, from what has been accomplished by the modern revolution: for the problem is nothing if not that of rendering the modern world spiritually significant.

Joseph Campbell

In 1856 A. Smythe Palmer, D. D., editor, *Oxford Essays*, could perceive that Max Müller's essay included in the volume, the essay on Comparative Mythology, was "a pioneer essay" which promised to open out "paths of research hitherto untrodden". Over the decades of the twentieth century comparative studies of religions and myth structures grew into an enormous corpus, developed into a discipline, a critical approach ready for application in the fields of the study of art and literature, sociology and culture studies. Max Müller's ideas took roots; and the religious sensibilities of man yielded to historical cartography. In this extending field of comparatist evaluation, in the expanding study of inter-relatedness, ancient India, discovered and codified by Western Indologists, remained a major culture profile on the "other" side of the divide.

Encounters with different faith structures, ritual patterns, codes of myths and symbols in far away unfamiliar lands in that season of receding frontiers, rolled out before the Westerners' gage chequered tapestries depicting amazing complexity, denoting unexpected depths. Archaeological explorations dug out remnants of lost civilizations; myths met reality. Freud and Jung provided newer clues, social anthropology opened out newer perspectives. Modernity's exploration into the story of man "here" and "there" (the "near-", the "middle-", and the "far-", loaded longitudinals all), "now" and "then", plunged into exciting adventures. All this, the adventure of relating and re-relating to the "prior", the "deeper down", Homi K. Bhabha and other scholars note, happened to be part of a process of the "self-inventions of modernity in the West". The eagerness to resume, almost the insistence on re-opening, a dialogue with the millennia-old mind of India came to constitute a chapter in this episode.

Terminology in comparatist parlance is important. To "compare" means placing different things side by side and observing, analysing the similarities and differences between them. This, the OED mentions as the primary meaning of the term; and this implies placing comparable items/terms at par. The OED mentions the idea of equality, parity in the Latin and French roots and gives meaning as 1. "to represent as similar, to liken"; 2. "to mark the similarities and differences of; to bring together for the purpose of noticing these". In grammar, OED mentions, "to compare" comes to mean an act of measuring by degrees – the "positive", the "comparative", the "superlative" – projecting a hierarchical structure. In the comparatist discourse, we note, the objective neutrality at the lexical level of signification – comparing things at par – yields to the signification at the grammatical level—relative evaluation of things, relative to an accepted/assumed referral, evaluation in relation to an accepted point of position. The referral un-questionably assumed, needless to mention, remains the conquering modern West.

At the time Max Müller formulated the comparative study of mythology, post-modernist perspectives of pluralism and multeity were more than a hundred years away; the idea of an earlier civilization in India, such as would be advanced by Bankim, Tilak, Aurobindo, would not matter; these could easily be ignored and pushed aside. The nineteenth-century narrative of unquestioned certitude, of definitive goals and linear progress, had a smooth run. The comparatist discourse growing through this period promoted not so much comparisons at par, as evaluatory designations erecting hierarchical alignments. The point of reference remaining the European module, "others", revealing similarities/kinship/variance, provided interesting, at times exciting, opportunities for value analysis. The "historical school" of thinking Max Müller had initiated, linking up the "others" in a sequential temporal order, provided the rational schema. The historical perspective, the order of the before and the after, simultaneously acknowledged other identities, accommodated them within the cognitive ken, and positioned them in a preparatory, aspirational role — preceding and paving the way towards, the one supreme moment, the modern West. The growth pattern deciphered extended to remote past; and the widening coverage increasingly proved gainful. The new knowledge born: factual knowledge of the identity of the "other" in obscure parts of the planet, and conceptual knowledge of inter-relations, opened up richer world-views even as it deepened the West's newer understanding of its own self, at maturity point in a long growth process.

Max Müller, in the Prefaces to his volumes of the Rig-veda, in his essay on Comparative Mythology, in his numerous series of lectures[1], had formulated his perception of an unbroken continuity that "connects our thoughts and our words with the first thought conceived and the first word uttered by the earliest ancestors of our race"[2]. The search for origins brought up the idea of shared ground and common stock. In the lecture on Mythology (XVI in the Gifford series), Max Müller mentioned that

> besides much that is peculiar to each, we find in all a common fund of mythology which we may look upon as the earliest stratum likely to contain the germs of religious thought.[3]

---

[1] *The Rig-veda Sanhita*, vol. III, pp. V-VI; "Essay on Comparative Mythology", p. 176; Lectures at the Royal Institute, "Introduction to the Science of Religion"(1870); Cambridge lecture, "India, What Can it Teach Us?"(1882); the Gifford lectures (1888) among others.

[2] Gifford lecture: "My Own Definition of Religion". Mircea Eliade notes how at that point of time "all Western historiography...was obsessed with the quest of origins" parallel to preoccupations in the fields of biology and even of geological researches. See, *The Quest for the Origins of Religion* (University of Chicago Press, 1969), p. 160.

[3] P. 411.

He explained how the historical approach "becomes more attractive when it leads us on to the discovery of general motives which alone can account for such similarities".[4]

The "common fund", the "general motives" and analogous phrasings, evoke the idea of a shared storehouse of perceptual insights. This is the idea that grows, through the troubled decades of the next century, into the premise of a "monomyth" that Joseph Campbell later comes to formulate. That, however, in Max Müller's time, had been far away. The tropes that recur in nineteenth-century discourse, the analogues that bear the impress of a dominant Euro-ego, induce the logic of temporal sequentiality and/or a gradation of vertical alignment, and effectively locate the "other" in the position of a "prior" and a "lower". The trope of the layers of encrustation forming the earth surface brings in the idea of a vertical alignment; the geologist digging down to "the petrified remains of a primeval" layer as a metaphor locates the "other" down below and generates the discourse of sub-structures and super-structures. In post-Freud parlance the verticality would acquire newer denominations; with Jung the "petrified primeval" that Max Muller had talked about, would come to denote a "substrate", potent, dark and mostly un-deciphered — despite nineteenth-century dexterity in docketing and codification.

II

In the introductory part of his essay on comparative mythology Max Müller had appreciatively mentioned the "inductive philosophy by which men like Columbus, Leonardo da Vinci, Copernicus, Kepler, Bacon and Galeleo had regenerated and invigorated the intellectual life of modern Europe". In the field

[4] Ibid., p. 429.

of comparative mythology J. G. Frazer, we note, undertakes the task of an inductive exploration into the story of human civilization. The mammoth adventure recorded in the twelve volumes of *The Golden Bough* published between 1890 and 1915, unfolds close field-work extending almost over the entire region of human habitation, old and new, under Hellenic and non-Hellenic culture coverage. Through unsparing scrutiny of details, the giant effort demonstrates, as it were, the premise in the historical school of thinking; it graphs a linear growth in human civilization. In Frazer's study it proceeds *from* magic *through* religion *to* science.

Reading the "dream like vision of the little woodland lake of Nemi" in Turner's piece of painting, the antique modalities detailed in it, Frazer delves into kindred lores around, far and near in space and time. Babylonia and Assyria, the kingdom of the Khazars in southern Russia, parts of Africa and other corners of the planet come under critical scanning.[5] He notes that the "rudeness and barbarity" of the custom (the succession through murder to the position of the Priest, the King of the wood), in contrast to the "polished Italian society" of "imperial times" can be explained only if parallels are found in the life of primitive communities, as

> recent researches into the early history of man have revealed the essential similarity with which, under many superficial differences, the human mind has elaborated its first crude philosophy of life.[6]

From the first crude philosophy of life recorded in various myth structures all over the world to the present moment, the moment of imperial times, Max Müller had been arguing, it is a consistent growth story. Frazer's explorations confirm it all in the details of a vast survey; he traces a consistent

[5] Abridged single volume, 1922, (Wordsworth Reference, 1993), pp. VI, 8.

[6] Ibid., p. 2.

successive pattern of growth. He brings his exploration to its close, bids farewell to Nemi, with the deliberation that

> We shall perhaps be disposed to conclude that the movement of the higher thought, so far we can trace it, has on the whole been from magic through religion to science.[7]

Similes recur; images, metaphors, tropes trace the growth-line. The journey of exploration, the inductive modality of collecting accounts of illustrative specificities that Frazer had undertaken, is recorded in the language of territorial expeditions; the major tropes are *sailing across uncharted seas*, *perilous voyages*, *discoveries*. His chosen task, Frazer anticipates in the beginning, would be arduous, the journey

> will be long and laborious, but may possess something of the interest and charm of a voyage of discovery in which we shall visit many strange foreign lands, with strange foreign peoples, and still stranger customs. The wind is in the shrouds: we shake out our sails to it.[8]

At the end of it all, when he brings the massive account to its close, drawing the curtain on one phase of enquiry into the growth of myths over the world, the experience is of the termination of a long, very long expedition; favoured tropes, recurring throughout, set the tune: "*our long voyage of discovery is over and our bark has dropped her weary sails in port at last*".

Geo-political acquisitions had established an inviolable global authority, installing modern Europe at the helm; the imperial experience operates as the point of reference. Adventures of the mind seek support and validation in the vocabulary of the triumphant adventure on the pragmatic, the territorial level. Odysseus, at the turn of the century, is a triumphant icon.

---

[7] Ibid., p. 711.

[8] Ibid., pp. 8-9.

2.

In 1919, in the Preface to *From Ritual to Romance*, Jessie Weston acknowledges that her work draws "initial inspiration" from the pioneering work of Frazer[9]; in a way Weston makes an extended, instance-specific application of the Frazer approach. She intends to find out whether the Grail Quest constitutes an isolated, unique event of perception, or whether, as contemporary investigations indicate, it relates to a common human aspiration cutting across faith lines and culture borders. She finds it incumbent to

> retrace our steps and turn back to the early tradition of our Aryan fore-fathers and see whether we cannot even in that remote antiquity lay our hands upon a clue, which, like the fabled thread of Ariadne, shall serve as guide through the mazes of a varying, yet curiously persistent tradition.[10]

Initially inspired by Frazer's adventurous expedition, Jessie Weston feels the need for the formation of a holistic view, the need for organizing the efforts into a planned purposive programme. She notes that the harvest gathered from the extensive field-work, path-breaking investigation as it had been, now must be deciphered and collected into a total design of meaningful relatedness and vital support. Weston comments,

> Valuable material has been collected, but the studies so far, have been individual, and independent, the much needed *travail de ensemble* has not yet appeared.[11]

---

[9] Jessie Weston notes, "Like many others, I owe to J.G. Frazer the initial inspiration which set me, as I may truly say, on the road to the Grail Castle". (Doubleday Anchor Books, New York, 1957), p. VII.

[10] Ibid., p. 24.

[11] Ibid., p. 81.

When it does, the later moments of human perception would present themselves as "re-statements" of the earlier ones. She assures,

> The study and the criticism of the Grail literature will possess an even deeper interest, a more absorbing fascination when it is definitely recognized that we possess in that literature a unique example of the re-statement of an ancient and august Ritual in terms of imperishable Romance.[12]

Valorization of the older, the earlier, is carried to newer heights. The "archaic" emerges as a category, a denomination; the "historical approach" propagated by Max Müller in the preceding century steadily individuates itself as a discipline. The wide irresistible influence of Jessie Weston's slender volume on the Modernists, the formation and the founding of the "archetypes" — the Waste Land, the Fisher King, the Chapel perilous, the bleeding lancet, the posing and the answering of questions, the freeing of the waters of life, along with the Indian sages' prayers for "Santih", in T. S. Eliot, the Homeric icons in James Joyce — almost lead to the construction of a new faith system, the cult of the "arche-". In images, symbols, verbal modules, in imaginative association, in emotional response it operates as the resonance, as T. S. Eliot phrases, "of the beating of an antique drum" in our spoken word of the day.

III

The discipline of comparative studies grew over the troubled decades of the twentieth century, decades in which the West faced in different denominations the challenge of questioning itself anew. As part of Europe's effort at re-defining its own

[12] Ibid., p. 209.

position, the comparative mode developed a complex process of handling the cultural "other". As at the time of Max Müller, it continued to operate as a dialectical strategy of integrating and keeping apart. Tropes changed and newer sets of binaries replaced the older ones in use, although, interestingly, the strategy retained its character defined in the season of imperial glory.

The "arche" in the back of the behind, in its essentials, got internalized, accommodated as the primary base in the structure of the human psyche. Freud and Jung, all the differences in between[13], rescued the "substrate", conceded it base priority. Jung expounded the modern man's elemental legacy of stored memories, experiences and impressions hidden beneath the layers of super-encrustation, and pleaded for a vital bonding of the surface and the sub-face. This bonding, he warned, is a precondition much neglected and neglected too long, for a healthy existence and full realization of the psychic potential.[14] In the discourse of comparative mythology and comparative religion Jung's "archaic", the "primal-original", assigned the status of the "pre-logical" by Levy Bruhl,[15] came to denote the primitive mentality and circulated as an antonym for the "modern". The pre-logical versus the logical, the unhistorical versus the historical, the cyclic versus the linear, the regressive versus the progressive — emerged as binaries, obviously loaded in the range of their signification. Mircea Eliade's "return" formulated a myth of the regress, the re-petition. The regressive, cyclic, non-linear, non-progressive modality now marked out the "archaic", the "pre-modern"— in Eliade's view including "both the world

[13] Explained, for instance, by Jung in *Modern Man in Search of a Soul* (New York, Harcourt, Brace and World, Inc., 1933), pp. 115-124.

[14] Ibid., p. 125ff.

[15] Jung cites and comments on Levy Bruhl's definition, Ibid., p. 126.

usually known as 'primitive' and the ancient cultures of Asia, Europe and America."[16] It all now came to pose as the "other" to the logical and progressive modern Occident. The archaic, Mircea Eliade believed, has to be "translated" in the language of modern perception, so that it can be understood.[17]

The effort, however, was felt to be urgent, Eliade assured, for several sets of reasons. First, in an age of comparatist culture (Eliade's own time), Eliade felt, Western philosophy would "provincialize" itself if not keeping in touch with the growing interest in Oriental thought.[18] Philosophical anthropology, Eliade with his long stretch of exposure to the mind of ancient India had to concede, might gain from the study of the modalities of perception in the life of the "pre-Socratic man". Second, "the cardinal problems of metaphysics (in the West's intellectual discourse) could be renewed through a knowledge of archaic ontology". Third, although a Western spiritual rebirth must happen within the framework of Western spiritual traditions, yet, Eliade noted, Westerners might need to be stimulated by ideas from non-Western cultures. A "genuine encounter" between cultures "might well constitute the point of departure for a new humanism upon a world-scale", he admitted in *Myths, Dreams and Mysteries.*[19]

---

16 *The Myth of the Eternal Return* (Bolingen, Princeton University Press, 1954, Paperback 1971), p. 3.

17 Ibid.

18 "First by jealously isolating itself in its own tradition and ignoring ... the problems and solutions of Oriental thought and second by its obstinate refusal to recognise any "situation" except that of the man of historical civilisations." Ibid., p. X.

19 (London, Harvil Press, 1960), pp. 244-45.
Eliade admits that modern man shorn of the defence coverage of myths and symbols, is exposed to the "terror of history", the tyranny of forward moving time, from whose iron grip no system of philosophy offers true release. His recommendation is a return to the Christian creed of faith and surrender as advised in the Gospel Mark II, 22-24.

Max Müller had assured that studies in Oriental culture needed to be expanded in the interest of the West for a fuller appreciation of its own privileged position. Eliade emphasizes the need for the study of archaic ontology in the interest of newer understanding of the modern West in crisis, terrorized by the profane and the pragmatic, and finding for it fresh guidelines for moving ahead. The metaphor changes from the geo-centric to the chrono-metric; however, "the continuist, progressivist myth of Man", as Bhabha mentions[20], marches ahead.

IV

In the late 20's and early 30's of the century Carl Jung had been talking of the peril at the brink the "modern man" stood facing. "The catastrophic results of the World War", he noted, had shattered "our faith in ourselves and in our own worth", it had rendered material "progress" a potential negative force. The modern West, in the situation, could no longer assume a towering profile.[21]

Heinrich Robert Zimmer (1890-1943), who had introduced Jung, a close friend, to the thoughts of Ramana Maharshi and acted as a major influence on young Joseph Campbell, lived through major part of the Second War, knew the intellectual-

---

This, Eliade believes, had for the first time "transcended" "the horizon of archetypes and repetition" and introduced the "new category of faith". Christianity, Eliade assures, is the religion of "the modern man and the historical man". See, *The Myth of Eternal Return*, pp.160-61. Bryan S. Rennie in *Reconstructing Eliade* (1996) examines whether Eliade had a Christian agenda; in his Introduction to *The Changing Religious Worlds*; *the Beginning and End of Mircea Eliade* (2001) he reviews the contribution made by Eliade to comparative discourse.

20 *The Location of Culture*, p. 340.

21 *The Modern Man in Search of a Soul,* pp. 203-213.

ethical crisis the Occident was going through and acknowledged the need for interacting afresh with "every possible antique tradition." In *The King and the Corpse* he noted how the religious fervor in the Christian faith, once fresh and vibrant, had fallen into decline and how

> a more primitive level of myth, abundant with timeless truth,... suddenly seems to have something very deep to say to us.[22]

Closely associated with Jung, Zimmer shared trust in the "substratum" below the conscious surface of the contemporary psyche,

> The spiritual heritage of archaic man ... has vanished to a large extent from the surface of the tangible and conscious realm, yet survives and remains ever present in the subterranean layers of the unconscious. It is the part of our being that links us to a remote ancestry and constitutes our involuntary kinship with archaic man and with ancient civilizations and traditions.[23]

Resuming conversation with this submerged heritage, bringing back "the long lost to our contemporary comprehension", Zimmer assured, is absolutely necessary. "To be a match for the new development", he said, "we must seek to penetrate the mythical contents of every possible antique tradition."[24]

The crisis happened to be so acute, the need for reaching out and reaching down so compulsive, that Zimmer advised Westerners, with their superior Hellenic aesthetic culture, to agree to listen to the tales told by Indian myths, even when the form of these oriental myths are un-poetical, "unattractive" and crude, compared to the work of Homer or Sophocles.[25]

---

[22] (Princeton University Press 1948; Indian edition, Delhi 1999), p. 310.

[23] Ibid.

[24] Ibid., p. 311.

[25] Ibid., p. 308.

2.

The crisis had been deepening in the other area: Science had been questioning itself. Quantum physics found the fundamental nature of the universe essentially different from the world of everyday perception and from the prevailing perception in classical physics. The nature of reality now revealed non-stability, unpredictability, indeterminacy. Capricious, shocking, bewildering, the new perception brought a revolutionary change in the understanding of the fundamental nature of reality. Reality turned out to be a series of probabilities of the results of observation. The enormously laden implications were a breaking down of barriers, dissolution of binaries. The mind/matter, subject/object divide began to break down, even as the opposition between particles and waves did in the recognition of the duality principle, the space denominator, the position here/there dissolved in the perception of the probability factor. It now seemed that Reality is as it is observed, as it is measured, as it turns out to be. The perceiver, the perceived and the perception seemed to blend; and if anything emerged as definitive – not so much to the universe as to man's understanding of it – it was consciousness. Beauty is in the act of beholding. James Jeans notes how the universe "begins to look more like a great thought than a great machine".[26] Eddington admits, "the stuff of the world is mind-stuff".[27] Max Planck, Niels Bohr, Werner Heisenberg, Edwin Shroedinger, over the first few decades of the twentieth century, notwithstanding initial resistance, bring out this other picture — demolishing the classical order, destabilizing the accepted schema, deleting the logic of definitive categorization.

---

[26] *The Mysterious Universe* (Cambridge University Press, 1930), p. 137.

[27] *The Nature of the Physical World* (Cambridge 1931), p. 332.

Amoury Reincourt in *The Eye of Shiva* notes how in a few decades science moves "many light years away from the classical physics of the nineteenth century". Fritjof Capra in "The Future of the New Physics: Afterward to the Third Edition" of *The Tao of Physics,* describes the change as a paradigm shift, "the shift from objective science to epistemic science".[28] Of course, no indication that the new science directly influenced newer approaches in the field of comparative studies in mythology or religion. The parallel movements reflect what might be considered as the temper of the age. Fritjof Capra, in his emotive idiom of expression, notes the strong interest in Eastern mysticism growing in the West "during the last twenty years"; in the Epilogue he affirms,

> The recognition of the similarities between modern physics and Eastern mysticism is part of a much larger movement, of a fundamental change of world-views, or paradigms, in science and society, which is now happening throughout Europe and North America and which amounts to a profound cultural transformation.[29]

Science does not need mysticism, mysticism does not need science; but Capra knows that man needs both—for a meaningful and harmonious and survival-ensured existence on earth. A meeting of the two and a total transformation, he feels, is urgent. The survival of our whole civilization, he thinks, depends on "whether we can bring about such a change."[30]

V

A transformation, a re-defining of the outlook, an act of consent to be re-born, is what Joseph Campbell pleads for in

---

28 (Flamingo, Harper Collins, 1982), p. 363.

29 Ibid., p. 357.

30 Ibid., p. 40.

his elaborate argumentation spread out over five volumes, laden with meticulous scrutiny of the long survival narrative of the human race, of the many phases in it, the many bends and turns on the way.

The compulsion was to effect a new start, the challenge was to retain the self-identity. Zimmer had faced the crisis. "We cannot borrow God. We must effect His new incarnation from within ourselves", he had announced. However, he felt convinced that studying "the mythical contents of every possible antique tradition", developing close acquaintance with, and an empathic understanding and absorption of, the essence of the myriad myth structures of all time and of all places, would help — as all these reveal "contents of our own being to which we consciously feel only scantily related".[31]

Joseph Campbell had in mind this kinship at deeper levels, when he borrowed the term "mono-myth" from Joyce's *Finnegan's Wake*. Deeply influenced by Jung and Zimmer, Campbell planned his epic effort in the Preface to *The Hero with a Thousand Faces* (1949); it was to read the hieroglyph of the myth idiom "from every corner of the world", a study which would reveal

> A vast and amazingly constant statement of the basic truths by which man has lived throughout the millenniums of his residence on the planet.

This, Campbell here had argued, is the "one, shape-shifting yet marvelously constant story", the basic substance of the experience of existence beneath surface variables. All the myths together, he proposed to demonstrate, "present in the form of one composite adventure the tales of a number of the

[31] *The King and the Corpse*, p. 311 f.n. 2.

world's symbolic carriers of the destiny of Everyman".[32] The "destiny" Campbell noted, was not to control the universe or to alter its system — as frequently argued — but to get attuned to it. All divergences, all instances of moving astray, rounded off in a return, a home coming of the individual soul to the essence of the universe.

This sense of being in unison which, we noted, had been the definitive perception in India in the days of yore, has been ruptured in the modern man's pattern of enlightened existence; "dead" had been "all the gods". The lost spirituality is the precious heritage urgent to recover. Jung had formulated, Zimmer had urged on and Joseph Campbell makes a heroic effort towards a recovery of, the "co-ordinated soul".

True, the locus of redemption had shifted to the inner arena of the individual's own identity, yet the inner redemption would be easier to access if the modern man discovers his own soul embedded in the collective soul of the race, of all living forms. At the biological level Campbell traces back the shared heritage to the survival instinct, the "innate releasing mechanism" operative in all forms of life. In the myth pattern he traces it to the image of the one tree "in the garden where God walks in the cool of the day", the tree that grows two branch limbs called the tree of Knowledge and the Tree of Immortal Life.[33] The old myth process, Campbell believes, had flown in two major channels: the Levantine and the Oriental. The Levant had developed a sense of separation between God and man; the Orient had retained its sense of unity with the universe, not excluding its maker. In India the primitive sense of being in unison with the physical cycle of birth, death and

---

[32] *The Hero with a Thousand Faces* (Bolingen, Princeton University Press, Paperback 1973), p. 36.

[33] *Oriental Mythology*, (1962; Penguin Books, 1976), pp. 8-9; *Occidental Mythology*, p. 106ff.

re-birth had been transformed into the transcendental metaphysics of the Upanishads. The Occident had explored the long, perilous pathways of the individual quester, a traveller on the "trackless way", separated from his Creator. The Western sojourner had tasted the giddy raptures of empirical achievements, also tasted the terror entailed. Now he waits for a newer revelation of some hidden inner resource which alone can redeem. Human history had witnessed recurring events of shape-shifting; the modern West waits for its own myth to emerge. The first step towards evoking a myth for the present time, towards what Campbell calls "rendering the modern world spiritually significant", is returning to the divinity/ humanity within, to the "*homo dei*" in Thomas Mann's fiction: "the way to become human is to recognize the lineaments of God in all the wonderful modulations of the face of man", he asserts.[34]

On completion of the volumes on the masks of God (five volumes written over nearly two decades, 1949–1968), Campbell feels confident in his assumption of "the unity of the race of man, not only in its biology but also in its spiritual history, which has everywhere unfolded in the manner of a single symphony."[35] Now that the themes and the forms can all be encompassed in the broader perspective of comparative scrutiny, the basic singleness, the underlying unity is easily discernible and claimable as common heritage. This claiming, owning of and conscious participation in, the "festival of passing forms", Campbell believes, would prepare modern man for the next leap in history. The event waited for would come as the emergence of a new myth-structure, broader, deeper, more fluid, more sophisticated, truly inclusive, offering an adequate spiritual sustenance to the hour. To attain this

---

[34] *The Hero with a Thousand Faces*., pp. 390; 391.

[35] *Creative Mythology* (1968, Penguin Books, 1974).

perhaps would be, to adapt T. S. Eliot's formulation in "Gerontion", the only "forgiveness" — after all the terrible "knowledge" acquired by man in modern times.

The larger gain from the study of the mono-myth and its appropriation in the modern mind – after the Wars, after the holocaust, under the threat of a nuclear apocalypse – Campbell believed, might be to realize that "the community today is the planet, not the bounded nation".[36] It might make possible some contribution, Campbell thought in 1949, to "the forces that are working in the present world for unification, not in the name of some ecclesiastical or political empire, but in the sense of human mutual understanding."[37]

Here, in the beginning of the venture (1949), Joseph Campbell almost enters the realm of the post-modernist urge to cross borders, to move towards the trans-national, the truly global. In the twenty-first century, at a point of time where the "post-" as a trope, though not dead, is on its way out, and the "trans-" tends to lead beyond borders — ethnic and political[38] — Campbell's "single symphony" is a promising metaphor.

---

36 *The Hero with a Thousand Faces*., p. 388.

37 Ibid. Preface.

38 See, for instance, Geoffrey Bennington, *'Inter', Post-Theory*, ed. M. mcQuillan (Edinburgh University Press, 2000); A. Appadurai, *Modernity at large: Cultural dimensions of Globalisation* (University of Minnesota Press, 1996); M. Pete Smith and L. Eduardo Guarnizo, *Transnationalism from Below* (New Brunswick and London: Transaction Publishers, 2004); Wolfgang Welsch, "Transculturality: the Puzzling Form of Cultures Today", M. Featherstone and S . Lash (eds) *Spaces of Culture*: *City, Nation, World*, (London, Sage, 1999); Krishna Sen and Sudeshna Chakravarti (eds), *Narrating the (Trans) Nation: the Dialectics of Culture and Identity*, (Kolkata: Dasgupta, 2008); Krishna Sen, "From "Post-" to "Trans-" : Signaling a Paradigm Shift?", A. Chakraborty and S. Aich Bhowmik eds., *Critical Perspectives in Postcolonialism*, (Kolkata, Booklore 2011).

However, with all his extensive exposure to Indian thoughts[39] and the Eastern modality in general, Joseph Campbell essentially belongs to the Occident; he shares the ecstasy and the agony of the modern Westerner. Attuned to the Modernist temperament, Campbell admires the hero portrayed in the novels of Thomas Mann and James Joyce. The hero at the gateway to a new era, waiting for a new shrine to open its doors and reveal a new visage, a new mask of God, in Campbell's vision is the Western man of the crisis moment, with the multitude of the racial lore behind.

Heinrich Zimmer, considered the greatest German Indologist after Max Müller, had drifted much closer to the Indian "shore". Zimmer had pronounced,

> We of the Occident are about to arrive at a cross-roads that was reached by the thinkers of India some seven hundred years before Christ. This is the real reason why we become both vexed and stimulated, uneasy yet interested, when confronted with the concepts and images of Oriental wisdom.[40]

Campbell cites with appreciation ancient India's formulations of spiritual experience, frequently falls back on the ancient wisdom; yet he remains basically rooted in the "historical" tradition defined more than a hundred years back by Max Müller. He surveys the story of human civilization in the neat order of the "crude", the "fine", the "super-fine" — gradations in the making of God's masks.[41] Earlier in time, India remains

---

[39] He had studied Sanskrit at the University of Paris and the University of Munich. Zimmer's lectures in the University of Columbia had deeply influenced him; editing Zimmer's Papers, he entered the world of Zimmers' ideas more deeply. He had met J. Krishnamurti in 1924 and formed a lifelong friendship with him, he had spent part of his sabbatical in India; with Swami Nikhilananda he had shared in the forties the work of translating from the Bengali original *The Gospel of Sri Ramakrishna* published in 1946.

[40] *Philosophies of India* (Routledge & Kegan Paul, 1952), pp. 1-2.

[41] *Creative Mythology*, p. 647.

closer to the crude and the primitive, to the "infancy" as Max Müller had known. Chronicity persists as measure. The earlier and the later, the archaic and the modern, take their position, once again, in a sequential order. Historicity, rather than multeity and simultaneity, reigns. Campbell's position stops short of an attitudinal readiness for the "spatial historiography" Frederick Jameson calls for, a readiness for the simultaneous validation required for moving beyond "the bounded national". Joseph Campbell himself, we noted, had stretched his vision to such a goal to reach at the outset, in the Preface to and in the concluding section of the *Hero with a Thousand Faces* (1949); yet it is the figure of the Western sojourner, the daring individual, that he stops with at the end of the last volume in the series, *Creative Mythology* (1968). The readiness to move into the "trans-local", the "trans-national" that the post-Said scholars think in terms of, is yet to evolve.

Contrary pulls persist in operation; cultural ethnicity conditions. The more sensitive the scholar's perception, stronger the empathic ability to share, more intriguing appears the play of contrarieties.

Talking about the event of Alexander's entry into India, Campbell notes how much ahead Indian thought had been at that point of time.[42] In the volumes on the "Masks of God" he repeatedly cites and refers to the cognition in the Rig-veda of a co-valence of the one and the many, the formulation: "Truth is one, sages call it by different names". With deep appreciation he cites passages from the Brihadaranyaka Upanishad expounding the nature of Truth as the Atman, the Self, and contrasts the perception with *Genesis* 3:22-24.[43] He devotes a whole section in the concluding chapter in *Creative*

---

[42] *Occidental Mythology*, p. 241.

[43] *Creative Mythology*, pp. 630-31.

Mythology analyzing the levels of consciousness systematically held together in the "mystic syllable AUM" as enunciated in the Mandukya Upanishad. Campbell locates here the Indian sages' perception of levels of consciousness, levels that would be deciphered in the West thousands of years later in the systems of Freud, Jung, Nietzsche, and sensitively handled in the novels of James Joyce and Thomas Mann. These are levels of consciousness, Campbell notes, that speak and levels of consciousness that constitute the unspeaking silence before and after.[44] His reading conveys a sense of awed admiration for the ancient gaze of penetration.

Yet, to him the vibrant moment in the long story of man's quest for Truth, the moment he truly relates to, is the time that begins with Bruno and Galileo, the time of the assertion of aspiration over authority, the era of the questing and the questioning individual. He eloquently expounds the assumption that this had been a beginning as important as man's acquisition, way back, of agrarian knowledge. Campbell is at home in the "fresh world of NOW and HERE—beyond the scattered remains still in fragments among us – of the old Sumerian mansion of five thousand years"[45]. He walks at ease down the "richly studded vale where stand the temples of the godly visions of the chief creative peoples of the Western World"[46]. The waiting, after all the stress and all ordeals, is for an opening, or a re-opening, of "the eye of the European man" to the divinity within, the hero in one's soul, as Nietzsche reminds the world, the divinity in man that Thomas Mann tries to bring under focus.

---

[44] Ibid., pp. 647-48.

[45] *Creative Mythology*, pp. 608-09.

[46] *Occidental Mythology*, p. 8.

Campbell closes the study in five volumes on this expectant note, waiting for yet another episode of dying into life,

> ... the criterion of achievement will be, ... the courage to let go the past, with its truths, its goals, its dogmas of 'meaning', and its gifts: to die to the world and to come to birth from within.[47]

The "shore" (one of the major tropes used in these volumes) that Campbell's heroic expedition over the long, many-phased story of man's imaginative-spiritual adventure on earth, studied in five volumes, reaches, is the vision of a reborn, open-eye West. This is the one section of the planet which is home to the one group of humanity that marches ahead, happens to be assigned the task of bearing the destiny of man from phase to phase, the one group that shapes and matters.

The rest of the human community, the non-West, rests where they are. Their journey along different paths are studied in detail, the masks of divinity they had devised, played with, and had discarded for others, are scrutinized, their sacred texts carefully recovered, critically edited and caringly preserved as the "Bibles of the World". It all forms a background-study, massive, unsparing, liberal, enlightened and of use.

VI

Even as the masks of God change, indeed, emphases in the modalities of the West's self-perception keep changing and discourse in culture studies alters.[48] The basics, however,

---

[47] *Creative Mythology*, p. 678.

[48] Bhabha analyses evolving idioms in "the colonial and postcolonial margins of modernity", *The Location of Culture*, p. 344. Robert Young argues how "the inscription of alterity within the self" in the case of the Western Modernism, allows new ethical relations. *White Mythologies: Writing, History and the West* (London, Routledge 1990), pp. 16-17.

remain the same. Max Müller's enquiry in his enormously painstaking engagement with India and her tradition had been "what India can teach" the West. Heinrich Zimmer felt it necessary to begin a conversation with ancient India as a "glance at the face of India", he believed, might "assist" the West to "discover and recover something in itself". Joseph Campbell explores the "way in which India might contribute ... to our rescue in the circumstances" of the spiritual crisis in the final decades of the twentieth century. In Indology this is the stable "site of enunciation", even though better informed modernist discourse, H. K. Bhabha notes, effectively "conceals" almost with an enchantingly graceful spirit of liberalism, "the fact that the hegemonic structures of power are maintained in a position of authority."[49] One remembers Said's distinction between "latent Orientalism" and "manifest Orientalism", the relatively naïve formulations in the nineteenth century and the enormously complex, highly sophisticated formulations in the twentieth.

Max Müller's interest in the future of India, the prospect of an India to emerge, India significantly altered under the impact of Westernization, had its imperial context; his live contact with the reformist groups and individuals, particularly the Brahmo intellectuals, in India record a keen interest in observing the result of the conquest of India at many levels. Joseph Campbell does not stretch his narration of the story of India to his own time; he stops much earlier. Influenced by the thoughts of Heinrich Zimmer, closely associated with Indian thinkers like Krishnamurti, Coomarswami, deeply engaged in the Ramakrishna wave of redefined spirituality, he presents the account in three chapters in *Oriental Mythology*. He wades through the decadence in late Vaishnavism — the

[49] *The Location of Culture*, p. 347.

erotic play of Krishna and the *gopinis* depicted by Joydeva — and leaves the subcontinent at the point it falls to the "blow of Islam", the last fortress of Vijaynagara empire succumbing to the triumphant sword. China is left to the Tao, Japan to its Shinto and the Way of Tea.

This certainly is not the full story.

Sure, humanity in this part of the world had not stopped questioning and questing. The "return" Eliade formulates or Campbell accepts is not, as the Westerners make it out to be, an actual retreat into mythical timelessness; it enshrines a metaphorical remembrance, a ritual modality of recollecting the myths and carrying along the tradition. Celebrating the worship of Durga, the ten-handed slayer of the demon, the Indian worshipper does not go back to the mythical time of the *Markandeya Purana* and engage with the buffalo demon; iconicity apart, he only reminds himself of the fact that evil exists, in myriad deceptive forms, in the universe and that man must assert his best self in resisting the same.

The idea of the cyclic perception negates growth, change and progress. Ascription of this to the Indian culture, in the period Jung onward, is in disregard of the movements in the history of ideas in India ancient and modern. Indian philosophy had split into the six schools of intellectual enquiry, the *Sharadarsan,* even in ancient times; the Vedic culture had been questioned by the anti-Vedic, *a-vaidika* streams of Buddhism, Jainism, the Charvaka principle. All these demonstrate a growth pattern, a live process of self-questioning and self-defining on many floors. Even in the times of Sastric orthodoxy, in the fourteenth century Vijaynagara empire for instance, Madhavacharya in his Collection of all Philosophies, the *Sarvadarshanasamgraha*, gives adequate space to alternative views, including atheism and materialism. Each chapter in the collection gives an exposition of a school of thought and then presents the counter-arguments. The dialectic brings out the inner resilience of the ancient tradition of debate, dissent and continuing quest.[50]

In more recent times the reforms and modifications brought in by leading thinkers, Dayananda Saraswati, Rammohan Roy, Keshabchandra Sen, take the ancient tradition ahead – re-forming, modernizing, re-relating it to changing times. The Ramakrishna-Vivekananda movement gives a new lease of life to the millennia-old spiritual tradition. Sri Ramakrishna opens up the arena of spiritual experience beyond dogma, acknowledges multeity and diversity among faith structures, accepts them all as pathways of pilgrimage leading to the same holy spot. Vivekananda re-orients the ancient tradition for the Indians even as he re-presents it to the West focusing on the inner essence which is non-sectarian, inclusive, all-accepting, all-embracing. The Ramakrishna-Vivekananda wave of reviving the Vedantic vision of non-divisive oneness truly opens out. At the cultural level the metaphysics welcome the vision in the critical concepts of the "trans-" position in the post-modernist, post-colonial, post-Said phase; it truly forms a gateway to the idea of the trans-National, the trans-local, the trans-denominational, the truly global. Sri Aurobindo's metaphysics of the Super Mind formulate a transcendent prospect for the entire humanity.

India does not stagnate nor move in cycles either. Burdened with centuries of colonial subjugation, perhaps India remains less self-possessed and self-focused, less articulate, less assertive than required.

---

[50] Amartya Sen makes appreciative note of this in *The Argumentative Indian*, p. 24.

The twentieth century had wrought vital changes in the realm of thought; the twenty-first century moves towards newer perceptions. History is perceived from below and the other chronicle of the subaltern existence surfaces; post-Said position in culture studies calls for deletion of borders and binaries. India, the land of the oldest continuous civilization on earth, the oldest country of multi-faith co-existence, of pluralistic inclusiveness, intellectually open to the borderless and the non-binary, can now project its essential identity and re-address the world.

The challenge perhaps is big. Ancient India is a massive corpus, a tradition distinct, full-grown with its own curve of growth and decay. Without written factual record, most of it is wrapped up as internal evidence in ancient texts scripted in an antique language. Again, colonized India is foreclosed, native enquirers hesitant and slow to come out.

Formidable as the task happens to be, the study of the confrontation between this ancient culture and the enlightened Occident is of cardinal importance in the field of post-colonial analyses; it is crucial to the understanding of the complex nature of colonial experience both sides of the divide. Discovering, re-discovering, re-rediscovering the self is part of the journey both in the West and in the East, in the case of the colonizer and the colonized.

As time moves ahead the East and the erstwhile colonized part of the planet find their voice. Humanity enslaved, repressed, ruled over and/or marginalized — in native habitat or in diaspora placement — steadily comes into visibility and becomes vocal, crosses over borders, moves along the path of translating, and trans-translating the message — the message(s) inevitably laden with the imprint of space-time pragmatics. To read and to re-read history, to trace and to retrace the footmarks of time, to decipher the cross-connectivity among forces at work, forces hegemonic and epistemic, is a need of increasing urgency. Glancing back in order to look forward, taking stock of the dynamics at work in the time-span behind as preparation for moving into time ahead, can etch out a broader and richer sense of perspective. A sense of perspective that takes into account the load of diverse, at times contrary positionalities, as Amartya Sen notes, can lead to an open-eyed perception, meta-positional, "a view from nowhere", as Thomas Nagel assures.

In such a discourse, free, evolving, bent on receptive cognition and transparency, might emerge the open-eyed perspection Joseph Campbell talks about — the perspection which the "Western Man", as much as the others, needs and the whole humanity waits for.

Appendix A

Commentators and their contexts : directions and diversions

Madhavacharya's conviction (cited earlier in Chapter 4) that the message of the Scriptures is to be interpreted anew in every age, operates in the variation in accent the commentator brings in. Madhava Acharya preparing under command of the Bukka monarch the annotated edition of Parashara Smriti — the Dharma Sastra text prescribed for the time prevailing, the *Kali Yuga*[1]—for instance, intends to keep his focus on the ethical rigour of the Sastra dictat in the interest of his community in his own time. He amasses the prescriptive enunciations on particular issues formulated by other Sastrakaras and presents to his own time the collective voice of the entire Dharma Sastra tradition. The *Parāshara-Mādhava* thus prepared is a compendium of the Sastra enunciations. Even when in the fragmentary text of the Parashara Smriti certain sections of Parashara text are missing, Madhava with his enormous scholarship presents the views of one Sastrakara after another in an argumentative sequence and competently fills up the void. Absorbed in the density of the ancient ethical discourse stretching over several centuries, we hardly notice the absence of the voice of Parashara. Presenting the ancient tradition with its massive weight and pervasive coverage is part of the mission in the context. The responsibility of the commentator is to bring the ancient text and the traditional ethos to bear upon the contemporary situation.

---

1 *"krite tu manavādharmāh tretāyām goutamāhsmritāh / dwāpare sankha-likhitāh kalau parāsarahsmritah" Āchāra Kāṇda*, 1: 24.

Parashara Smriti is the most liberal of all the Smriti texts. Iswarchandra Vidyasagara in times much closer to us, cited Parashara in support of his movement in favour of the marriage of widows. Most acutely aware of the passage of time, the Parashara text accepts the inevitable decline at the end of a cycle (covering the Krita, Treta, Dwapara and the Kali Yuga) and assumes a permissive attitude in the context of human frailties. *Prāyascitta*, penal performances prescribed for diverse forms of fallings off from the ethical norm, Parashara says, have to be lessened in the contemporary time in view of the diminishing abilities of men in the Kali Yuga, this being no aspersion, as the measure of human abilities changes with the change of time—" *teshām nindā na kartavyā, yuga-rupāh hi te dwijāh*".

The vision in the Sastra text glances over the passing of the four *yugas* extending over thousands of years; the commentator Madhava is primarily concerned with his own time, the time of a revival of Brahmanic orthodoxy. He has to ensure that Parashara's permissive attitude does not yield a lightening of the ethical seriousness. The Vijaynagara Acharya of the fourteenth century CE in the prefatory verse to his Commentary, the "*Tikākāropakramaṇikā*", carefully assures that this generosity, *dayāluta*, in Parashara does not affect, oppose or negate the more stringent enunciations of the other Sastrakaras[2], which he cites in profusion. Parashara's leniency, Madhava assures, is to be taken as a mere recognition of larger moral vulnerability—"*pāpabāhulyam*"—in present times[3].

---

2 "*Na Parāsharavākyasya bādhah smrityantare kvachit*".

3 "*kaling pratipravrittatvāt prayascittam prapanchitam // kalau hi pāpabāhulyang drishyate smaryate api*".

Commenting on the Parashara text, Āchāra Kāṇda, 1: 23, which stipulates that *tapah* is for the *Krita Yuga*, *jnāna* is for the *Tretā*, *yajna* is for *Dwāpara* and simply *dāna* for the *Kali Yuga*, Madhava hastens to explain that this is just to indicate a minimum, nothing rules out or excludes nothing[4], none of the modalities, *tapah*, *jnāna* etc., is ever denied relevance. The celebrated Parashara dictum: "*teshām nindā na kartavyā, yugarupāh hi te dwijāh*" ("they / people are not to be blamed, their abilities vary according to the times"), Āchāra Kāṇda, 1:33, is too liberal, too generous, to be left alone. Madhava marshals Sastra enunciations condemning the symptoms Parashara mentions in the sloka text and poses the question: "*tatah katham anindā*?" ("how then, not to blame?").

Parashara speaks eloquently on serving the guest, the *atithi*, and his views are most humanitarian. He places the *atithi*, the *yati*— the *brahmachārin* engaged in studies—and the *bhikshuka* in the same category and forcefully adds that attending to the needs of a *bhikshuka* is the top priority – failure to serve a *bhikshuka* is more reprehensible than failure to serve other guests. If one fails to serve a guest, one can atone for it by serving a *bhikshuka*, but failing to serve a *bhikshuka* cannot be atoned for by any other act, Āchāra Kāṇda, 1:55.[5] Madhava at this point asserts that the term *bhikshuka* here refers to those engaged in studies–" *atra bhikshushabdo vidyārthinām upalakshakah*". Beggars in Madhava's view would be too low in the social hierarchy to enjoy priority.

As to the position of women and their responsibilities, the views of Sastrakara Parashara are remarkably liberal. He permits re-marriage of widows in five critical situations:

---

4 "*yugasāmarthang kebalam atra nirupyate // yathā 'vasante pushpaprāchuryang grishme santāpabāhulyam*" *ityādi*.

5 "*Vaishyadeva-kritang pāpang shakto vikshurvyāpohitum // na hi vikshu-kritāndoshān vaishydevovyāpohati*".

"*nastemritepravrajiteklibecha patite patau // panchasu āpatsu nārināng patiranyo bidhiyate*" ("in cases where the husband is lost, dead, gone off for good, impotent or fallen in corruption, women may take another husband / marry again") Āchāra Kāṇda, 4:28. The commentator Madhava points out that this permissiveness is a matter of Parashara's own time, "*yugāntaravishayah*", not to be followed in general. The traditional Sastric enunciation is always against re-marriage of women once married. He cites codes laid down in the Adi Purana and draws our attention to the alternatives mentioned in the next two Parasharaslokas: one recommends the adoption of the life of *brahmacharya*, the other of *anugamana*, burning on the pyre with the husband — as higher moral options. He profusely quotes *sastravākyas*, sastra enunciations from the vast orthodox tradition. Parashara says, in Āchāra Kānda, 4; 31, that the virtues of a good wife can redeem the evil deeds and propensities of the husband and lift him up to a high moral-spiritual level, even as a snake-catcher grips and pulls out a snake from its hole. Madhava cites enunciations from other Sastra texts highlighting the recommendations of *anugamana*, wives following the husband in death. Subjugation is to be validated again, and again.

Parashara says that penance for women of all the four *varnas* (castes) should be very light, nominal, like *chāndrāyana*, because women, like the earth, are never degraded, corrupted or tainted— "*yathābhumistathā nāri tasmāt tāng na dushayet*", Prāyascitta Kāṇda, 10:22. Madhava hastens to assure that the intention here is to make the point that for women aversion to transgression should operate as innate moral revulsion and not follow from a fear of severe forms of penance. The focus on the essential purity of women and of the earth, a beautiful formulation in the Parashara text, is shifted to penal prospects.

As an analogous instance we might recollect the text-commentary situation in *Yājnavalkya Smriti*, Striprakarana section, and Vijnaneswara Misra's explicatory comments. Yajnavalkya, the Sastrakara, says, "*lokānantyang divahprāptih putra-pautra-praputrakaih//yasmāt tasmāt striyah sevyāh kartavyāscha surakshitāh*", ("survival through procreation in this world, prospect of attaining the heavenly abode through progeny –sons, grandsons, great grandsons—all these are gifts of our wives; hence service to wives and their protection are bounden duties"), Āchāra Adhyāya, 78. The commentator around the 9th century CE explains: "*striyahsevyāh : upabhogyāhprajārtham*" ("wives should be enjoyed for begetting off-springs"). Here, as in sloka 81, the Yajnavalkya text had assured happiness, pleasure and protection to the wife, whereas the commentary concentrates on the objective of procreation and male prerogation.

In the context of the *Parāshara-Mādhava* we note that if Parashara had been a Sastrakara of the *Kali Yuga*, a time of diminishing, *hrāsa / sankocha*, shrinkage, Madhava Acharya is a commentator of times of identity crisis and threatened survival. Parashara accepts the shrinkage and places his trust in the basics of a tradition, a value-system which, he assures, remains and continues in spite of inevitable decline, lessening, minimizing in external details of daily practice, *āchāra.*[6] The trust in the essentials, the inner spirit, the in-built resilience of the system, lends a confidence and a quality of broadness and an attitude of acceptance in Parashara; he glances at the passage of time with the relaxed patience of an observer from within. The fourteenth-century CE commentator Madhava Acharya is a figure of more difficult times, times of a crisis of faith. He

---

[6] "*kalpekalpe kshayotpattau Brahmā-Vishnu-Maheswarah //shruti-smriti-sadāchāra-nirnetārascha sarbadā*" *Āchara Kāṇda,* 1: 20.

spends his giant erudition in an effort at holding on to the externals, to all that is supposedly sanctified through usage, practice and unbroken ancestry.

Sayana Acharya explicates the Rig-veda, Madhava Acharya presents Smriti texts — in their own time. The times dictate; positionality defines.

Appendix B

Indology and its reception in India

The Indian response to the West's interest in Indian antiquity in the nineteenth century, the response particularly to Max Müller's mammoth venture, brings out shades and nuances in the native sensibility shaping and re-shaping itself under the colonial rule.

Max Müller mentions in the Cambridge lecture, in *Chips from a German Workshop* and in other contexts the orthodox resistance of native Veda scholars to intervention in Veda studies by foreigners from the West, the *mlecchhas*.

Orthodox Veda scholarship in India, however, at the time had been much weakened. Raja Radhakanta Dev mentions with a wry sense of irony, and Swami Vivekananda glances back with a sense of regret to, the situation of decline in Veda studies in the country, the situation in which the East India Company's venture to get the Rig-veda edited could not be undertaken in Calcutta. Naturally the orthodox resistance had proved feeble and futile. Enlightened Indians welcomed the Westerners' interest and collaborated with their ventures of exploration. We would remember that in 1788 Jagannath Tarkapanchanan had joined the Asiatic Society to assist William Jones in his project of compiling the "Digest of Hindu and Mahammadan Laws"; in 1885 Dr Rajendralal Mitra had been the first Indian President of the Society. Interaction between the Western scholars and the enlightened, critically alert, forward-looking Indian intellects grew into a live channel of communication.

In the Preface to the second volume of his *Rig-veda Sanhita with Sayana Bhasya* (Christmas 1853) Max Müller mentioned the valuable gift of the *Sabdakalpadruma*, "a large thesaurus of the Sanskrit language in seven large quarto volumes", from Raja Radhakanta Deva,

> I have been also honoured by that distinguished scholar and noble patron of Sanskrit literature, Raja Radhakanta Deva of Calcutta with a most valuable present, the *Sabdakalpadruma*, a work which by its comprehensive range and its excellent arrangement stands unrivalled in Indian philology.[1]

Sending this gift in 1851, the Raja had mentioned that the appreciation of his painstaking job by "a Mueller and a Wilson, who have won golden opinions by their profound scholarship in Sanskrit", if forthcoming, would truly make him feel proud. The Raja mentions the copy of the first volume of Max Müller's *Rig-veda Sanhita* he had received from the Court of Directors of the East India Company, also the pre-publication version before that sent personally by the scholar himself:

> I have lately been honoured by the Honourable the Court of Directors with the present of the first volume of your noble and excellent edition of the Rig Veda, published under their patronage. Some time ago when I received your specimen copy of it, which you had so politely desired Dr Roer to send me, I read it with eagerness and, although I was obliged to return it sooner than I could have wished, I saw enough to convince me that you would go far beyond all expectation, and your present publication has confirmed this opinion.

He welcomes the progress of the scholar's work which will

> furnish the Vedic Pandits with a complete collection of the holy *Sanhitas* of the first Veda, only detached portions of which are to be found in the possession of a few of them, and enable the

[1] P. LIX.

> student of antiquity 'to snatch the veil that hung her face before', supply materials for the history of the ancient East – nay, ancient world, and rear up for you a monument more durable than brass.

He notes the irony in the situation:

> It is surely a very curious reflection on the vicissitudes of human affairs that the descendants of the divine rishis should be studying on the banks of the Bhagirathi, the Yamuna and the Sindhu their Holy scriptures as published on the banks of the Thames by one whom they regard as a distant *mlechchha*... who will ere long rise to the rank of a Veda-Vyasa of the *Kali-Yuga.*

When the gift of the second volume of the *Rig-veda Sanhita* arrived, Radhakanta Deva Raja Bahadur, on 5 March 1855, wrote to acknowledge,

> I have lately received through the Bengal Government a copy of the second volume of the Rig Veda, as a present from the Honourable the Court of Directors, and I can ill express the feelings of mingled joy and admiration with which I grasped this most precious gift.... Great is the obligation under which you have laid the learned world. By your successfully embarking on such an arduous undertaking, you have done to the Hindus an inestimable benefit, supplying them a correct and superb edition of their Holy Scriptures. Accept therefore my most grateful and sincere thanks, which, in common with my countrymen I owe you, and my special acknowledgments for the very kind and obliging manner in which you have noticed my name and work in the preface to the second volume of the Rig Veda.[2]

Radhakanta Deva, Max Müller knew, had been one of the leading intellectuals in the conservative section in contemporary India. It is interesting to note that with his enlightened attitude, critical perception of the space for cross-cultural engagement and genuine appreciation of the fruits of

---

[2] Raja Radhakanta's letters quoted by Max Müller cited in N. Mookerjee (ed) *I Point to India: Selected Writings of Max Müller 1823-1900* (Ramakrishna Mission Institute of Culture 1970, reprint, 2012).

the foreigner's labour, the Raja extends grateful thanks on behalf of the entire community and places the German scholar in the position of Veda Vyasa, the mythical systematizer of the Veda.

By the mid-fifties of the century the first volume of the *Rig-veda Sanhita with Sayana Bhasya* had sold out and other volumes were almost running out of print. To the deep dismay of Max Müller the Literary Committee of the India Council declined the proposal of sponsoring the publication of a second edition. A "Sovereign Prince" from India, Ananda Gajapati Raju of Vizianagaram or Vijaynagaram, came forward to donate more than £ 64,000 for the purpose; an agreement was signed on 10 September 1887. Rimi B. Chatterjee tells the story in detail in "Dealing with a 'Sovereign Prince', Friedrich Max Müller, Oxford University Press and the second edition of the Rig Veda."

Max Müller got interested in the reform movements in India, particularly in the programmes undertaken by the Brahmo Samaj; regular exchange of opinion with Indian reformists took place. Max Müller quotes a letter dated 27 December 1884 from Debendranath Thakur, a leading exponent of the Brahmo Samaj; Debendranath happened to be more critically aware of the positioning of the East and the West and his emphasis was on the opening up of the East to the West. He wrote,

> There are branches of knowledge and art in which the East is deficient, and which she must learn from foreign sources. But there are things all her own, and even your enlightened countrymen may turn with pleasure and profit to a leaf or two out of the books of the East to learn something new, to get a glimpse of vistas of thought with which they are not familiar. And you, Sir, have done not a little to open out before the world treasures of Oriental wisdom which only the diligence of scholars

> like you could unfold. By the publication of the Rig Veda and the Upanishads you have brought within the reach of European scholars the thoughts and aspirations of our ancient rishis, hitherto hidden in inaccessible manuscripts.[3]

Swami Vivekananda in the 1890's deeply appreciated the dedicated engagement of the Western scholar in the study of the Veda and the Vedic culture, his enormous toil in mastering an alien language. And Vivekananda whole-heartedly acknowledged the debt of the contemporary Indians, the native inheritors of the ancient tradition, to this European scholar. In the 1896 article on Paul Deussen for the *Brahmavadin,* Vivekannada talking with wonder and admiration of the European scholar's struggle with an antique language, noted,

> We Hindus certainly owe more to him (Max Müller) than to any other scholar in the West, and I am simply astonished when I think of the gigantic task which he in his enthusiasm, undertook as a young man and brought to a successful conclusion in his old age. Think of this man without any help, poring over old manuscripts, hardly legible to the Hindus themselves, and in a language to acquire which takes a lifetime even in India .... This one man has done a thousand times more for the preservation, spreading, and appreciation of the literature of our forefathers than any of us can ever hope to do, and he has done it all with a heart which is full of the sweet balm of love and veneration.[4]

On 6 June 1896 from London he reported to the *Brahmavadin* his visit to Max Müller who by that time had published an article on Sri Ramakrishna in the *Nineteenth Century* and was looking forward to writing a book on the Indian Saint. The visit, Vivekananda said, had been "a revelation" to him. He had felt like meeting the rishis of ancient India; the ambience of the scholar's habitat, he wrote,

---

[3] *I Point to India*, p. 54.

[4] *The Complete Works of Swami Vivekananda* (Advaita Ashram, Calcutta, eleventh edn., 1978), Vol. 4, pp. 275-76.

> sent me back in imagination to the glorious days of ancient India, the days of our Brahmarshis and Rajarshis, the days of the great Vanaprasthas, the days of Arundhatis and Vasisthas.[5]

Above all he deeply appreciated the scholar's dedication: "And what love he bears towards India! I wish I had a hundredth part of that love for my own motherland!" In a letter to Mary Hale (30 May 1896), he again wrote, "I wish I had half his love for India".[6]

In the review article (*Udbodhan*, 14 March 1899) on Max Müller's book, *Ramakrishna: his Life and Sayings*, Vivekananda reminded his countrymen the debt of gratitude they owed to the foreigners. He noted how, in times of decline of Veda scholarship in India, at a time when the whole of the Rig-Veda Samhita "no one could even get at", the ancient text came out, "now very neatly printed and made accessible to the public, thanks to the munificent generosity of the East India Company and to the Professor's prodigious labours extending over years".[7]

Vivekananda here appreciates the scholar's unfailing interest in the reform movements in India. Well-acquainted with the reformist groups, the scholar comes to focus on Sri Ramakrishna as the one iconic sage personality embodying the entire ancient tradition. Vivekananda raises the question: how many Indians share this perception?[8] Placing the German scholar within the framework of the Vedic culture and using Vedic terminology, Vivekananda notes that the huge erudition in the case of the scholar was but the *aparāvidyā*, lower knowledge which had led the man to the *parāvidyā*, a

---

[5] Ibid., p. 280.

[6] Ibid., p. 281; Vol. 8, p. 378.

[7] Ibid., Vol. 4, p. 409.

[8] Ibid.

Vedantist realization of the *atman*, the inner self, as the ultimate. He designates Max Müller "a Vedantist of Vedantists"[9].

The analogues and the traditional associations used extend warm welcome from the leading intellects in India, most of whom by the end of the nineteenth century happened to get engaged in the assertion of a national identity — laden with the glory of a hoary antiquity.

The critical voices of Bankim, Dayananda, Tilak, Aurobindo, had been pushed back. The nineteenth century admiration of the Westerners' interest in India's past, on the other hand had been very much on the surface and had proved a much stronger force. The appreciation of the brave rescue operation of the Vedic lore from behind the phase of Islamic domination and decadence of the Hindu culture, conveys a sense of grateful gratulation and this constitutes the mainstream culture interface. Recognition from the modern West at the time had acted as a confidence-booster; so it does even at the close of the twentieth century and the beginning of the twenty-first.

In a Seminar on "Max Müller and His Contemporaries" commemorating the death centenary of the scholar, held in the Ramakrishna Mission Institute of Culture in 2000, Swami Prabhanandaji in his welcome address mentions that

> Indians cherish his (Max Müller's) name with a fervor near to that of hero-worship.

that his monumental work and "his contact with the best minds of contemporary India made him 'the truest friend of India…"[10].

---

[9] Ibid., p. 281.

[10] *Max Müller and His Contemporaries* (Ramakrishna Mission Institute of Culture, Calcutta, 2001), pp. 1-2

D. P. Chattopadhyay notes, "In what a high esteem the scholar was being held by the leading Indians like R. G. Bhandarkar and R. C. Dutt of the time is evident from their glowing tributes paid to him on his passing away". Visvanath Chatterjee, adapting Vivekananda's phrase "Vedantist of Vedantists", designates Max Müller the Sanskritist of Sanskritists and the Indologist of Indologists and feels tempted to call him a *rishi*, a sage.[11]

Kapil Kapoor in his paper captioned "Vyāsa Paramparā, Text Renewal Mechanisms, Max Müller and Contemporary European Scholarship", refers to the numerous points of text recovery in the oral tradition in ancient India mentioned in the Puranas, the "operation of various text renewal mechanisms" and the recovery of seminal texts. He places the nineteenth-century Westerners' effort in this sequence, considers this as the major text renewal achievement after "the great disruption in India in the 11th century and the vandalism and oppression that followed"[12]. Analysing the long history of the *Vyāsaparamparā*, the Vyasa tradition, he places the German scholar's editorial achievement in place,

> We may recognize Prof. Max Müller's place in the Indian intellectual traditions as the 33rd Vyasa.

In his enumeration, 'Yaska of the 9th Century BC' 'ranks as the 31st and 'Adi Sankara of the 7th Century AD' as the 32nd. Kapil Kapoor appreciates the rescue work by Max Müller as an event in the sequence after several centuries.

Appropriating is a gesture of multiple meaning, operating at altered and altering levels of perception.

---

[11] Ibid., pp. 12-13; p. 48.

[12] Ibid., p. 123-24; 133.

Bibliography

Sanskrit texts :

Rig-veda Sanhita with Sayana Bhasya, vols. I–VI (ed.) Max Müller, 1849–1875.

_____, (2nd edn.), vols. I–IV, 1890–1891.

Rig-veda, hymns to the Maruts, Rudra, Vāyu and Vāta, (tr.) Max Müller, *The Sacred Books of The East,* vol. 32; 1891.

Rigveda Specimen,(ed.) F. Rosen, London, 1830.

Rig Veda, The Vedic Samsodhanamandala, Pune, 1933.

Rikveda Samhita (with Bengali trans., based on the tr. by Rameshchandra Dutta), : vols. I & II, Calcutta, Haraph Prakashani, 1976.

Samaveda Samhita, (with Bengali trans., ed.), Paritosh Thakur, Calcutta, Haraph Prakashani, 1975.

Yajurveda Samhita (with Bengali trans., ed.), Bijanbehari Goswami, Calcutta, Haraph Prakashani 1975.

Atharvaveda Samhita (Bengali trans., ed.), Haraph Prakashani, 1978.

The Rig-veda Saṁhita, vol. 1: Vāsanti Bhāṣya, (tr., ed.), Basanta Kumar Ganguly, Calcutta, The Asiatic Society, 2004.

The Rig Veda, one hundred and eight Hymns (selected, tr.,) O'Flaherty, W. D., Penguin, 1981.

Sayanacharya, *Veda Bhasyopakramaṇikasaṁgraha* (ed.), Baladeva Upadhyaya, Varanasi, Chawkhamba Sanskrit series, 1985.

—Sayaṇacharya, *Vedārthaprakāsh, Rigveda-saṁ hita Srimat-sayaṇacharya Bhasya-sameta,* vols. I-IV, Baladeva Upadhyaya (ed.), Varanasi, Chawkhamba Sanskrit series, Vaidikasamsodhana Mandala, Pune 1933-1946.

Yaska, *Nirukta* : *Nighaṇtu and the Nirukta* (tr., ed.), L. Sarup, Delhi, Motilal Banarasidass, 1962.

Aitareya Brahmaṇa, (ed., tr., Martin Haug, Superintendent of Sanskrit Studies, Poona College), London, Trubner & Co. 1863. (ed.) Keith, A.B., Delhi, Motilal Banarasidass 1920.

Shatapatha Brahmaṇa (ed.) Weber, A., Berlin, 1849. (Repr.), Varanasi Chowkhamba Sanskrit Series, 1964.

Āpastambiya Paribhāsā Sutra (Dharma and Grihya Sutras), translated by various scholars, (ed.), Ramanuja Achari, online: srimatham.com (accessed 20/2 2016).

Upanishad Granthavali (with Bengali trans.), vols. 1-3, (ed.) Swami Gambhirananda, Calcutta, Udbodhan 1941.

Eight Upanishads, (with English tr.), vols. 1 & 2, Swami Gambhirananda, Calcutta, Adwaita Ashram, 1957.

The Brihadaraṇyaka Upanishad (with English tr.), vols. 1 & 2, Swami Madhavananda, Calcutta, Adwaita Ashram, 1934.

The Principal Upanishads (with English tr.), Radhakrishnan, S., UK, Harper Collins, 1953.

Mahabharatam, the Critical Edition, vols. 1-19, Pune, The Bhandarkar Oriental Research Institute, 1919-1966.

Mahabharata (with Bengali trans. in prose), Kaliprasanna Sinha, serialized 1860–1866, 1886 text online, https// archive.org, (accessed, 20/2/2016).

Mahabharata, 43 vols., (with Bengali trans., ed.), Srimad Haridas Siddhanta-bagish Bhattacharya, Calcutta, Visva-vani, 1931.

Vyasa's Mahabharatam (summary trans.) Bharadwaja Sharma, Calcutta, Academic Publishers, 2008.

Bhagavadgita (Tr., Swami Prabhavananda and Christopher Isherwood), Signet Classic 2002.

Bhagavadgita (with Bengali trans., Swami Jagadiswarananda, ed. Swami Jagadishananda), Calcutta, Udbodhan, 1939.

Manu Samhita (ed., with Bengali trans. and commentary), S. Bandyopadhyay, Kolkata, Ananda Publishers, 1999.

Yājnavalkya Smriti, Vijnāneswarapraneeta Mitāksharā-vyākshayā... sanāthakrita, (ed.) Narayana Rama Acharya, Nirnayasagara Mudranalayam, (N.S. Prakashan), Mumbai, 1949.

Parāshara Smriti, Sriman Mādhavāchārya-krita-vyākhyā-sahitā, vol. I, (ed.) Mahamahopadhyaya Sri Chandrakanta Tarkalankara, Kolkata, The Asiatic Society, 1974.

Parashara Smriti, Sriman Madhavacharya-krita-vyakhya-sahita, vols. II & III, Kolkata, the Asiatic Society, 1973.

Vishnu Smriti, online text : hinduonline.co/scriptures/smriti/Vishnu smriti.html., (accessed, 21/2/2016).

Nārada Smriti, online text : https/arch.org., (accessed, 21/2/2016).

The Dharma Sastras – Hindu Religious Code, 6 vols., Datta, M.N., online text : https//arch.org/the hindudharmasastras., (accessed, 21/2/2016).

....

Agarwala, V. S. "Yaska and Panini", *The Cultural Heritage of India* vol. I, (ed.) Sarvepalli Radha Krishnan, Calcutta, The Ramakrishna Institute of Culture, 1937, Paperback 2001.

Anandabardhana and Abhinavagupta, *Dhanyaloka O Lochana*, (trans.) S.C. Sengupta and K. Bhattacharyya, Calcutta, A. Mukherjee, 1950; second edn. 1968.

Appadurai, A., *Modernity at Large : Cultural Dimensions of Globalisation*, University of Minnesota Press, 1996.

Apte, V. M., "The Vedangas", *The Cultural Heritage of India* vol. I. Calcutta, The Ramakrishna Institute of Culture, 1937, Paperback 2001.

Ashcroft, Bill, *Key Concepts in Post-Colonial Studies*, London, Routledge, 1998.

______, *Post-Colonial Transformation,* London, Routledge, 2001.

______, "Globalization, Transnation and Utopia", (eds.) Sen, K. and Chakravarti, S., *Narrating the (Trans) Nation: the Dialectics of Culture and Identity*, Calcutta, Das Gupta & Co., 2008.

Ashcroft, Bill, Griffiths, G., Tiffin, H., *The Empire Writes Back*, London, Routledge, 1989.

______, (eds.) *Post-Colonial Reader*, London, Routledge, 1995.

Aurobindo (Sri), *Works*, SABCL vols. 1-30. Pondicherry Ashram, 1972–1976.

______, *The Secret of the Veda*, Pondicherry Ashram, 1956.

______, *Essays on the Gita,* Pondicherry Ashram, 1922.

______, *The Upanishads,* Pondicherry Ashram, 1971.

Aurobindo (Sri) Archives and Research, Pondicherry Ashram, April 1977 – December, 1994.

Bandyopadhyay, S., (ed.) *Harinath De : Select Papers, mainly Indological*, Calcutta, Sanskrita Pustak Bhandar, 1972.

Bannerjee, B., (ed.) *Future of Indology*, Calcutta, The Asiatic Society, 2003.

Basham, L., *The Wonder that was India*, Calcutta, Rupa, 1954.

______, *Aspects of Ancient Indian Culture*, London, Asia Publishing House, 1963.

Bennington, G., "Inter", (ed.) M. macQuillan, *Post-Theory*, Edinburgh University Press 2000.

Bhabha, H. K., *The Location of Culture*, NY, Routledge, 1994.

______, (ed.) *Nation and Narration*, London, Routledge 1990.

Bhattacharya, N., "Remaking Custom: the Discourse and Practice of Colonial Codification", (eds.) R. Champakalakshmi and S. Gopal, *Tradition, Dissent and Ideology*, OUP, 1996.

Bierlein, J. F., *Parallel Myths*, N.Y., Ballantyne Publishing, 1994.

Campbell, J., *The Hero With a Thousand Faces*, Princeton University Press, 1949, second edn. 1968.

Campbell, J., *Creative Mythology*, Viking, 1968.

______, *Occidental Mythology*, Penguin, 1964.

______, *Oriental Mythology*, Penguin, 1962.

______, *Primitive Mythology*, Penguin, 1959.

Capra, F., *The Tao of Physics*, London, Fontana, 1976, Flamingo 1983.

Chakrabarti, D. K., *India, an Archaeological History*, OUP 1999.

Chakrabarti, D. K., *The Archaeology of Ancient Indian Cities*, OUP 1995.

_____, *Archaeological Geography of the Ganga Plain*, Delhi, Permanent Black, 2001.

_____, *Archaeology in the Third World, a history of Indian archaeology since 1947,* Delhi, Printworld, 2003.

_____, *The Oxford Companion to Indian Archaeology*, 2006.

Chakraborty, A. and Aich Bhowmik (eds.), *Critical Perspectives in Postcolonialism*, Kolkata, Booklore, 2011.

Chakravorty Spivak, G., *A Critique of Postcolonial Reason*, Harvard University Press, 1999.

_____, *Nationalism and the Imagination*, University of Chicago Press, 2010.

_____, *Other Asias,* Blackwell 2008.

_____, *Death of a Discipline,* Columbia University Press, 2003.

_____, and Butler, Judith, *Who Sings in Nation-State?* 2007.

_____, Ranajit Guha and, *Selected Subaltern Studies*, OUP 1988.

Champakalakshmi, R. and Gopal, S. (eds.) *Tradition, Dissent and Ideology,* Essays in honour of Romila Thapar. Delhi, OUP, 1996.

Chatterjee, B. (ed.), *Bankimchandra : Essays in Perspective*. Calcutta Sahitya Akademi 1994.

Chatterjee, S. *Sri Aurobindo : a Postcolonial Reader*, Centre for Sri Aurobindo Studies, Jadavpur University in association with National Council of Education, Bengal. Calcutta Mahabodhi Book Agency, 2015.

Chatterjee, S., *Smriti Samhita : Phire Dekha* (Smriti Samhita in retrospect) Calcutta, National Council of Education, Bengal 1997.

______, "Social Philosophy in the Smriti Samhitas", *Fusion of Horizons : Socio-Spiritual Heritage of India*, J.U., Department of Philosophy, Calcutta, Allied Publishers 2000.

______, "Ontological Status of Women in the Dharmasastras", *Feminism, Tradition and Modernity*, Indian Institute of Advanced Studies, Shimla, 2002.

______, "Indology and the Empire(s) of the Mind : a 19th Century Perspective", Journal of the Asiatic Society, Vol. LI, no. 3, 2009.

Chaudhuri, Nirad C., *Scholar Extraordinary*, the life of Friedrich Max Müller. Delhi, Orient Paperbacks 1974.

Conrad, J., *The Heart of Darkness*, London 1946; Wordsworth 1995.

______, *Lord Jim*, London, Blackwoods, 1900.

______, *The Collected Short Stories of Joseph Conrad*, Halcyon Classics.

Coward, H. G., *The Sphota Theory of Language*, Delhi, Motilal Banarasidass, 1980.

De, Amalendu, *Introduction to the Early Correspondence of the Asiatic Society. Calcutta,* The Asiatic Society, 2003.

Duff, A., "The State of Education in Bengal", *Calcutta Review*, 1844.

Eddington, Sir A. S., *The Nature of the Physical World*, Cambridge 1931.

Eliade, M., *Patterns in Comparative Religion* (tr., R. Sheed), NY, New American Library 1958.

——, *The Myth of Eternal Return* (tr., W. R. Trask), Princeton University Press 1954.

——, *Myths, Dreams and Mysteries* (tr., Philip Mairet), London Harvil Press 1960.

——, *The Sacred and the Profane* (tr., W. R. Trask), London, Harcourt 1959.

——, "The Quest for the Origins of Religion", *History of Religions*, vol. 4:1, summer 1964 University of Chicago Press.

Eliot, T. S., *Four Quartets* 1942.

——, *The Waste Land* 1922.

——, *Complete Poems and Plays*. London Faber & Faber 1969.

Featherstone, M. and Lash, S. (eds.), *Spaces of Culture: City, Nation, World*. London, Sage 1999.

Feuerstein,G., Kak, S., Frawley, D., *In Search of the Cradle of Civilization*. USA 1995, Indian edn., 1999.

Foucault, M., *The Archaeology of Knowledge*. 1969; London, Routledge 1972.

——, *Madness and Civilization.* NY, Pantheon Books 1965.

Frawley, D., *The Myth of Aryan Invasion*. Delhi, Voice of India 1994.

——, *Rig Veda and the History of India*. Delhi, Aditya Prakashan, 2001.

Frazer, J. G., *The Golden Bough*. (12 vols. 1890–1915); single vol. 1922; London Wordsworth edn. 1993.

Ganguly, Basanta, *The Rigveda Samhita: Vasanti Bhasya* vol.I., Calcutta, The Asiatic Society 2004.

Goswami, Sitanath, *Riksamhita* Calcutta 1974.

Guha, Ranajit and Chakravarti Spivak, G., *Selected Subaltern Studies*, OUP 1988.

Guenon, R., *Introduction to the Study of Hindu doctrines*. London, Luzac 1945.

Gupta, S. P., "Longer Chronology of the Indus-Saraswati civilization", *Puratatwa*, Bulletin of The Indian Archaeological Society, no. 23 ; 1992-93.

Hancock, G., *Underworld : Flooded Kingdoms of the Ice Age*, Penguin 2002.

Hegel, F., *The Phenomenology of Spirit,* 1807.

———, *Encyclopaedia of the Philosophical Sciences,* 1816.

———, *Lectures on the Philosophy of History,* 1822-1830.

Horace, *Satires*.

Inden, R., *Imagining India*. London, Blackwell 1990.

———, "Orientalist Constructions of India", *Modern Asian Studies*, vol. 20, no. 3 (1986).

Indramitra, *Karunasagar Vidyasagar*, Kolkata, Ananda Publishers 1969.

Jana, Satyasaurav, *Mehergarh Harappa Savyatar Gramin Patabhumi*. Calcutta, Punascha 2005.

Jarrige, J. F., Du neolithique a la civilisatione de l'Indean cienne 1995.

Jarrige, J. F., (ed.), La prehistoire et la civilisatione de l'Inde. 1990.

Jarrige, J. F., (ed.), *The early Architectural traditions of the greater Indus valley as seen from Mehergarh*, 1993.

Jeans, Sir James, *The Mysterious Universe*, Cambridge University Press 1930.

_____, *The Universe Around Us*, 1929.

_____, *Through Space and Time*, 1934.

Jones, Sir William, *The Collected Works of Sir William Jones*, Cambridge Books Online.

Jung, C. G., *Modern Man in Search of a Soul*, (tr. W.S. Dell and C.F. Baynes) NY, Harcourt Brace 1933.

_____, *Four Archetypes* (tr., R. F. C. Hull), 1953.

_____, *Psychology of the Unconscious* (tr., B. M. Hinkle), NY, Dover Publication 1912.

_____, *The Basic Writings* (tr., R. F. C. Hull), Princeton, 1959.

Kane, P. V., *The History of the Dharmasastras*, vols. 1-5, Pune, Bhandarkar Oriental Research Institute, 1930–1962.

Kant, E., *Critique of Pure Reason* 1781.

_____, *Critique of Practical Reason* 1788.

_____, *Critique of Judgement* 1790.

Kennoyer, J. M., *Ancient Cities of the Indus Valley Civilization*, American Institute of Pakistan Studies, Oxford, 1998.

Kitagawa, J. M. and Long, C. H. (eds.), *Myths and Symbols : essays in honour of Mircea Eliade,* University of Chicago Press 1998.

Levi-Strauss, C., *Structural Anthropology*. N.Y., Basic Books 1963.

Levi-Strauss, C., *The Savage Mind*, 1962.

Levi-Strauss, *Myth and Meaning*, 1978.

Loomba, A., *Colonialism / Postcolonialism*, Routledge, 1998.

Loomba, A., Kaul, S., Bunzl, M., Burton, A., Esty, J. (eds.), *Postcolonial Studies and Beyond*, Permanent Black, 2005.

Loomba, A. and Martin Orkin, *Postcolonial Shakespeares*, Routledge, 2013.

Macaulay, T. B., "Minute on Education", 1835.

Majumdar, R. C., *An Advanced History of India*, Macmillan, 1946.

———, (General editor), *History and Culture of the Indian People*, vol. IX: *British Paramountcy and Indian Renaissance*, Part 1 and Part 2. Bharatiya Vidya Bhawan, Mumbai 2002 and 2007.

Mallory, J. P., *In Search of the Indo-Europeans: Language, Archaeology and Myth*, N.Y., Thames and Hudson, 1991.

Marx, C., *The Communist Manifesto*, 1848.

———, *Das Kapital*, 1867.

———, *Critique of Political Economy*, 1859.

Mukhopadhyay, Manik (ed.), *The Golden Book of Vidyasagar*, a commemorative volume, All Bengal Vidyasagar Death Centenary Committee, Calcutta 1993.

Müller, Max, *Rig-veda Sanhita with Sayana Bhasya*, vols. I-VI, 1849–1875.

Müller, Max, *Comparative Mythology*, Edinburg, Ballantyne Press, 1856.

Müller, Max, *A History of Ancient Indian Sanskrit Literature: so far as it illustrates the primitive religion of the Brahmans*, London, Williams and Norgate 1859.

_____, *India, What Can it teach Us?* (Cambridge lectures 1882), Longmans Green & Co., new edition, 1892.

_____, *Introduction to the Science of Religion* (lectures at Royal Institute 1870), Longmans Green & Co. 1882.

_____, *Introduction to the Science of Language*, Longmans, Green & Co. 1885.

_____, *Gifford Lectures* 1888-92.

_____, *Natural Religion,* Longmnas, Green & Co. 1889.

_____, *Anthropological Religion,* 1892.

_____, *Contributions to the Science of Mythology* (Oxford lectures 1896), 1898.

_____, *Origin and Growth of Religion* (Hibbert lectures 1878), 1878.

_____, *Ramakrishna, His Life and Sayings*, 1898.

_____, *My Autobiography, a Fragment*, 1901.

_____, *Collected Works* 18 vols. Longmans, 1898.

_____, (ed.) *The Sacred Books of the East, translated by various Oriental Scholars* Vols. 1-50; 1879-1910. (Max Müller's trans. : vols. 1, 10, 15, 30, 32, 49).

Müller, Georgiana (ed.), *The Life and Letters of Right Hon'ble F. Max Müller*, Longmans 1902.

Nagel, T. *The View from Nowhere*, N.Y., OUP, 1986.

_____, *Mind and Cosmos*, N.Y., OUP, 2012.

_____, *Other Minds,* N.Y., OUP, 1999.

Ngugi, wa Thiongo, *Decolonizing the Mind*, 1981. Indian edn., Worldview Publications, 2007.

(Swami) Nikhilananda, *The Gospel of Sri Ramakrishna*, N.Y., Ramakrishna-Vivekananda Centre 1942.

Piggott, S., *Pre-historic India*, Penguin Books, 1950.

Possehl, G. L., *Indus Age: the Beginnings*, University of Pennsylvania Press, 1999.

Purani, A. B., *The Life of Sri Aurobindo*, Pondicherry Ashram 1958.

Ramakrishna Mission Institute of Culture, The, *The Cultural History of India*, (Second edn.) vols. I–VI, Calcutta 1958-86.

———, *Indological Studies and Research in India*, Calcutta 1992.

———, *Max Müller and his Contemporaries*, Calcutta 2001.

———, *I Point to India : selected writings of Max Müller,* Calcutta 1970; 2012.

Rao, S. R., *The Lost City of Dwarka*, National Institute of Oceanography, Delhi 1999.

———, *The Decipherment of the Indus Script*, Bombay, Asia Publishing, 1982.

———, *Lothal and the Indus Civilization*, Bombay, Asia Publishing, 1973.

———, *Dawn and Devolution of the Indus Civilization*, Delhi, Aditya Prakashan, 1991.

———, *New Frontiers of Archaeology*, Bombay, Popular Prakashan, 1994.

———, *Reminiscences of an Archaeologist*, Delhi, Aryan Books International, 2008.

Rao, S. R., Felicitation volume, Society of Marine Archaeology in India, Publications Division, 2001.

Reincourt, A. de, *The Eye of Shiva*, Souvenir Press Ltd. 1980.

_____, *The Soul of India*, NY, Harper and Brothers Publishers, 1960.

Renfrew, C., *Archaeology and Language : the Puzzle of Indo-European Origins*, Cambridge University Press, 1987.

Rennie, B. S., *Reconstructing Eliade*, University of New York Press, 1996.

_____ (ed.), *Changing religious Worlds : the Beginning and End of Mircea Eliade*, Sunny Press, 2001.

Roy, Raja Rammohan, *Correspondence of*, vols. I and II (ed.), D. K. Biswas, Saraswat Library, Calcutta 1992; 1997.

Said, Edward, *Orientalism*, Routledge 1978; Penguin Books 1991.

_____, *Culture and Imperialism*, NY, Vintage Books, 1993.

_____, *Representations of the Intellectual*, NY, Pantheon Books 1994.

Samet, E. D., "A Prosewriter and a Gentleman: Edward Burke's idiom of impeachment", ELH 68; no. 2, 2001.

Sartre, Jean-Paul, Preface to F. Fanon's *Wretched of the Earth* 1961.

Sastri, Gouri Nath, "Sanskrit Poetics", *The Cultural History of India*, vol. V. Calcutta, Ramakrishna Mission Institute of Culture 1978.

Sen, Amartya, *The Argumentative Indian*, Penguin 2005.

_____, *On Interpreting India's Past*, Calcutta, the Asiatic Society 1996.

Sen, Krishna, "From 'Post-' to 'trans-' : Signaling a Paradigmshift?", Chakraborty, A. and Aich-Bhowmik, S. (eds.), *Critical Perspectives in Postcolonialism*, Kolkata, Booklore 2011.

_____, and Chakravarti Sudeshna (eds.), *Narrating the (Trans) Nation*, Kolkata, Das Gupta 2008.

Sharp, J. P., *Geographies of Postcolonialism*, London, Sage 2009.

Smith, M. P. and Guarnizo, L.E., *Transnationalism from Below*, London, Transaction Publishers 2004.

Tilak, Balagangadhara, *The Orion*, 1893; Delhi Cosmo Repr. 1984.

Valery, Paul, *Oeuvres*, Jean Hytier (ed.), Paris Gallimard 1960.

Viswanathan, G., "The beginning of English literary study in British India", *Oxford Literary Review*, 9; nos. 1 & 2.

(Swami) Vivekananda, *Complete Works*, vols. 1-8. (Mayavati Memorial Edn.), Calcutta, Adwaita Ashram.

Welsch, W., "Transculturality : the Puzzling Form of Cultures Today", Featherstone, M. and Lash, S. (eds.), *Species of Cultures: City, Nation, World London*, Sage, 1999.

Weston, J., *From Ritual to Romance*, N.Y., Doubleday 1956.

Young, R., *White Mythologies: Writing, History & the West*. Routledge 1990.

Zimmer, H., *Myths and Symbols in Indian Art and Civilization*, (ed.) Joseph Campbell, Princeton, 1972.

Zimmer, H., *The King and the Corpse*, (ed.) Joseph Campbell, Princeton, 1948.

_____, *Philosophies of India*, Princeton, 1952.

Index